HARNESS

Prophetic Gates, Apostolic Foundations,
Kingdom Economics and Dimensions

Kenneth Walley

CIBUNET
Publishing

Published by
Cibunet Publishing
Email: admin@cibunet.com
Website: www.cibunet.com

TABLE OF CONTENTS

SECTION 2

SECTION 3

INTRODUCTION

"And it came to pass, when Pharaoh had let the people go, that God led them not through the way of the land of the Philistines, although that was near; for God said, lest peradventure the people repent when they see war, and they return to Egypt. But God led the people about, through the way of the wilderness of the red sea: and the children of Israel went up harnessed out of the land of Egypt" Exodus 13:17&18. The Israelites were freed from bondage in Egypt through the leadership of Moses the servant of God. They did not leave Egypt in a disorganized manner but were harnessed in orderly ranks as a family of tribes. The reasons for this order were for relaying instructions, leadership, advancement, warfare, and blessings. These five reasons were fundamental to their progress as they journeyed through the wilderness to the Promised Land.

Under the auspices of God's glory, the entire Israelite community journeyed to the Promised Land and possessed their allotments. Ultimately no one was left disenfranchised because their corporate progress fostered individual progress. Can that be said about the Body of Christ today? Many strange and worldly premises shroud the Christian faith today, and that has turned the Church into a wilderness for the survival of the fittest. If there was a manner by which approximately a million Israelites were delivered from bondage and ended up with a promised possession, then there is certainly a model for the Church today.

Jesus Christ unveiled this model to John the apostle at the island of Patmos. "Then one of the seven angels who had the seven bowls filled with the seven last plagues came to me and talked with me, saying, "Come, I will show you the bride, the Lamb's wife." And he carried me away in the Spirit to a great and high mountain, and showed me the great city, the holy Jerusalem, descending out of heaven from God, having the glory of God. Her light was like a most precious stone, like a jasper stone, clear as crystal. Also she had a great and high wall with twelve gates, and twelve angels at the gates, and names written on them, which are the names of the twelve tribes of the children of Israel: three gates on the east, three gates on the north, three gates on the south, and three gates on the west. Now the wall of the city had twelve foundations, and on them were the names of the twelve apostles of the Lamb. And he who talked with me had a gold reed to measure the city, its gates, and its wall" Revelation 21:9-15. In this revelation, the Church is the bride, and Jesus Christ is the bridegroom. Jerusalem is our spiritual habitation where there is a manifestation of God's glory. This city has twelve gates and twelve foundations. The twelve gates are assigned to the twelve tribes of Israel and signify their prophetic destinies. These gates are the access ways into the city of God, so our access is contingent upon our prophetic identity. The twelve foundations of the city are assigned to the twelve apostles of Jesus Christ. This signifies their role as witnesses of His life, death and resurrection. "Therefore, of these men who have accompanied us all the time that the Lord Jesus went in and out among us, beginning from the baptism of John to that day when He was taken up from us, one of these must become a witness with us of His resurrection" Acts

1:21&22. As the designation implied, the apostle was an ambassador, one sent to represent. These twelve apostles saw, heard and experienced Jesus in unique ways for which they became witnesses who passed on the gospel to us.

Though all the potentials of the twelve tribes were in Jacob, each of his sons enshrined a unique potential. Furthermore, through the unique way by which the tribes were harnessed, as well as the design of the holy Jerusalem, we can identify and engage our dominant potentials as well as our recessed potentials to foster our corporate and individual progress in Christ.

Jesus Christ said that the beginning of the spiritual kingdom was announced by John the Baptist and has continued to gain ground through the propagation of the gospel. "From the time of John the Baptist until now, the kingdom of heaven has been forcefully advancing, and forceful people have been laying hold of it" Matthew 11:12 (GWT). In this book, we shall learn how the twelve tribes provide insight into our prophetic purposes and the corresponding apostolic foundations for a grasp of basic kingdom economics as well as the dimensions of how God works.

SECTION ONE

Prophetic Gates And Apostolic Foundations

PART ONE:

Eastern Tribes

COMPETITIVE PROGRESS

In their movement from Egypt towards the Promised Land, the Israelites were organized with three tribes, Judah, Zebulun and Issachar positioned at the eastern side of the tabernacle. The tribe of Judah was the head of this group of tribes, and their ensign was a lion. Whenever Israel was to move forward during their journey toward the Promised Land, the glory cloud will lift from the tabernacle and the Levites would dismantle it to follow the leading of the cloud. The eastern tribes were the first to follow the tabernacle and so they represented competitive progress. The glory cloud initiated the path of Israel to conquer new territory, and this entailed warfare. "And the cloud of the Lord was above them by day when they went out from the camp. So it was, whenever the ark set out, that Moses said: "Rise up, O Lord! Let Your enemies be scattered and let those who hate You flee before You." And when it rested, he said: "Return, O Lord, To the many thousands of Israel" Numbers 10:34-36.

By their prophetic dispositions, these three tribes were endowed with the ability to engage the enemy and take new territory for the kingdom. As their ensign denotes, the dominant potential of these tribes was warfare. "For I consider that the sufferings of this present time are not worthy to be compared with the glory which shall be revealed in us. For the earnest expectation of the creation eagerly waits for the revealing of the sons of God. For the creation was subjected to futility, not willingly, but because of Him who subjected it in hope; because the creation itself also will be delivered from the bondage of corruption into the glorious liberty of the children of God. For we know that the whole creation groans and labors with birth pangs together until now. Not only that, but we also who have the firstfruits of the Spirit, even we ourselves groan within ourselves, eagerly waiting for the adoption, the redemption of our body. For we were saved in this hope, but hope that is seen is not hope; for why does one still hope for what he sees? But if we hope for what we do not see, we eagerly wait for it with perseverance. Likewise, the Spirit also helps in our weaknesses. For we do not know what we should pray for as we ought, but the Spirit Himself makes intercession for us with groanings which cannot be uttered. Now He who searches the hearts knows what the mind of the Spirit is, because He makes intercession for the saints according to the will of God" Romans 8:18-27.

Though the Adamic curse withholds blessings that are due to us, the eastern tribes are divinely burdened to foster their release through travailing prayer. This burden entails the revelatory blessing of Judah, the supernatural endowments of Zebulun and the spiritual senses of Issachar. Their dominant potential is how we take new territory for the kingdom. "If you should say in your heart, 'These nations are greater than I; how can I dispossess them?' you shall not be afraid of them, but you shall remember well what the Lord your God did to Pharaoh and to all Egypt: the great trials which your eyes saw, the signs and the wonders, the mighty hand and the outstretched arm, by which the Lord your God brought you out. So shall the Lord your God do to all the peoples of whom you are afraid. Moreover, the Lord your God will send the hornet among them until those who are left, who hide themselves from you, are destroyed. You shall not be terrified of them; for the Lord your God, the great and awesome God, is among you. And the Lord your God will drive out those nations before you little by little; you will be unable to destroy them at once, lest the beasts of the field become too numerous for you. But the Lord your God will deliver them over to you and will inflict defeat upon them until they are destroyed. And He will deliver their kings into your hand, and you will destroy their name from under heaven; no one shall be able to stand against you until you have destroyed them. You shall burn the carved images of their gods with fire; you shall not covet the silver or gold that is on them, nor take it for yourselves, lest you be snared by it; for it is an abomination to the Lord your God. Nor shall you bring an abomination into your house, lest you be doomed to destruction like it. You shall utterly detest it and utterly abhor it, for it is an accursed thing" Deuteronomy 7:17-26. There was a divine strategy by which Israel possessed the Promised Land which serves as our scriptural model. God did not give them all the Promised Land rapidly because it would have overwhelmed Israel to maintain such victory. He scheduled it in such a way that they could maintain whatever territory they conquered. Think of the world in which we live today, the sophistications of the global economy, the various industries and complexities of geopolitical alliances. Though this is promised in the scriptures, it is never going to be an easy feat to turn over world systems to become kingdom systems overnight. "Then the seventh angel sounded: And there were loud voices in heaven, saying, "The kingdoms of this world have become the kingdoms of our Lord and of His Christ, and He shall reign forever and ever!" Revelation 11:15. According to the model which God used with Israel at the threshold of the Promised Land, God gave them the land 'little by little'. Similarly, the kingdoms of our world would be conquered using divine strategies and tactics. Revelation, endowments and divine timing must be engaged to determine where we have been mandated and favored to advance against the systems of the world.

Harness

Chapter One

Tribe of

Judah

"And she conceived again, and bare a son: and she said, now will I praise the Lord: therefore she called his name Judah; and left bearing" Genesis 29:35. Leah, the mother of Judah had given birth to three sons while going through the turmoil of emotional frustrations. This was because Jacob, her husband, was not as loving as she expected. She craved the obvious endearment that Jacob demonstrated towards her rival Rachael. Though God compensated for this lack of endearment from Jacob by making her fruitful while Rachael was barren, Leah did not acknowledge her blessings until she conceived her fourth son and named him Judah meaning 'Praise'.

Leah's praise triggers a very significant blessing that comes upon her fourth son. "Judah, you are he whom your brothers shall praise; Your hand shall be on the neck of your enemies; Your father's children shall bow down before you. Judah is a lion's whelp; From the prey, my son, you have gone up. He bows down, he lies down as a lion; And as a lion, who shall rouse him? The scepter shall not depart from Judah, nor a lawgiver from between his feet, Until Shiloh comes; And to Him shall be the obedience of the people. Binding his donkey to the vine, And his donkey's colt to the choice vine, He washed his garments in wine, And his clothes in the blood of grapes. His eyes are darker than wine, And his teeth whiter than milk" Genesis 49:8-12. Jacob pronounces this astounding blessing on Judah that foretells his lineage as the one for the coming Messiah. Judah would be a revelatory king, worshipper and warrior.

Revelatory King

As a revelatory king, Judah diligently seeks to be equipped with divine mysteries. "There is therefore now no condemnation to those who are in Christ Jesus, who do not walk according to the flesh, but according to the Spirit. For the law of the Spirit of life in Christ Jesus has made me free from the law of sin and death. For what the law could not do in that it was weak through the flesh, God did by sending His own Son in the likeness of sinful flesh, on account of sin: He condemned sin in the flesh, that the righteous requirement of the law might be fulfilled in us who do not walk according to the flesh but according to the Spirit. For those who live according to the flesh set their minds on the things of the flesh, but those who live according to the Spirit, the things of the Spirit. For to be carnally minded is death, but to be spiritually minded is life and peace. Because the carnal mind is enmity against

21

God; for it is not subject to the law of God, nor indeed can be. So then, those who are in the flesh cannot please God" Romans 8:1-8. There are two laws governing our world. First is the law of sin and death, while the second is the law of the Spirit of Life.

The law of sin and death is the literal logos that is delivered to us in the scriptures. While these are legitimate principles given by God, they are so broad in literal terms that it is impossible to appropriate them in the varied dynamics that real life issues present. For this reason, the Israelites practiced these principles in such a dysfunctional way that made the religious leaders feel justified to persecute and crucify Jesus. A lot of the wickedness practiced in religious circles and society at large today are predicated on the literal interpretations of the law of sin and death.

The law of the Spirit of life is the revelation of Christ Jesus. It is how God's word sanctifies, redeems, anoints and justifies us. "But of Him you are in Christ Jesus, who became for us wisdom from God, and justice and sanctification and redemption" 1 Corinthians 1:30. Without divine inspiration the scriptures can be weaponized to perpetuate all forms of evil, detrimental to our humanity. "And we have such trust through Christ toward God. Not that we are sufficient of ourselves to think of anything as being from ourselves, but our sufficiency is from God, who also made us sufficient as ministers of the new covenant, not of the letter but of the Spirit; for the letter kills, but the Spirit gives life" 2 Corinthians 3:4-6.

The blessing Jacob conferred upon Judah entailed bearing a scepter that symbolizes the reign of a king. This blessing also states that He rides a donkey with its colt. Several years later, Zechariah the prophet foretells the triumphant entry of Jesus Christ into Jerusalem as the manifestation of this blessing. "Rejoice greatly, O daughter of Zion! Shout, O daughter of Jerusalem! Behold, your King is coming to you; He is just and having salvation, Lowly and riding on a donkey, A colt, the foal of a donkey" Zechariah 9:9. In the account of the triumphant entry into Jerusalem, Jesus and the disciples arrive at Bethpage a town nearby. Jesus sends two of his disciples: "saying to them, "Go into the village opposite you, and immediately you will find a donkey tied, and a colt with her. Loose them and bring them to Me. And if anyone says anything to you, you shall say, 'The Lord has need of them,' and immediately he will send them." All this was done that it might be fulfilled which was spoken by the prophet, saying: "Tell the daughter of Zion, 'Behold, your King is coming to you, Lowly, and sitting on a donkey, A colt, the foal of a donkey.'" So the disciples went and did as Jesus commanded them" Matthew 21:2-6.

The donkey and colt were raised by the owner for this special moment. The owner never rode on them and had tied them to a tree awaiting this prophetic moment. Interesting is that Matthew the author of the text, referred to the prophecy of Zechariah saying 'that it might be fulfilled'. Throughout the synoptic gospels we notice that most of the significant manifestations in the life and ministry of Jesus Christ, were a fulfillment of scriptures that had been penned down years before He was born. It is quite interesting that His life fitted a puzzle that was set up to manifest Him. This is an important essence of royalty where we ought to seek God's mind, embrace it and plug ourselves into the divine puzzle. "My frame was not hidden from You, when I was made in secret, and skillfully wrought in the lowest parts of the earth. Your eyes saw my substance, being yet unformed. And in Your book they all were written, the days fashioned for me, when as yet there were none of them" Psalms 139:15&16. Here, the psalmist speaks of how Jesus Christ operated in the revelation of God that symbolized royalty. It is therefore expedient that we seek to know what God has designed for our life of royalty. King Solomon said: "It is the glory of God to conceal a matter, but the glory of kings is to search out a matter" Proverbs 25:2.

Interestingly, our adversary the devil knows so much detail concerning God's covenant with us than we are often aware of. "Moreover, the word of the Lord came to me, saying, "Son of man, take up a lamentation for the king of Tyre, and say to him, 'Thus says the Lord God: "You were the seal of perfection, full of wisdom and perfect in beauty. You were in Eden, the garden of God; every precious stone was your covering: the sardius, topaz, and diamond, beryl, onyx, and jasper, Sapphire, turquoise, and emerald with gold. The workmanship of your timbrels and pipes was prepared for you on the day you were created. "You were the anointed cherub who covers; I established you; you were on the holy mountain of God; you walked back and forth in the midst of fiery stones. You were perfect in your ways from the day you were created, till iniquity was found in you" Ezekiel 28:11-15. Here the prophet Ezekiel uses the king of Tyre as a metaphor for Lucifer while he was an archangel in heaven. God created him with all the precious stones listed in this scripture which signify divine covenants. When Moses was given the assignment of building the tabernacle, we find these same precious stones were positioned in the breastplate of the High Priest. ""You shall make the breastplate of judgment. Artistically woven according to the workmanship of the ephod you shall make it: of gold, blue, purple, and scarlet thread, and fine woven linen, you shall make it. It shall be doubled into a square: a span shall be its length, and a span shall be its width. And you shall put settings of stones in it, four rows of stones: The first row shall be a sardius, a topaz, and an emerald; this shall be the first row; the second row shall be a turquoise, a sapphire, and a diamond; the third row, a jacinth, an agate, and an amethyst; and the fourth row, a beryl, an onyx, and a jasper. They shall be set in gold settings. And the stones shall have the names of the sons of Israel, twelve according to their names, like the engravings of a signet, each one with its own name; they shall be according to the twelve tribes" Exodus 28:15-21. Notice that the breastplate of the High Priest's mantle was decked with the same stones that God decked the devil with. This tells us that the devil is aware of God's covenant with the twelve tribes of Israel.

Fast-forward to what was revealed to John the apostle by our Lord Jesus Christ concerning His bride which is the Church. "Then one of the seven angels who had the seven bowls filled with the seven last plagues came to me and talked with me, saying, "Come, I will show you the bride, the Lamb's wife." And he carried me away in the Spirit to a great and high mountain, and showed me the great city, the holy Jerusalem, descending out of heaven from God, having the glory of God. Her light was like a most precious stone, like a jasper stone, clear as crystal. Also, she had a great and high wall with twelve gates, and twelve angels at the gates, and names written on them, which are the names of the twelve tribes of the children of Israel: three gates on the east, three gates on the north, three gates on the south, and three gates on the west. Now the wall of the city had twelve foundations, and on them were the names of the twelve apostles of the Lamb. And he who talked with me had a gold reed to measure the city, its gates, and its wall. The city is laid out as a square; its length is as great as its breadth. And he measured the city with the reed: twelve thousand furlongs. Its length, breadth, and height are equal. Then he measured its wall: one hundred and forty-four cubits, according to the measure of a man, that is, of an angel. The construction of its wall was of jasper; and the city was pure gold, like clear glass. The foundations of the wall of the city were adorned with all kinds of precious stones: the first foundation was jasper, the second sapphire, the third chalcedony, the fourth emerald, the fifth sardonyx, the sixth sardius, the seventh chrysolite, the eighth beryl, the ninth topaz, the tenth chrysoprase, the eleventh jacinth, and the twelfth amethyst" Revelations 21:9-20.

Notice here that the Church that is the bride of our Lord Jesus Christ, is the holy Jerusalem. This city has twelve gates that are assigned to each of the twelve tribes of Israel. Most importantly, the foundations are twelve and they correspond to the twelve apostles of the Lamb. Each of these foundations is a distinct precious stone which were those by which the devil was decked. Here again we notice that the devil has some knowledge of our covenant provisions with God. The challenge here is that if the devil knows some things about us while most of us know so little about our identity in Christ, then that gives the devil an advantage over us. With his knowledge of our destiny, he orchestrates an unwelcome environment so we don't appreciate what pertains to our divine destiny. This is the reason for which the religious leaders during the ministry of Jesus opposed His ministry and constantly laid traps for Him.

However, Jesus fortified Himself with the disciples whom God had given Him by revelation. Their assertiveness of His identity was a fortress. "When Jesus came into the region of Caesarea Philippi, He asked His disciples, saying, "Who do men say that I, the Son of Man, am?" So they said, "Some say John the Baptist, some Elijah, and others Jeremiah or one of the prophets." He said to them, "But who do you say that I am?" Simon Peter answered and said, "You are the Christ, the Son of the living God." Jesus answered and said to him, "Blessed are you, Simon Bar-Jonah, for flesh and blood has not revealed this to you, but My Father who is in heaven. And I also say to you that you are Peter, and on this rock I will build My church, and the gates of Hades shall not prevail against it. And I will give you the keys of the kingdom of heaven, and whatever you bind on earth will be bound in heaven, and whatever you loose on earth will be loosed in heaven" Matthew 16:13-19. In this dialogue between Jesus and the disciples, He intended to gauge how people perceived His identity. Peter got it right and Jesus acknowledged that it was an attribute of revelation. Furthermore, Jesus said that revelation was key to how the Church would prevail over the kingdom of darkness.

Revelatory Worshipper

As a revelatory worshipper, Judah acknowledges the Sovereignty of God. David is a key figure from the tribe of Judah who exemplifies this blessing in a profound way. He is delegated to take care of the family sheep in the wilderness and survives by trusting God through a lifestyle of worship. This way, he is inspired with many of the prophecies concerning the coming Messiah, Jesus Christ. Through worship David is assigned the duty of changing the atmosphere of King Saul's condition of torment by evil spirits. When he became king of Israel, David instituted a new order of tabernacle worship that included adoration of God with musical instruments alongside the prescribed Mosaic order.

The account of the triumphant entry of Jesus Christ into Jerusalem where his disciples brought Him the donkey with its colt, and they spread their garments on the donkey for Jesus to sit on, triggered a celebration of praise. People cut palm branches and spread on the path where Jesus rode and sang Hosannah! This was a prophetic moment underscoring how Judah was named by his mother Leah, and his father Jacob ratified this by a blessing declaring: "Judah, you are he whom your brothers shall praise..." On this occasion of the triumphant entry, the people started praising God on account of Jesus Christ, thereby fulfilling His prophetic purpose. "They brought the donkey and the colt, laid their clothes on them, and set Him on them. And a very great multitude spread their clothes on the road; others cut down branches from the trees and spread them on the road. Then the multitudes who went before and those who followed cried out, saying: "Hosanna to the Son of David! 'Blessed is He who comes in the name of the

Lord!' Hosanna in the highest!" And when He had come into Jerusalem, all the city was moved, saying, "Who is this?" So the multitudes said, "This is Jesus, the prophet from Nazareth of Galilee." Then Jesus went into the temple of God and drove out all those who bought and sold in the temple and overturned the tables of the money changers and the seats of those who sold doves. And He said to them, "It is written, 'My house shall be called a house of prayer,' but you have made it a 'den of thieves.'" Then the blind and the lame came to Him in the temple, and He healed them. But when the chief priests and scribes saw the wonderful things that He did, and the children crying out in the temple and saying, "Hosanna to the Son of David!" they were indignant and said to Him, "Do You hear what these are saying?" And Jesus said to them, "Yes. Have you never read, 'Out of the mouth of babes and nursing infants You have perfected praise'?" Matthew 21:7-16.

The religious leaders became apprehensive about the praise of the people and requested that Jesus silence the crowd. In response Jesus invoked Psalms 8:2, "Out of the mouth of babes and nursing infants You have ordained praise, because of Your enemies, that You may silence the enemy and the avenger." We get an outstanding insight of the purpose of praise, and that is to silence the enemy. Lucifer the devil was created by God as an embodiment of musical instruments to praise God. "Moreover, the word of the Lord came to me, saying, "Son of man, take up a lamentation for the king of Tyre, and say to him, 'Thus says the Lord God: "You were the seal of perfection, full of wisdom and perfect in beauty. You were in Eden, the garden of God; every precious stone was your covering:

the sardius, topaz, and diamond, beryl, onyx, and jasper, sapphire, turquoise, and emerald with gold. The workmanship of your timbrels and pipes was prepared for you on the day you were created. "You were the anointed cherub who covers; I established you; you were on the holy mountain of God; you walked back and forth in the midst of fiery stones. You were perfect in your ways from the day you were created, till iniquity was found in you" Ezekiel 28:11-15.

Lucifer was given the function to praise God in such a way as no human being could ever mimic. All the instruments of music were inherent in his praise like a well-directed orchestra of music. The splendor of God's glory that manifested with this praise made Lucifer think of himself as deserving of this glory for himself. "How you are fallen from heaven, O Lucifer, son of the morning! How you are cut down to the ground, you who weakened the nations! For you have said in your heart: 'I will ascend into heaven, I will exalt my throne above the stars of God; I will also sit on the mount of the congregation On the farthest sides of the north; I will ascend above the heights of the clouds, I will be like the Most High.' Yet you shall be brought down to Sheol, to the lowest depths of the Pit" Isaiah 14:12-15. It is for this same reason that those who refuse to give God praise, often seek to be acknowledged by people and punish those who fail to do so. Scripture records in the book of Esther of Haman who was offended because Mordecai the Jew did not praise him. Haman got the king to enact a decree to annihilate all jews across the empire because of this. It is obvious that Haman was under the inspiration of the devil for his actions. The devil wishes that no human being should praise God, because our praise delegitimizes him. Whenever we praise God, we are freed from self-will which corrupts us and gives us the devil's resemblance. Our praise takes away any significance the devil claims and so he hates our praise and often inspires people to silence us. "As the fining pot for silver, and the furnace for gold; so is a man to his praise" Proverbs 27:21.

In the same way that fire is the agent that purifies silver and gold, praise purges us of the tendency to think of ourselves being the source of abilities to succeed and prosper in life. Though one cannot compare the momentary feeling of pleasure from a sporting event with God's goodness, it is an interesting observation of how many men who attend sporting events would often sing and display all forms of cheering support for their team, and yet when they attend a Church service, they refuse to acknowledge God with demonstrative praise. "Therefore, by Him let us continually offer the sacrifice of praise to God, that is, the fruit of our lips, giving thanks to His name" Hebrews 13:15. In similar manner as on the triumphant entry, we ought to always acknowledge the victory of Christ our Lord in praise to God. Praise is our victory over the self-aggrandizement nature of the devil. Here, we often tend to bump ourselves to the spotlight where everyone can acknowledge us. It is God who promotes us as a function of His judgment in due time, so we must continue faithfully in our divine assignment without being perturbed by any illegitimate craving.

Revelatory Warrior
As a revelatory warrior, Judah wages war by the leading of the Holy Spirit. Jesus Christ whose biological birth is

from the lineage of Judah is described as a lion. "And I saw in the right hand of Him who sat on the throne a scroll written inside and on the back, sealed with seven seals. Then I saw a strong angel proclaiming with a loud voice, "Who is worthy to open the scroll and to loose its seals?" And no one in heaven or on the earth or under the earth was able to open the scroll, or to look at it. So I wept much, because no one was found worthy to open and read the scroll, or to look at it. But one of the elders said to me, "Do not weep. Behold, the Lion of the tribe of Judah, the Root of David, has prevailed to open the scroll and to loose its seven seals." And I looked, and behold, in the midst of the throne and of the four living creatures, and in the midst of the elders, stood a Lamb as though it had been slain, having seven horns and seven eyes, which are the seven Spirits of God sent out into all the earth. Then He came and took the scroll out of the right hand of Him who sat on the throne" Revelation 5:1-7. In this scenario in heaven, there is a scroll whose contents are sealed. John the apostle wept because no one was found worthy to access the contents of this scroll until one of the elders proclaimed that the lion of the tribe of Judah had prevailed to access the contents. This victory is through submission to the cross as a lamb and the roar of a lion. The lion is a strong warrior yet its secret for victory lies in the inherent dependency on God. "The young lions roar after their prey and seek their food from God" Psalm 104:21. The lion has significant hunting prowess that is notable among animals in the jungle. For this reason, there is a conspiracy by which potential prey stays away from a lion lurking in their vicinity. This makes it difficult for the lion to track prey so the lion roars as a prayer for God to reveal the location of prey. When the lion roars, the animals in its vicinity know not to panic and flee. However, the lion is persistent and intensifies its roar until the earth shakes and the prey in its vicinity panic and flee. In this way, their flight away from the lion gives it a sense of direction. The lion pursues in this direction and spots one of them which it determines as prey. It focuses on this animal and continues in relentless pursuit until the prey is conquered.

This is the essence of warfare that we ought to wage to take what is rightfully due to us. "If a trumpet is blown in a city, will not the people be afraid? If there is calamity in a city, will not the Lord have done it? Surely the Lord God does nothing, Unless He reveals His secret to His servants the prophets. A lion has roared! Who will not fear? The Lord God has spoken! Who can but prophesy? "Proclaim in the palaces at Ashdod, And in the palaces in the land of Egypt, and say: 'Assemble on the mountains of Samaria; See great tumults in her midst, And the oppressed within her. For they do not know to do right,' Says the Lord, 'Who store up violence and robbery in their palaces." Therefore, thus says the Lord God: "An adversary shall be all around the land; He shall sap your strength from you, and your palaces shall be plundered" Amos 3:6-11. When Judah roars, it is the trumpet sound of divine revelation that shakes the earth, triggering a tumult in the demonic realm. All demonic and human entities panic at the roar of the lion, because it is a judgment against their robberies and illegitimate holdings. Creation was subjected to the Adamic curse and so it is possible for the kingdom of darkness to illegally hold on to what is not theirs. "For the earnest expectation of the creation eagerly waits for the revealing of the sons of God. For the creation was subjected to futility, not willingly, but because of Him who subjected it in hope; because the creation itself also will be delivered from the bondage of corruption into the glorious liberty of the children of God. For we know that the whole creation groans and labors with birth pangs together until now. Not only that, but we also who have the firstfruits of the Spirit, even we ourselves groan within ourselves, eagerly waiting for the adoption, the redemption of our body. For we were saved in this hope, but hope that is seen is not hope; for why does one still hope for what he sees? But if we hope for what we do not see, we eagerly wait for it with perseverance. Likewise the Spirit also helps in our weaknesses. For we do not know what we should pray for as we ought, but the Spirit Himself makes intercession for us with groanings which cannot be uttered. Now He who searches the hearts knows what the mind of the Spirit is, because He makes intercession for the saints according to the will of God" Romans 8:19-27. Judah wars with revelation knowledge to release creation that is with oppressors because of the Adamic curse. The Holy Spirit intercedes through the groaning of the believer to release creation from the bondage of the Adamic curse. This groaning is symbolic of the roar of the lion that is inherent in the believer and must be unleashed through intercession. Most times the enemy stimulates distractions to discourage the groanings of the believer. Common distractions include the feeling of an infirmity, opposition of people, or furnishing with a false opportunity that is not related with our divine inheritance. Many believers end up silenced by the distractions orchestrated by the kingdom of darkness and so they never possess their inheritance in Christ.

Satan the head of the kingdom of darkness is a thief whose mission is to steal from people, their legitimate possessions. "The word of the Lord came again to me, saying, "Now, son of man, take up a lamentation for Tyre, and say to Tyre, 'You who are situated at the entrance of the sea, merchant of the peoples on many coastlands, thus says the Lord God: "O Tyre, you have said, 'I am perfect in beauty.' Your borders are in the midst of the seas. Your builders have perfected your beauty. They made all your planks of fir trees from Senir; they took a cedar from Lebanon to make you a mast. Of oaks from Bashan they made your oars; the company of Ashurites have inlaid your planks with ivory from the coasts of Cyprus. Fine embroidered linen from Egypt was what you spread for your sail; Blue and purple from the coasts of Elishah was what covered you" Ezekiel 27:1-7. "The ships of Tarshish were carriers of your merchandise. You were filled and very glorious in the midst of the seas. Your oarsmen brought you into many waters, but the east wind broke you in the midst of the seas" Ezekiel 27:25&26. Satan knows what God has assigned to people as their legitimate inheritance and so he burdens them differently to steer them away. Notice that he tasks every nation on earth with what they are to supply to global commerce. Many third world nations are relegated to producing raw materials for the global supply chain system. This way they earn minimal revenue for their exports and end up importing added-value versions of these products at very high prices. Both the prices of raw materials exported by third world nations and their imports are determined by the economics of the advanced nations, and so poverty continues unabated in third world nations. Another dynamic responsible for so much economic frustration among people today is the advice offered by career counselors to students, who are encouraged to follow the trends of job hiring instead of pursuing their purpose. After training for an industry and gaining experience, assuming the trend changes and an industry is in decline, people lose their jobs and end up with menial jobs for survival.

However, the prophet Ezekiel foretells that Tyre who is a metaphor for Satan, would be broken at sea by an east wind. 'You were filled and very glorious in the midst of the seas. Your oarsmen brought you into many waters, but the east wind broke you in the midst of the sea.' Judah leads the eastern tribes of Israel's harness and so their movement that follows immediately after the tabernacle stimulates the east wind. Obedience to revelation knowledge by Judah triggers the east wind by which the global economic systems inspired by Satan ultimately fails. We all have a measure of Judah in us either as a dominant or recessed potential. Assuming your dominant potential is that of the tribe of Judah, your travail would often result in downloads of deep revelation knowledge that unveils where God has opened doors for His people. However, those of us who have Judah as a recessed potential also receive limited downloads of revelation knowledge to guide our endeavors. God's covenant relationship with the believer has seven seals that can be unlocked by the roar of the lion of the tribe of Judah. This is the travail that unleashes the seven Spirits of God. "There shall come forth a Rod from the stem of Jesse, and a Branch shall grow out of his roots. The Spirit of the Lord shall rest upon Him, the Spirit of wisdom and understanding, the Spirit of counsel and might, the Spirit of knowledge and of the fear of the Lord" Isaiah 11:1&2.

These seven spirits are a working of the Holy Spirit in the believer to unlock the seven seals. Intense prayer causes the Spirit of Knowledge to furnish us with a dream, vision or prophetic word that may be coded. Prayer for insight causes the Spirit of Understanding to decode the revelation. If we continue being prayerful, the Spirit of Wisdom micromanages our role to play for the manifestation of the vision. As we walk in the direction of the Spirit of Wisdom, the enemy notices we are breaking out of his trap of disenfranchisement, so he obstructs us. With increased prayer, the Spirit of the Lord encourages us with divine testimonies. Though the advances of the enemy may not be thwarted immediately, we must not be discouraged but rather continue in the diligence of our divine assignments upholding the Spirit of Reverence. At this point, the Spirit of Counsel inspires us to consult with specific people divinely positioned to help us. Applying such counsel triggers the Spirit of Might by which we overcome the obstacles to moving forward.

It is interesting how the seven spirits work in us to overcome 'self' which is the nature of the devil. Though a spiritually laborious process, dependency on the Holy Spirit unseals revelation hidden from the believer. "…The effective, fervent prayer of a righteous man avails much" James 5:16b. It is for this reason that the believer must develop an intense prayer life and never waver from the course of divine revelation.

Chapter two

The Tribe of

Zebulun

"Then Leah conceived again and bore Jacob a sixth son. And Leah said, "God has endowed me with a good endowment; now my husband will dwell with me, because I have borne him six sons." So she called his name Zebulun" Genesis 30:19&20. The name Zebulun means 'gifted'. It is profound because it predicts the great role that spiritual gifts would play in the New Testament Church. The blessing that Jacob imparts upon Zebulun is equally prophetic of their role in identifying Jesus as the Messiah. "Zebulun shall dwell by the haven of the sea; he shall become a haven for ships, and his border shall adjoin Sidon" Genesis 49:13. Zebulun inherits coastal lands which determines his vocation as a mariner. Today, we have technologically advanced navigation systems that are powered by the Global Positioning System (GPS) software, so it is easier to navigate the oceans. However, in the past mariners depended on the constellations to determine their position at sea. So, it was those who had the gifted ability to understand the constellations that endeavored in this vocation.

It was this gifted ability that enabled Peter, Andrew, James and John who were mariners to quickly recognize Jesus as the Messiah. "And leaving Nazareth, He came and dwelt in Capernaum, which is by the sea, in the regions of Zebulun and Naphtali, that it might be fulfilled which was spoken by Isaiah the prophet, saying: "The land of Zebulun and the land of Naphtali, By the way of the sea, beyond the Jordan, Galilee of the Gentiles: The people who sat in darkness have seen a great light, And upon those who sat in the region and shadow of death Light has dawned." From that time Jesus began to preach and to say, "Repent, for the kingdom of heaven is at hand." And Jesus, walking by the Sea of Galilee, saw two brothers, Simon called Peter, and Andrew his brother, casting a net into the sea; for they were fishermen. Then He said to them, "Follow Me, and I will make you fishers of men." They immediately left their nets and followed Him. Going on from there, He saw two other brothers, James the son of Zebedee, and John his brother, in the boat with Zebedee their father, mending their nets. He called them, and immediately they left the boat and their father, and followed Him?" Matthew 4:13-22.

After the death and resurrection of Jesus, He instructed the disciples to tarry in Jerusalem until they were endued with the power of the Holy Ghost. "When the Day of Pentecost had fully come, they were all with one accord in one place. And suddenly there came a sound from heaven, as of a rushing mighty wind, and it filled the whole house where they were sitting. Then there appeared to them divided tongues, as of fire, and one sat upon each of them. And they were all filled with the Holy Spirit and began to speak with other tongues, as the Spirit gave them utterance. And there were dwelling in Jerusalem Jews, devout men, from every nation under heaven. And when this sound occurred, the multitude came together, and were confused, because everyone heard them speak in his own language. Then they were all amazed and marveled, saying to one another, "Look, are not all these who speak Galileans? And how is it that we hear, each in our own language in which we were born? Parthians and Medes and Elamites, those dwelling in Mesopotamia, Judea and Cappadocia, Pontus and Asia, Phrygia and Pamphylia, Egypt and the parts of Libya adjoining Cyrene, visitors from Rome, both Jews and proselytes, Cretans and Arabs, we hear them speaking in our own tongues the wonderful works of God." So they were all amazed and perplexed, saying to one another, "Whatever could this mean?" Others mocking said, "They are full of new wine." But Peter, standing up with the eleven, raised his voice and said to them, "Men of Judea and all who dwell in Jerusalem, let this be known to you, and heed my words. For these are not drunk, as you suppose, since it is only the third hour of the day. But this is what was spoken by the prophet Joel: 'And it shall come to pass in the last days, says God, That I will pour out of My Spirit on all flesh; Your sons and your daughters shall prophesy, your young men shall see visions, your old men shall dream dreams. And on My menservants and on My maidservants, I will pour out My Spirit in those days; And they shall prophesy.

I will show wonders in heaven above And signs in the earth beneath: Blood and fire and vapor of smoke. The sun shall be turned into darkness, And the moon into blood, Before the coming of the great and awesome day of the Lord. And it shall come to pass That whoever calls on the name of the Lord shall be saved'" Acts 2:1-21. The manifestations that characterized the outpouring of the Holy Spirit on the Day of Pentecost were prophesied by the prophet Joel several years earlier. However, on that day, the Jews who had come to Jerusalem from wherever they were dispersed, supposed that the disciples of Jesus were drunk with alcohol. Peter who was one of the disciples that was first to identify Jesus Christ as the Messiah, rises to the occasion and makes scriptural reference, that Joel prophesied about this occurrence. This became the occasion of the birth of the New Testament Church.

The Apostle Paul elaborates about the spiritual gifts which begun to manifest on the Day of Pentecost in 1 Corinthians 12:1–11, "Now concerning spiritual gifts, brethren, I do not want you to be ignorant: You know that you were Gentiles, carried away to these dumb idols, however you were led. Therefore, I make known to you that no one speaking by the Spirit of God calls Jesus accursed, and no one can say that Jesus is Lord except by the Holy Spirit. There are diversities of gifts, but the same Spirit. There are differences of ministries, but the same Lord. And there are diversities of activities, but it is the same God who works all in all. But the manifestation of the Spirit is given to each one for the profit of all: for to one is given the word of wisdom through the Spirit, to another the word of knowledge through the same Spirit, to another faith by the same Spirit, to another gifts of healings by the same Spirit, to another the working of miracles, to another prophecy, to another discerning of spirits, to another different kinds of tongues, to another the interpretation of tongues. But one and the same Spirit works all these things, distributing to each one individually as He wills." Gordon Lindsey, the revivalist preacher, author, and founder of Christ for the Nations Institute in Dallas, Texas categorized the spiritual gifts as revelatory, power and utterance.

The **revelatory gifts** are, Word of Knowledge, Discerning of Spirits and Word of Wisdom. Word of knowledge is the supernatural ability to know things that have taken place in the past or occur in the present but hidden from our regular senses. Discerning of spirits is the supernatural ability to know which spirits are present in an environment. The word of wisdom is the supernatural ability to know what will happen in the future. The revelatory gifts furnish us with a measure of the omniscience of God.

The **power gifts** are, Gift of Faith, Gift of Healing and Working of Miracles. The gift of faith is the supernatural ability to believe God for great accomplishments. The gift of healing is the supernatural ability to heal the sick. The working of miracles is the supernatural ability to disrupt natural laws and trigger an unusual manifestation. The power gifts furnish us with a measure of the omnipotence of God.

The **utterance gifts** are Tongues, Interpretation of Tongues and Prophecy. Tongues is the supernatural ability to communicate with God in an unknown language. Interpretation of tongues is the supernatural ability to interpret a tongue. Prophecy is the supernatural ability to comfort, edify and exhort. The utterance gifts furnish us with a measure of the omnipresence of God.

Travailing prayer unleashes the manifestation of spiritual gifts. Zebulun travails to unleash the spiritual gifts for outwitting the oppressive demonic schemes of the kingdom of darkness. Usually those whose dominant potential is Zebulun manifest the gifts of the Holy Spirit in a profound way. For those who have this tribe as a recessed potential, the manifestation of the gifts of the Holy Spirit is usually limited.

Harness

Chapter Three

The Tribe of

Issachar

"Now Reuben went in the days of wheat harvest and found mandrakes in the field, and brought them to his mother Leah. Then Rachel said to Leah, "Please give me some of your son's mandrakes." But she said to her, "Is it a small matter that you have taken away my husband? Would you take away my son's mandrakes also?" And Rachel said, "Therefore he will lie with you tonight for your son's mandrakes." When Jacob came out of the field in the evening, Leah went out to meet him and said, "You must come in to me, for I have surely hired you with my son's mandrakes." And he lay with her that night. And God listened to Leah, and she conceived and bore Jacob a fifth son. Leah said, "God has given me my wages, because I have given my maid to my husband." So she called his name Issachar" Genesis 30:14-18. Jacob was married to

Leah and Rachel by a devious scheme of their father. However, Jacob loved Rachel and only furnished Leah with conjugal rights which was scheduled by Rachel. At this point, Leah had stopped conceiving with Jacob and so Rachel did not schedule her to sleep with Jacob. One day, Reuben brought home mandrakes to his mother Leah, and when Rachael requested some of the mandrakes, Leah demanded to be placed on the schedule to sleep with Jacob. Issachar was conceived as a result and named 'there is recompense'.

The blessing Jacob imparts on this tribe reflects the name given to Issachar at birth. "Issachar is a sturdy donkey, resting between two saddle packs. When he sees how good the countryside is and how pleasant the land, he will bend his shoulder to the load and submit himself to hard labor" Genesis 49:14&15 (NLT). Issachar signifies human resources and takes on tasks to earn wages. Later, this lineage of Issachar demonstrates an unusual capability. "Of the sons of Issachar who had understanding of the times, to know what Israel ought to do, their chiefs were two hundred; and all their brethren were at their command" 1 Chronicles 12:32. Think of a manager who diligently schedules tasks for the appropriate times. Issachar is aligned with divine timing through highly exercised senses. Issachar engages divine timing that is the 'Kairos', to determine physical timing which is the 'Chronos'. He is intuitive, instinctive, perceptive and resolute.

Intuition is sourced from the value system of the conscience. A good and pure conscience is the bedrock of a functional intuition. A weak, defiled, and seared

49

conscience results in a dysfunctional intuition. Intuition is the ability to know something immediately, without the need for conscious reasoning. It is one of the ways by which the Holy Spirit communicates to us. Here, we experience a quick knowing of right and wrong, good or bad through contact and without a vivid declaration of the Holy Spirit. People often refer to it as a hunch or use some other words to describe this. An example is a carpenter buying wood in bulk that is classified as first grade by the vendor, but then there is rotten stock hidden in the stack. Intuition furnishes this carpenter with an uncomfortable nudge, so he declines the allotment. This way he is saved from the inconveniences of returning the wood when the rotten stock is uncovered. A scripture instance of intuition is recorded in John 8:3-11, "Then the scribes and Pharisees brought to Him a woman caught in adultery. And when they had set her in the midst, they said to Him, "Teacher, this woman was caught in adultery, in the very act. Now Moses, in the law, commanded us that such should be stoned. But what do You say?" This they said, testing Him, that they might have something of which to accuse Him. But Jesus stooped down and wrote on the ground with His finger, as though He did not hear. So when they continued asking Him, He raised Himself up and said to them, "He who is without sin among you, let him throw a stone at her first." And again He stooped down and wrote on the ground. Then those who heard it, being convicted by their conscience, went out one by one, beginning with the oldest even to the last. And Jesus was left alone, and the woman standing in the midst. When Jesus had raised Himself up and saw no one but the woman, He said to her, "Woman, where are those accusers of yours? Has no one condemned you?" She said, "No one, Lord." And Jesus said to her, "Neither do I condemn you; go and sin no more." Notice that though these religious leaders had brought a legitimate case against the woman caught in adultery, the adjudication of Jesus using the same standard of the law convicted them in their conscience. Without pointing a finger at any of them, these religious leaders intuitively excused themselves. Issachar consciously develops a good and pure conscience to awaken this sense of intuition.

Instinct is spontaneous access to hidden insights of genetic related issues, ancestral potentials, bloodline blessings and curses. The emotion is the seat of our instincts. People often use the term 'gut feeling' for their instinct. Animals do not have a sophisticated mind like humans, however their distinct characteristics such us how they mate, care for their young, hunt for food, adapt to weather changes and so on are a function of their instincts. Instincts convey genetic information of the bloodline. We inherit traits of our ancestors through the bloodline. The apostle Paul mentions in 2 Timothy 1:5 concerning Timothy's unusual faith. "When I call to remembrance the genuine faith that is in you, which dwelt first in your grandmother Lois and your mother Eunice, and I am persuaded is in you also". In any aspect of life where our ancestors upheld divine values, there is a great chance that we may also uphold such values because they often get imprinted in the genetic composition. In the same way that values can turn into bloodline virtues, we all have the tendency to manifest some of the vices of our ancestors that are in our instincts. Stable or unstable emotions define our level of instinctiveness. A stable emotion is a clear conduit for the Holy Spirit to convey divine promptings. Unstable emotions blur such divine nudges. People have often received nudges of advance warning for certain occurrences such as accidents and unexplainable phenomena that are related to judgement or demonic activity. Those who often escape such tragedies understand that the prompts of the instinct are not just weird feelings to be ignored but are legitimate signals of the Holy Spirit.

Perception of the intellect is how the anointing equips us to perform complex tasks. It relies on conscience and emotions as well as available facts to compute solutions. The anointing prompts us when a given method or solution is legitimate or illegitimate. An instance in the scripture was when David was considered a fugitive in Israel and King Saul was seeking to kill him. "Now it happened, when Saul had returned from following the Philistines, that it was told him, saying, "Take note! David is in the Wilderness of En Gedi." Then Saul took three thousand chosen men from all Israel, and went to seek David and his men on the Rocks of the Wild Goats. So he came to the sheepfolds by the road, where there was a cave; and Saul went in to attend to his needs. (David and his men were staying in the recesses of the cave.) Then the men of David said to him, "This is the day of which the Lord said to you, 'Behold, I will deliver your enemy into your hand, that you may do to him as it seems good to you.'" And David arose and secretly cut off a corner of Saul's robe. Now it happened afterward that David's heart troubled him because he had cut Saul's robe. And he said to his men, "The Lord forbid that I should do this thing to my master, the Lord's anointed, to stretch out my hand against him, seeing he is the anointed of the Lord." So

David restrained his servants with these words, and did not allow them to rise against Saul. And Saul got up from the cave and went on his way" 1 Samuel 24:1-7. David's men considered this encounter with King Saul as a divine opportunity to assassinate him and advised David accordingly. However, David was prompted by the anointing inversely because that was not the divinely ordained way.

Resolute of the will is our decision-making prowess. The will is the faculty of the mind for conscious and deliberate action. This is where our actions are initiated so whatever direction our will dictates is where we follow. The will is where we make our determinations after processing our values, sentiments, and facts. "For it is God who works in you both to will and to do for His good pleasure" Philippians 2:13. Ultimately it is the direction of our inclinations that determines what we do. The outcome of our endeavoring in life is often a direct consequence of how we invest ourselves on a consistent basis. If our determinations and what we do begin to flourish, then multiplication or branching out becomes our next inclination. We develop manuals from the processes by which we have experienced results so that others who join us can apply these same processes. If the root inspiration for any of our systemic processes is godly or demonic, then it gets perpetuated from generation to generation.

Using his highly developed spiritual senses, Issachar wages war against **intellectual oppression.** "Then the Pharisees and Sadducees came and testing Him asked that He would show them a sign from heaven. He answered and said to them, "When it is evening you say,

'It will be fair weather, for the sky is red'; and in the morning, 'It will be foul weather today, for the sky is red and threatening.' Hypocrites! You know how to discern the face of the sky, but you cannot discern the signs of the times. A wicked and adulterous generation seeks after a sign, and no sign shall be given to it except the sign of the prophet Jonah." And He left them and departed" Matthew 16:1-4. Our world today is besieged by enterprises that make products based on quack science. The latest scheme of the technology industry is prognostication by Artificial Intelligence. Issachar's burden is to reverse the common trend where our decision making is based on what is known in the human realm. This tribe are all those who are burdened with the essence of knowing the mind of God to determine how to relate to the issues of life. Issachar travails to unleash highly developed spiritual senses for outwitting the intellectual schemes of oppressors.

Issachar understands **manifestations of challenges and opportunities**. "To everything there is a season, A time for every purpose under heaven: A time to be born, And a time to die; A time to plant, And a time to pluck what is planted; A time to kill, And a time to heal; A time to break down, And a time to build up; A time to weep, And a time to laugh; A time to mourn, And a time to dance; A time to cast away stones, And a time to gather stones; A time to embrace, And a time to refrain from embracing; A time to gain, And a time to lose; A time to keep, And a time to throw away; A time to tear, And a time to sew; A time to keep silence, And a time to speak; A time to love, And a time to hate; A time of war, And a time of peace. What profit has the worker from that in which he labors? I have seen the God-given task with which the sons of men are to be occupied. He has made everything beautiful in its time" Ecclesiastes 3:1-11. Some people schedule when they should attain certain ambitious objectives in life. While it may seem expedient to have such a projection, life often throws us a curve ball that tends to derail scheduled objectives. When this happens, we tend to judge ourselves as having failed. Though not everyone feels this way, it is clear from the scriptures that God schedules the occurrences of our existence so that we can align our ways accordingly.

Issachar has an unusual **insight of cycles, patterns and disruptions**. "The words of the Preacher, the son of David, king in Jerusalem. "Vanity of vanities," says the Preacher; "Vanity of vanities, all is vanity." What profit has a man from all his labor in which he toils under the sun? One generation passes away, and another generation comes; But the earth abides forever. The sun also rises, and the sun goes down, and hastens to the place where it arose. The wind goes toward the south and turns around to the north; The wind whirls about continually and comes again on its circuit. All the rivers run into the sea, Yet the sea is not full; To the place from which the rivers come, there they return again. All things are full of labor; Man cannot express it. The eye is not satisfied with seeing, Nor the ear filled with hearing. That which has been is what will be, That which is done is what will be done, And there is nothing new under the sun. Is there anything of which it may be said, "See, this is new"? It has already been in ancient times before us" Ecclesiastes 1:1-10. Nature functions in a way that makes the human mind anticipatory. We expect certain occurrences at certain times and prepare ourselves accordingly. Regardless of how sophisticated these occurrences may manifest, they are fundamentally based on certain premises that are already enshrined in our existence. Those who can unlock these to bear in their work are able to lead the way for others to follow. The latest gadget, fashion and others that become trending is because someone designed by considering cycles, patterns and disruptions. Many good ideas and inventions that did not factor in the time element, often failed only to succeed later at a time of relevance. Relevance is essential because it is the quest to align an endeavor with the times. "But you, beloved, remember the words which were spoken before by the apostles of our Lord Jesus Christ: how they told you that there would be mockers in the last time who would walk according to their own ungodly lusts. These are sensual persons, who cause divisions, not having the Spirit. But you, beloved, building yourselves up on your most holy faith, praying in the Holy Spirit" Jude 1:17-20. Prayer is the key that unlocks the spiritual senses of Issachar. This is not casual prayer, rather it is an intense and persistent prayer lifestyle.

PART TWO:

Southern Tribes

ADMINISTRATIVE PROGRESS

The southern tribes were the second group of tribes that followed the ark of the covenant in their movement from Egypt towards the Promised Land. These three southern tribes were Reuben, Simeon and Gad. The tribe of Reuben was the head of this group of tribes and their ensign was a man. When new territory is secured by the eastern tribes, the next objective is to establish an administrative framework. In the same way a government is set up to consist of an emergency medical unit, administration and security force, the southern tribes established this framework for order.

The dominant potential of these tribes is compassion, which is the core attribute of our humanity. Our Lord Jesus Christ demonstrated compassion as the womb from which His miracles were birthed. Jesus manifested the compassion of Reuben, "And when Jesus went out He saw a great multitude; and He was moved with compassion for them, and healed their sick" Matthew 14:14. Jesus manifested the compassion of Simeon, "But when He saw the multitudes, He was moved with compassion for them, because they were weary and scattered, like sheep having no shepherd" Matthew 9:36. "Now Jesus called His disciples to Himself and said, "I have compassion on the multitude, because they have now continued with Me three days and have nothing to eat. And I do not want to send them away hungry, lest they faint on the way" Matthew 15:32. Jesus manifested the compassion of Gad, "How God anointed Jesus of Nazareth with the Holy Spirit and with power, who went about doing good and healing all who were oppressed by the devil, for God was with Him" Acts 10:38.

Chapter Four

The Tribe of

Reuben

"And when the Lord saw that Leah was hated, he opened her womb: but Rachel was barren. And Leah conceived, and bare a son, and she called his name Reuben: for she said, Surely the Lord hath looked upon my affliction; now therefore my husband will love me" Genesis 29:31&32. Jacob was in love with Rachael and served her father Laban for seven years as the agreed dowry for marriage. However, when Jacob expected to be given Rachael, Laban substituted her with Leah with the excuse that their culture did not allow for the younger to be given off in marriage before the elder. Laban therefore required Jacob to serve for an additional seven years to complete the dowry for his two daughters. Though Jacob served for fourteen years, and married both daughters of Laban, he was not affectionate towards Leah. God saw that Leah was not loved by Jacob and compensated her with the fruit of the womb, while Rachael was restrained from childbirth. Leah named her firstborn son Reuben, after her neglect from Jacob which had degenerated into an affliction.

Prior to his death, Jacob summoned his sons to impart blessings upon them. This was what he said concerning Reuben, "Reuben, you are my firstborn, My might and the beginning of my strength, The excellency of dignity and the excellency of power. Unstable as water, you shall not excel, because you went up to your father's bed; Then you defiled it, He went up to my couch" Genesis 49:3&4. The name given to Reuben tremendously impacted his lifestyle and he caused his father pain. As a result, Jacob did not impart the blessing of the firstborn on Reuben. Usually, the firstborn is the key heir and inherits a double portion of the estate. Furthermore, the descendants of Reuben noticeably suffered from the plague of infirmities that resulted in premature death. Moses interceded for the Reubenites and turned their affliction into a blessing. "Let Reuben live and not die; and let not his men be few" Deuteronomy 33:6. This tribe became the health and medical industry of Israel. "And this land, which we possessed at that time, from Aroer, which is by the river Arnon, and half mount Gilead, and the cities thereof, gave I unto the Reubenites and to the Gadites" Deuteronomy 3:12. The Reubenites inherited portions of mount Gilead where the prophet Jeremiah acknowledges as the source of medicines. "Is there no balm in Gilead; is there no physician there? why then is not the health of the daughter of my people recovered?" Jeremiah 8:22. We can trace the medical potential of Reuben to how he found mandrakes and brought them home. "Now Reuben went in the days of wheat harvest and found mandrakes in the field, and brought them to his mother Leah. Then Rachel said to Leah, "Please give me some of your son's mandrakes" Genesis 30:14. It is significant that at a time of wheat harvest when everyone brought in the wheat, Reuben brought home mandrakes. According to the online dictionary Wikipedia, "The mandrake root is hallucinogenic and narcotic. In sufficient quantities, it induces a state of unconsciousness and was used as an anesthetic for surgery in ancient times. In the past, juice from the finely grated root was applied externally to relieve rheumatic pains. It was used internally to treat melancholy, convulsions, and mania. Reuben's instinctiveness drew him to bring home the mandrakes.

Someone asked Jesus Christ what would grant his access to eternal life. "He said to him, "What is written in the law? What is your reading of it?" So he answered and said, "'You shall love the Lord your God with all your heart, with all your soul, with all your strength, and with all your mind,' and 'your neighbor as yourself.' And He said to him, "You have answered rightly; do this and you will live." But he, wanting to justify himself, said to Jesus, "And who is my neighbor?" Then Jesus answered and said: "A certain man went down from Jerusalem to Jericho, and fell among thieves, who stripped him of his clothing, wounded him, and departed, leaving him half dead. Now by chance a certain priest came down that road. And when he saw him, he passed by on the other side. Likewise a Levite, when he arrived at the place, came and looked, and passed by on the other side. But a certain Samaritan, as he journeyed, came where he was. And when he saw him, he had compassion. So he went to him and bandaged his wounds, pouring on oil and wine; and he set him on his own animal, brought him to an inn, and took care of him. On the next day, when he departed, he took out two denarii, gave them to the innkeeper, and said to him, 'Take care of him; and whatever more you spend, when I come again, I will repay you.' So which of these three do you think was neighbor to him who fell among the thieves?" And he said, "He who showed mercy on him." Then Jesus said to him, "Go and do likewise" Luke 10:26-37. Notice how the Levite and Priest walked by this victim and did not stop to take care of him. The Samaritan arrived where this victim lay down wounded and was burdened to attend to this situation. He dressed the wounds and administers wine and oil as well as paid for his care at the inn. This Samaritan inherently demonstrated the compassion of Christ by sanctifying, redeeming, anointing and justifying the wounded person. (1 Corinthians 1:30)

Chapter Five

The Tribe of

Simeon

"Then she conceived again and bore a son, and said, "Because the Lord has heard that I am unloved, He has therefore given me this son also." And she called his name Simeon" Genesis 29:33. Leah was not consoled by her blessings that fostered her childbearing and was more concerned with her need for Jacob's endearment. She named her second son Simeon, which means 'unloved'. Leah perpetuated her emotional disposition in how she named Simeon, and it impacted his character in a negative way. Like Reuben, Simeon did not receive a blessing from Jacob. "Simeon and Levi are brothers; Instruments of cruelty are in their dwelling place. Let not my soul enter their council; Let not my honor be united to their assembly; For in their anger they slew a man, And in their self-will they hamstrung an ox. Cursed be their anger, for it is fierce; And their wrath, for it is cruel! I will divide them in Jacob And scatter them in Israel" Genesis 49:5-7.

An occurrence that highlights Simeon's disposition of hatred is when Dinah his sister was raped by Shechem. "And when Shechem the son of Hamor the Hivite, prince of the country, saw her, he took her and lay with her, and violated her. His soul was strongly attracted to Dinah the daughter of Jacob, and he loved the young woman and spoke kindly to the young woman. So Shechem spoke to his father Hamor, saying, "Get me this young woman as a wife." And Jacob heard that he had defiled Dinah his daughter. Now his sons were with his livestock in the field; so Jacob held his peace until they came. Then Hamor the father of Shechem went out to Jacob to speak with him. And the sons of Jacob came in from the field when they heard it; and the men were grieved and very angry, because he had done a disgraceful thing in Israel by lying with Jacob's daughter, a thing which ought not to be done. But Hamor spoke with them, saying, "The soul of my son Shechem longs for your daughter. Please give her to him as a wife. And make marriages with us; give your daughters to us, and take our daughters to yourselves. So you shall dwell with us, and the land shall be before you. Dwell and trade in it, and acquire possessions for yourselves in it." Then Shechem said to her father and her brothers, "Let me find favor in your eyes, and whatever you say to me I will give. Ask me ever so much dowry and gift, and I will give according to what you say to me; but give me the young woman as a wife." But the sons of Jacob answered Shechem and Hamor his father, and spoke deceitfully, because he had defiled Dinah their sister. And they said to them, "We cannot do this thing, to give our sister to one who is uncircumcised, for that would be a reproach to us. But on this condition we will consent to you: If you will become as we are, if every male of you is circumcised, then we will give our daughters to you, and we will take your daughters to us; and we will dwell with you, and we will become one people. But if you will not heed us and be circumcised, then we will take our daughter and be gone." And their words pleased Hamor and Shechem, Hamor's son. So the young man did not delay to do the thing, because he delighted in Jacob's daughter. He was more honorable than all the household of his father. And Hamor and Shechem his son came to the gate of their city, and spoke with the men of their city, saying: "These men are at peace with us. Therefore let them dwell in the land and trade in it. For indeed the land is large enough for them. Let us take their daughters to us as wives, and let us give them our daughters. Only on this condition will the men consent to dwell with us, to be one people: if every male among us is circumcised as they are circumcised. Will not their livestock, their property, and every animal of theirs be ours? Only let us consent to them, and they will dwell with us." And all who went out of the gate of his city heeded Hamor and Shechem his son; every male was circumcised, all who went out of the gate of his city. Now it came to pass on the third day, when they were in pain, that two of the sons of Jacob, Simeon and Levi, Dinah's brothers, each took his sword and came boldly upon the city and killed all the males. And they killed Hamor and Shechem his son with the edge of the sword, and took Dinah from Shechem's house, and went out. The sons of Jacob came upon the slain, and plundered the city, because their sister had been defiled. They took their sheep, their oxen, and their donkeys, what was in the city and what was in the field, and all their wealth. All their little ones and their wives they took captive; and they plundered even all that was in the houses. Then Jacob said to Simeon and Levi, "You have troubled me by making me obnoxious among the inhabitants of the land, among the Canaanites and the Perizzites; and since I am few in number, they will gather themselves together against me and kill me. I shall be destroyed, my household and I." But they said, "Should he treat our sister like a harlot?" Genesis 34:2-31.

Jacob did not bless Simeon, and this manifested as a zero allotment for Simeon when the Promised Land was being allocated by means of casting lots. Simeon had no inheritance! However, Judah his brother comes to the rescue. "Out of the portion of the children of Judah was the inheritance of the children of Simeon: for the part of the children of Judah was too much for them: therefore the children of Simeon had their inheritance within the inheritance of them" Joshua 19:9. Judah made a deal with Simeon where they partnered to conquer their inheritance. "And Judah said unto Simeon his brother, Come up with me into my lot, that we may fight against the Canaanites; and I likewise will go with thee into thy lot. So Simeon went with him" Judges 1:1-3. Though Judah is king, he needs an administrator to administer the affairs of the kingdom. The core potential in Simeon happens to be the opposite of how he was named. Simeon's potential is an administrator of love. There are three Greek words that are all translated as love in the New Testament. Phileo is the love between friends. Eros is the love between husband and wife. Agape is God's kind of love. "Love suffers long and is kind; love does not envy; love does not parade itself, is not puffed up; does not behave rudely, does not seek its own, is not provoked, thinks no evil; does not rejoice in iniquity, but rejoices in the truth; bears all things, believes all things, hopes all things, endures all things. Love never fails" 1 Corinthians 13:4-8. Developing God's kind of love is a very long maturing process which explains the timeframe at which Simeon appreciates partnering with Judah. "By this we know love, because He laid down His life for us. And we also ought to lay down our lives for the brethren. But whoever has this world's goods, and sees his brother in need, and shuts up his heart from him, how does the love of God abide in him?" 1 John 3:16&17. Simeon demonstrates God's love from the womb of compassion.

Jesus Christ demonstrated this potential of Simeon to manifest the miraculous providence of God. "And Jesus, when He came out, saw a great multitude and was moved with compassion for them, because they were like sheep not having a shepherd. So He began to teach them many things. When the day was now far spent, His disciples came to Him and said, "This is a deserted place, and already the hour is late. Send them away, that they may go into the surrounding country and villages and buy themselves bread; for they have nothing to eat." But He answered and said to them, "You give them something to eat." And they said to Him, "Shall we go and buy two hundred denarii worth of bread and give them something to eat?" But He said to them, "How many loaves do you have? Go and see." And when they found out they said, "Five, and two fish." Then He commanded them to make them all sit down in groups on the green grass. So they sat down in ranks, in hundreds and in fifties. And when He had taken the five loaves and the two fish, He looked up to heaven, blessed and broke the loaves, and gave them to His disciples to set before them; and the two fish He divided among them all. So they all ate and were filled. And they took up twelve baskets full of fragments and of the fish. Now those who had eaten the loaves were about five thousand men" Mark 6:34-44.

This is a scenario where Jesus had been ministering to a crowd numbering thousands of people. At some point, the disciples suggested that the crowd be dismissed so everyone could go and fend for themselves. Out of compassion for the people, Jesus instructs the disciples to carry out a financial and logistical impossibility. The amount 'two hundred denarii' suggests the amount of money in their treasury that could not procure the amount of bread to feed this crowd. Furthermore, the bakeries would have required advance notice to prepare the quantity of bread required to feed such a crowd. However out of the womb of compassion springs forth supernatural miracles, so Jesus provided step-by-step guidance for such a manifestation. He instructed the disciples to find out if there was a token of food with anyone in the crowd. After stocktaking the disciples came back with an answer of five loaves and two fishes. This was the food in the lunch pack of a little boy. Jesus instructed that the crowd be organized into groups. He lifted the five loaves and two fishes, gave thanks and broke the break among the disciples who distributed to the crowds according to the order in which they had been arranged. Everyone was fed with this divine providence until they were full, and the leftovers were twelve backets full. From the womb of compassion there was a supernatural manifestation of

73

such a phenomenal miracle that is a core potential of Simeon.

Chapter Six

The Tribe of

Gad

"When Leah saw that she had stopped bearing, she took Zilpah her maid and gave her to Jacob as wife. And Leah's maid Zilpah bore Jacob a son. Then Leah said, "A troop comes!" so she called his name Gad" Genesis 30:9-11. Zilpah, the maid of Leah conceived a son and he was named Gad. Leah took consolation in the several sons she had provided Jacob and designated this child as an army. At the time when he is blessing his sons, Jacob ratifies the name Leah gave Gad as his blessing. "Gad, a troop shall tramp upon him, but he shall triumph at last" Genesis 49:19. Gad overcomes mediocrity, failure and defeat to become victorious.

Moses imparted a blessing on this tribe, "And of Gad he said: "Blessed is he who enlarges Gad; He dwells as a lion and tears the arm and the crown of his head. He provided the first part for himself, because a lawgiver's portion was reserved there. He came with the heads of the people; he administered the justice of the Lord, and His judgments with Israel" Deuteronomy 33:20&21. Gad is a soldier who secures the territorial integrity of a nation or a cop who keeps the peace of the community. For this reason, he is trained as a skillful warrior and armed to accomplish the mission. "Some Gadites joined David at the stronghold in the wilderness, mighty men of valor, men trained for battle, who could handle shield and spear, whose faces were like the faces of lions and were as swift as gazelles on the mountains" 1 Chronicles 12:8. The Gadites had inherent capabilities to handle insurrections as well as whatever disrupts the peace and tranquility of a space.

Gad enshrines the victory of the believer over the schemes of darkness. "For whatever is born of God overcomes the world. And this is the victory that has overcome the world, our faith. Who is he who overcomes the world, but he who believes that Jesus is the Son of God?" 1 John 5:4&5. The key here is faith in Jesus Christ our Lord. Faith is how we overcome the forces of darkness. Basic faith and rich faith are two kinds of faith that the scripture teaches.

Basic faith releases our commonwealth blessings in an instant way. "Therefore remember that you, once Gentiles in the flesh, who are called Uncircumcision by what is called the Circumcision made in the flesh by hands, that at that time you were without Christ, being aliens from the commonwealth of Israel and strangers from the covenants of promise, having no hope and without God in the world. But now in Christ Jesus you who once were far off have been brought near by the blood of Christ" Ephesians 2:11-13. Our salvation in Christ makes us a part of spiritual Israel and grants us access to the covenant blessings promised to Israel. Through faith in our Lord Jesus Christ, we can experience various blessings associated with redemption. "Christ has redeemed us from the curse of the law, having become a curse for us (for it is written, "Cursed is everyone who hangs on a tree"), that the blessing of Abraham might come upon the Gentiles in Christ Jesus, that we might receive the promise of the Spirit through faith" Galatians 3:13&14. "But He was wounded for our transgressions, He was bruised for our iniquities; the chastisement for our peace was upon Him, and by His stripes we are healed" Isaiah 53:5. "For you know the grace of our Lord Jesus Christ, that though He was rich, yet for your sakes He became poor, that you through His poverty might become rich" 2 Corinthians 8:9. These blessings associated with redemption can be accessed instantly by the believer's faith. However, not all our life expectations are designed to be released by basic faith.

Rich faith is how we experience blessings associated with our divine destiny. It involves all the unique experiences that mature us for the promises of God. There is no quick fix as to how any believer is prepared to function in their purpose to arrive at their destiny. Any attempt by the believer to bump themselves to manifest blessings associated with destiny prematurely, results in evil schemes. Believers who become weary of the divine process resort to all sorts of manipulation and corrupt practices to achieve their goals. Rich faith is a process furnished by God's grace until we experience the divine promise, "Therefore, having been justified by faith, we have peace with God through our Lord Jesus Christ, through whom also we have access by faith into this grace in which we stand, and rejoice in hope of the glory of God. And not only that, but we also glory in tribulations, knowing that tribulation produces perseverance; and perseverance, character; and character, hope. Now hope does not disappoint, because the love of God has been poured out in our hearts by the Holy Spirit who was given to us" Romans 5:1-5. Notice the process begins with faith in God's Word that promises us the manifestation of His glory. We can continue under the auspices of grace to endure tribulations that produce in us perseverance. Perseverance molds our godly character which translates into hope that never disappoints.

Gad is the tribe that keeps us in check where there is a proclivity to become reckless, ignoring our true path to prosperity in Christ.

Harness

PART THREE:

Western Tribes

EXCELLENCE PROGRESS

The western tribes were the third group of tribes that followed the ark of the covenant in their movement from Egypt towards the Promised Land. These three western tribes were Ephraim, Manasseh and Benjamin. The tribe of Ephraim was the head of this group of tribes, and their ensign was an ox.

The ox is a symbol of humility that fostered excellence progress. Ephraim represents the diligence of Joseph who submitted to the heritage training of Jacob. Manasseh represents the endurance of Joseph, and Benjamin depicts the essence of initiative. Joseph's name meant 'addition to fruitfulness'. "Then God remembered Rachel, and God listened to her and opened her womb. And she conceived and bore a son, and said, "God has taken away my reproach." So she called his name Joseph, and said, "The Lord shall add to me another son" Genesis 30:22-24. Together these three tribes are the bedrock of Israel's productivity. At some point during the era of the kings of Israel, God was appalled by the attitude of his people and compared them to an ox. "Hear, O heavens, and give ear, O earth! For the Lord has spoken: "I have nourished and brought up children, and they have rebelled against Me; The ox knows its owner and the donkey its master's crib; but Israel does not know, My people do not consider" Isaiah 1:2&3. Though the ox and donkey were beasts of burden they acknowledged their human owners, while Israel was living in abject rebellion toward God. God's dealings with Ephraim, Manasseh and Benjamin signify how we mature through humility. "Wherefore lay apart all filthiness and superfluity of naughtiness, and receive with meekness the engrafted word, which is able to save your souls" James 1:21.

Humility is the character that accepts God's dealings without disputing or resisting. Often the process of humility takes us in a path that is inconvenient and shrouded with trials, but then this is how Jesus Christ secured a name above all names. "Let this mind be in you which was also in Christ Jesus, who, being in the form of God, did not consider it robbery to be equal with God, but made Himself of no reputation, taking the form of a bondservant, and coming in the likeness of men. And being found in appearance as a man, He humbled Himself and became obedient to the point of death, even the death of the cross. Therefore God also has highly exalted Him and given Him the name which is above every name, that at the name of Jesus every knee should bow, of those in heaven, and of those on earth, and of those under the earth, and that every tongue should confess that Jesus Christ is Lord, to the glory of God the Father" Philippians

2:5-11. Joseph the patriarch developed the character of humility through the trials that he went through. He ended up as the Prime Minister of Egypt and administered their economy using divine principles. While the world has its standards of excellence based on their ungodly premises, our standard of excellence is predicated upon divine premises. Our principles, purposes, plans and pursuits are totally different to those of the world, so our competence process is distinct.

Chapter Seven

The Tribe of

Ephraim

"And Joseph took them both, Ephraim with his right hand toward Israel's left hand, and Manasseh with his left hand toward Israel's right hand, and brought them near him. Then Israel stretched out his right hand and laid it on Ephraim's head, who was the younger, and his left hand on Manasseh's head, guiding his hands knowingly, for Manasseh was the firstborn. And he blessed Joseph, and said: "God, before whom my fathers Abraham and Isaac walked, The God who has fed me all my life long to this day, The Angel who has redeemed me from all evil, bless the lads; Let my name be named upon them, And the name of my fathers Abraham and Isaac; And let them grow into a multitude in the midst of the earth." Now when Joseph saw that his father laid his right hand on the head of Ephraim, it displeased him; so he took hold of his

86

father's hand to remove it from Ephraim's head to Manasseh's head. And Joseph said to his father, "Not so, my father, for this one is the firstborn; put your right hand on his head." But his father refused and said, "I know, my son, I know. He also shall become a people, and he also shall be great; but truly his younger brother shall be greater than he, and his descendants shall become a multitude of nations" Genesis 48:13-19.

God blessed Rachael after she had endured a period of barrenness, and she conceived Joseph. Joseph had two sons, namely Ephraim and Manasseh, to whom Jacob imparted the blessings that were due to Reuben, so they are counted as two tribes. Ephraim was Joseph's second born. "And the name of the second he called Ephraim: "For God has caused me to be fruitful in the land of my affliction" Genesis 41:52. Ephraim means 'fruitful', so he inherited part of the blessings Jacob imparted upon Joseph. "Joseph is a fruitful bough, a fruitful bough by a well; his branches run over the wall. The archers have bitterly grieved him, shot at him and hated him. But his bow remained in strength, and the arms of his hands were made strong by the hands of the Mighty God of Jacob (From there is the Shepherd, the Stone of Israel), by the God of your father who will help you, and by the Almighty who will bless you with blessings of heaven above, blessings of the deep that lies beneath, blessings of the breasts and of the womb. The blessings of your father have excelled the blessings of my ancestors, up to the utmost bound of the everlasting hills. They shall be on the head of Joseph, and on the crown of the head of him who was separate from his brothers" Genesis 49:22-26.

Among the sons of Jacob, it was Joseph who paid attention to the family legacy to become diligent. His father made him a coat of many colors to reflect all the areas where he excelled. One of the prominent instances in the life of Jacob that manifested the blessing of fruitfulness, is while he was working for his uncle Laban. "Now Jacob heard the words of Laban's sons, saying, "Jacob has taken away all that was our father's, and from what was our father's he has acquired all this wealth." And Jacob saw the countenance of Laban, and indeed it was not favorable toward him as before. Then the Lord said to Jacob, "Return to the land of your fathers and to your family, and I will be with you." So Jacob sent and called Rachel and Leah to the field, to his flock, and said to them, "I see your father's countenance, that it is not favorable toward me as before; but the God of my father has been with me. And you know that with all my might I have served your father. Yet your father has deceived me and changed my wages ten times, but God did not allow him to hurt me. If he said thus: 'The speckled shall be your wages,' then all the flocks bore speckled. And if he said thus: 'The streaked shall be your wages,' then all the flocks bore streaked. So God has taken away the livestock of your father and given them to me. "And it happened, at the time when the flocks conceived, that I lifted my eyes and saw in a dream, and behold, the rams which leaped upon the flocks were streaked, speckled, and gray-spotted. Then the Angel of God spoke to me in a dream, saying, 'Jacob.' And I said, 'Here I am.' And He said, 'Lift your eyes now and see, all the rams which leap on the flocks are streaked, speckled, and gray-spotted; for I have seen all that Laban is doing to you. I am the God of Bethel, where you anointed the pillar and where you made a vow

to Me. Now arise, get out of this land, and return to the
land of your family'" Genesis 31:1-13. Joseph learned from
Jacob how to be successful and employed this skill as a
slave in Potiphar's house. Ephraim is imparted from this
ancestral heritage to become fruitful.

Joshua from the tribe of Ephraim was chosen to
understudy Moses. "Then the Lord said to Moses, "Come
up to Me on the mountain and be there; and I will give you
tablets of stone, and the law and commandments which I
have written, that you may teach them" So Moses arose
with his assistant Joshua, and Moses went up to the
mountain of God" Exodus 24:12&13. Joshua had
submitted wholeheartedly to the mentoring of Moses. He
served Moses and was present when the Ten
Commandments were delivered to Moses on the mount.
When the tabernacle was erected, after fellowshipping
with God, Moses would usually leave Joshua to tarry in
the presence of the Lord while he went home to be with
his family. This way, Joshua experienced the way by
which Moses encountered God. Prior to the death of
Moses, God instructed him to anoint Joshua as leader of
Israel.

Joshua led the Israelites to possess the Promised Land
and shared it among the tribes. Through the guidance of
Joshua, the tribe of Ephraim became immediately
prosperous. They submitted to divine nurturing and so
were taught by God. "Whom will he teach knowledge?
And whom will he make to understand the message?
Those just weaned from milk? Those just drawn from the
breasts? For precept must be upon precept, precept upon
precept, line upon line, line upon line, here a little, there a

little" Isaiah 28:9&10. Several years after they occupied the Promised Land, the prophet Isaiah spoke of the ancestral heritage by which the tribe of Ephraim became prosperous. "Give ear and hear my voice, listen and hear my speech. Does the plowman keep plowing all day to sow? Does he keep turning his soil and breaking the clods? When he has leveled its surface, does he not sow the black cummin and scatter the cummin, plant the wheat in rows, the barley in the appointed place, and the spelt in its place? For He instructs him in right judgment, his God teaches him. For the black cummin is not threshed with a threshing sledge, nor is a cartwheel rolled over the cummin; but the black cummin is beaten out with a stick, and the cummin with a rod. Bread flour must be ground; therefore he does not thresh it forever, break it with his cartwheel, or crush it with his horsemen. This also comes from the Lord of hosts, Who is wonderful in counsel and excellent in guidance" Isaiah 28:23-29. Through the diligence of instruction, Ephraim develops excellence in cultivating seeds to become fruitful. This way they prospered in the vocation of agriculture.

The diligence of Ephraim's submission to divine nurturing was the same process that prepared Timothy the protégé of the Apostle Paul for ministry. "But you have carefully followed my doctrine, manner of life, purpose, faith, longsuffering, love, perseverance, persecutions, afflictions, which happened to me at Antioch, at Iconium, at Lystra, what persecutions I endured. And out of them all the Lord delivered me. Yes, and all who desire to live godly in Christ Jesus will suffer persecution. But evil men and impostors will grow worse, deceiving and being deceived. But you must continue in the things which you have learned and been assured of, knowing from whom you have learned them, and that from childhood you have known the Holy Scriptures, which are able to make you wise for salvation through faith which is in Christ Jesus. All Scripture is given by inspiration of God, and is profitable for doctrine, for reproof, for correction, for instruction in righteousness, that the man of God may be complete, thoroughly equipped for every good work" 2 Timothy 3:10-17. The apostle Paul reminds his protégé Timothy of his faith, doctrine, purpose, manner of life as well as the experiences he suffered for being a witness of Christ. He encourages Timothy to model this same mentorship with those under his leadership.

Instruction in righteousness – This is where a protégé is taught basic truths of scripture. A protégé is assigned to learn the various books, principles and characters of the scriptures. "Therefore, laying aside all malice, all deceit, hypocrisy, envy, and all evil speaking, as newborn babes, desire the pure milk of the word, that you may grow thereby" 1 Peter 2:12.

Doctrine – A doctrine is a spiritual topic that entails an assembly of scripture instances that all projects a truth. "Therefore, leaving the discussion of the elementary principles of Christ, let us go on to perfection, not laying again the foundation of repentance from dead works and of faith toward God, of the doctrine of baptisms, of laying on of hands, of resurrection of the dead, and of eternal judgment. And this we will do if God permits" Hebrews 6:1-3. Here, we see a list of doctrines which are among several others that provide insights into the various spiritual disciplines.

Correction – A protégé who violates scriptures they have been taught must be admonished with reference to the scriptures. Assuming they did not understand how to apply this premise of the scripture, it gives them an opportunity to realign themselves.

Reproof – Assuming a protégé who has been previously corrected over a fault repeatedly violates this premise of scripture, there would be need to apply a measure of discipline. Such discipline serves as a reminder of the consequences of violating this scripture premise.

These are the four processes that furnish us to be equipped for every good work. Spiritual mentoring is somewhat different from secular mentoring. "So Elihu, the son of Barachel the Buzite, answered and said: "I am young in years, and you are very old; Therefore I was afraid, and dared not declare my opinion to you. I said, 'age should speak, and multitude of years should teach wisdom.' But there is a spirit in man, and the breath of the Almighty gives him understanding" Job 32:6-8. When Job suffered from the trials he encountered, three of his friends gave lengthy discourses to fault Job for his situation. Elihu, who was a younger friend, noticed that their criticism of Job was baseless. However, because they were elderly, which was equated with being intellectual, he allowed them to be first in rendering their opinion of Job's situation. Elihu then makes a profound assertion of truth. "But there is a spirit in man, and the breath of the Almighty gives him understanding." Spiritual truths are not learned in the way secular truths are passed on to others. They are given by divine inspiration and their insights streamed by divine transmission. In John 6:63 Jesus said, "It is the Spirit who gives life; the flesh profits nothing. The words that I speak to you are spirit, and they are life." Ephraim acquired the skill to be fruitful by learning the heritage passed down from his ancestor Abraham. He symbolizes how God's word tutors us to be competent for any vocation, assignment or industry where we are given the opportunity.

Chapter Eight

The Tribe of

Manasseh

"And Joseph took them both, Ephraim with his right hand toward Israel's left hand, and Manasseh with his left hand toward Israel's right hand, and brought them near him. Then Israel stretched out his right hand and laid it on Ephraim's head, who was the younger, and his left hand on Manasseh's head, guiding his hands knowingly, for Manasseh was the firstborn. And he blessed Joseph, and said: "God, before whom my fathers Abraham and Isaac walked, the God who has fed me all my life long to this day, The Angel who has redeemed me from all evil, bless the lads; let my name be named upon them, and the name of my fathers Abraham and Isaac; and let them grow into a multitude in the midst of the earth." Now when Joseph saw that his father laid his right hand on the head of Ephraim, it displeased him; so he took hold of his father's hand to remove it from Ephraim's head to Manasseh's head. And Joseph said to his father, "Not so, my father, for this one is the firstborn; put your right hand on his head." But his father refused and said, "I know, my son, I know. He also shall become a people, and he also shall be great; but truly his younger brother shall be greater than he, and his descendants shall become a multitude of nations" Genesis 48:13-19.

Manasseh is the firstborn of Joseph and together with his brother Ephraim, they inherited the blessings of the grandfather Jacob that was due to their father Joseph. "And to Joseph were born two sons before the years of famine came, whom Asenath, the daughter of Poti-Pherah priest of On, bore to him. Joseph called the name of the firstborn Manasseh, "For God has made me forget all my toil and all my father's house" Genesis 41:50&51. Manasseh is named after the suffering Joseph endured until the promise of God was manifested. "He remembers His covenant forever, The word which He commanded, for a thousand generations, the covenant which He made with Abraham, and His oath to Isaac, and confirmed it to Jacob for a statute, to Israel as an everlasting covenant, saying, "To you I will give the land of Canaan as the allotment of your inheritance," when they were few in number, indeed very few, and strangers in it. When they went from one nation to another, from one kingdom to another people, He permitted no one to do them wrong; yes, He rebuked kings for their sakes, saying, "Do not touch My anointed ones, and do My prophets no harm." Moreover He called for a famine in the land; He destroyed all the provision of bread. He sent a man before them, Joseph, who was sold as a slave. They hurt his feet with fetters, he was laid in irons. Until the time that his word came to pass, the word of the Lord tested him. The king sent and released him, the ruler of the people let him go free. He made him lord of his house, and ruler of all his possessions, to bind his princes at his pleasure, and teach his elders wisdom" Psalm 105:8-22. God entered into a covenant with Abraham the great ancestor of Joseph, and this entailed Abraham's descendants going into Egypt for four hundred years. God chose Joseph to lead the way into Egypt. The process of suffering was how he was transformed to play the role of Prime Minister of Egypt. By his given name, Manasseh is tested through suffering to have enduring life, wealth and fruitfulness.

Enduring Life is depicted as silver in the scriptures. "Take away the dross from silver, and it will go to the silversmith for jewelry" Proverbs 25:4. Purifying silver entails purging the dross. "The words of the Lord are pure words, like silver tried in a furnace of earth, purified seven times" Psalms 12:6. God's word by which we are tried is never an unproven theory. "For You, O God, have tested us; You have refined us as silver is refined. You brought us into the net; You laid affliction on our backs. You have caused men to ride over our heads; we went through fire and through water; but You brought us out to rich fulfillment" Psalms 66:10-12. The challenges that we go through as we apply God's word to our lives, transforms us into pure and enduring silver that is the essence of eternal life.

Enduring Wealth is depicted as gold in the scriptures. "Elect according to the foreknowledge of God the Father, in sanctification of the Spirit, for obedience and sprinkling of the blood of Jesus Christ: grace to you and peace be multiplied. Blessed be the God and Father of our Lord Jesus Christ, who according to His abundant mercy has begotten us again to a living hope through the resurrection of Jesus Christ from the dead, to an inheritance incorruptible and undefiled and that does not fade away, reserved in heaven for you, who are kept by the power of God through faith for salvation ready to be revealed in the last time. In this you greatly rejoice, though now for a little while, if need be, you have been grieved by various trials, that the genuineness of your faith, being much more precious than gold that perishes, though it is tested by fire, may be found to praise, honor, and glory at the revelation of Jesus Christ" 1 Peter 1:2-7. Purifying gold entails removing the impurities by fire. As believers, our wealth is an inheritance from Jesus Christ, that manifests as we endure the trials associated with walking by faith in the vocation to which we are called. "Bondservants, obey in all things your masters according to the flesh, not with eyeservice, as men-pleasers, but in sincerity of heart, fearing God. And whatever you do, do it heartily, as to the Lord and not to men, knowing that from the Lord you will receive the reward of the inheritance; for you serve the Lord Christ. But he who does wrong will be repaid for what he has done, and there is no partiality" Colossians 3:22-25.

Enduring Fruit is the third essence of Manasseh. Jesus told His disciples, "You did not choose Me, but I chose you and appointed you that you should go and bear fruit, and that your fruit should remain, that whatever you ask the Father in My name He may give you" John 15:16. Whatever assignment we are called to fulfil in the Church or for the Body of Christ, our impact must never be wishy washy. The impact of our work must transcend our lives. "Most assuredly, I say to you, unless a grain of wheat falls into the ground and dies, it remains alone; but if it dies, it produces much grain" John 12:24. The seed of our works is predicated upon divine conviction. Like a seed sown into the soil, it must die to the acidic conditions of the soil and geminate with the presence of water. Prior to harvest, the ripening of a fruit entails neutralizing the acids to become sweet. "My brethren, count it all joy when you fall into various trials, knowing that the testing of your faith produces patience. But let patience have its perfect work, that you may be perfect and complete, lacking nothing" James 1:2-4.

Manasseh inherited from Joseph that virtue of endurance that brings us into maturity in all that we are called. He is transformed through the suffering of perseverance to be purged as silver and gold, and become ripe as a fruit.

Chapter Nine

The Tribe of

Benjamin

"Then they journeyed from Bethel. And when there was but a little distance to go to Ephrath, Rachel labored in childbirth, and she had hard labor. Now it came to pass, when she was in hard labor, that the midwife said to her, "Do not fear; you will have this son also." And so it was, as her soul was departing (for she died), that she called his name Ben-Oni; but his father called him Benjamin" Genesis 35:16-18. Benjamin is so named because of the circumstances surrounding his birth. His mother Rachel travailed in hard labor for him and died in the process. She named him Benoni after this experience of her struggle for survival. Having noticed how the names given by Leah to her three sons impacted their character, Jacob staged an intervention, and with light depth of thought, named him Benjamin, meaning son of my right hand. These two names shape the character of Benjamin. He is blessed with initiatives that furnish him with royal opportunities but struggles with character flaws. Prior to his death, Jacob imparts the following blessings on Benjamin, "Benjamin is a ravenous wolf; in the morning he shall devour the prey, and at night he shall divide the spoil" Genesis 49:27. Benjamin is like a merchant who identifies merchandise of great value with a vendor but then degrades the value to acquire it at a cheap price. After procuring and reselling it at its true value, he celebrates his success!

At some point when Israel had settled in the Promised Land, they begun to pressurize the prophet Samuel to institute a monarchy like the neighboring countries. "Then all the elders of Israel gathered together and came to Samuel at Ramah, and said to him, "Look, you are old, and your sons do not walk in your ways. Now make us a king to judge us like all the nations." But the thing displeased Samuel when they said, "Give us a king to judge us." So Samuel prayed to the Lord. And the Lord said to Samuel, "Heed the voice of the people in all that they say to you; for they have not rejected you, but they have rejected Me, that I should not reign over them" 1 Samuel 8:4-7. Saul from the tribe of Benjamin was chosen as the first king of Israel. This was because of how Jacob had named him at birth by conferring upon him the firstborn blessings. However, this royal blessing was short-lived as Saul struggled with the character required to sustain it. During his reign as king, Saul was given a divine assignment to annihilate the Amalekites. "Samuel also said to Saul, "The Lord sent me to anoint you king over His people, over Israel. Now therefore, heed the voice of the words of the Lord. Thus says the Lord of hosts: 'I will punish Amalek for what he did to Israel, how he ambushed him on the way when he came up from Egypt. Now go and attack Amalek, and utterly destroy all that they have, and do not spare them. But kill both man and woman, infant and nursing child, ox and sheep, camel and donkey.'" So Saul gathered the people together and numbered them in Telaim, two hundred thousand foot soldiers and ten thousand men of Judah. And Saul came to a city of Amalek, and lay in wait in the valley. Then Saul said to the Kenites, "Go, depart, get down from among the Amalekites, lest I destroy you with them. For you showed kindness to all the children of Israel when they came up out of Egypt." So the Kenites departed from among the Amalekites. And Saul attacked the Amalekites, from Havilah all the way to Shur, which is east of Egypt. He also took Agag king of the Amalekites alive, and utterly destroyed all the people with the edge of the sword. But Saul and the people spared Agag and the best of the sheep, the oxen, the fatlings, the lambs, and all that was good, and were unwilling to utterly destroy them. But everything despised and worthless, that they utterly destroyed" 1 Samuel 15:1-9.

King Saul carried out this assignment in a way that fits the description Jacob imparted to him. Instead of destroying all that pertained to Amalek as he was instructed, behaving like a hungry wolf, he only destroyed what was worthless and spared the valuable things. From that point onwards he lost favor with God and spiraled downwards until his death. Benjamin has a conflicted personality. As King Saul, he conducts himself as carnal and an opportunist. However, we notice his spiritual nature in Jonathan, the son of King Saul. Jonathan initiates godly action to tackle challenges. "Now it happened one day that Jonathan the son of Saul said to the young man who bore his armor, "Come, let us go over to the Philistines' garrison that is on the other side." But he did not tell his father. And Saul was sitting in the outskirts of Gibeah under a pomegranate tree which is in Migron. The people who were with him were about six hundred men. Ahijah the son of Ahitub, Ichabod's brother, the son of Phinehas, the son of Eli, the Lord's priest in Shiloh, was wearing an ephod. But the people did not know that Jonathan had gone. Between the passes, by which Jonathan sought to go over to the Philistines' garrison, there was a sharp rock on one side and a sharp rock on the other side. And the name of one was Bozez, and the name of the other Seneh. The front of one faced northward opposite Michmash, and the other southward opposite Gibeah. Then Jonathan said to the young man who bore his armor, "Come, let us go over to the garrison of these uncircumcised; it may be that the Lord will work for us. For nothing restrains the Lord from saving by many or by few." So his armorbearer said to him, "Do all that is in your heart. Go then; here I am with you, according to your heart." Then Jonathan said, "Very well, let us cross over to these men, and we will show ourselves to them. If they say thus to us, 'Wait until we come to you,' then we will stand still in our place and not go up to them. But if they say thus, 'Come up to us,' then we will go up. For the Lord has delivered them into our hand, and this will be a sign to us." So both of them showed themselves to the garrison of the Philistines. And the Philistines said, "Look, the Hebrews are coming out of the holes where they have hidden." Then the men of the garrison called to Jonathan and his armorbearer, and said, "Come up to us, and we will show you something."

Jonathan said to his armorbearer, "Come up after me, for the Lord has delivered them into the hand of Israel." And Jonathan climbed up on his hands and knees with his armorbearer after him; and they fell before Jonathan. And as he came after him, his armorbearer killed them. That first slaughter which Jonathan and his armorbearer made was about twenty men within about half an acre of land. And there was trembling in the camp, in the field, and among all the people. The garrison and the raiders also trembled; and the earth quaked, so that it was a very great trembling" 1 Samuel 14:1-15.

Jonathan initiated a preemptive strike against the Philistines based on his faith in God and was supernaturally helped to become victorious. While this victory predicated by the faith of Jonathan was manifesting, King Saul initiated a carnal fast that placed their army at a disadvantage. "And the men of Israel were distressed that day, for Saul had placed the people under oath, saying, "Cursed is the man who eats any food until evening, before I have taken vengeance on my enemies." So none of the people tasted food. Now all the people of the land came to a forest; and there was honey on the ground. And when the people had come into the woods, there was the honey, dripping; but no one put his hand to his mouth, for the people feared the oath. But Jonathan had not heard his father charge the people with the oath; therefore he stretched out the end of the rod that was in his hand and dipped it in a honeycomb, and put his hand to his mouth; and his countenance brightened. Then one of the people said, "Your father strictly charged the people with an oath, saying, 'Cursed is the man who eats food this day.'" And the people were faint. But Jonathan said, "My father has troubled the land. Look now, how my countenance has brightened because I tasted a little of this honey. How much better if the people had eaten freely today of the spoil of their enemies which they found! For now would there not have been a much greater slaughter among the Philistines?" Now they had driven back the Philistines that day from Michmash to Aijalon. So the people were very faint. And the people rushed on the spoil, and took sheep, oxen, and calves, and slaughtered them on the ground; and the people ate them with the blood. Then they told Saul, saying, "Look, the people are sinning against the Lord by eating with the blood!" So he said, "You have dealt treacherously; roll a large stone to me this day" 1 Samuel 14:24-33.

As king of Israel, Saul was obviously sleepwalking through his reign. He constantly held back Jonathan whenever Jonathan offered an initiative. "Do you see a man wise in his own eyes? There is more hope for a fool than for him. The lazy man says, "There is a lion in the road! A fierce lion is in the streets!" As a door turns on its hinges, so does the lazy man on his bed. The lazy man buries his hand in the bowl; it wearies him to bring it back to his mouth. The lazy man is wiser in his own eyes than seven men who can answer sensibly" Proverbs 26:12-16. This is the reason for which Jonathan sneaked out of the camp to execute an initiative based on his faith in God. Jonathan was not happy with his father and so he identified David as Godsent to fix the dysfunctional leadership condition of Israel. He initiated a covenant with David that ultimately preserved his heritage. The tribe of Benjamin signify how we initiate action in the face of opportunity. We are either inclined to follow divine prompting or become opportunistic.

PART FOUR:

Northern Tribes

INHERITANCE PROGRESS

The northern tribes were the fourth group of tribes that followed the ark of the covenant in their movement from Egypt towards the Promised Land. These three northern tribes were Dan, Asher and Naphtali. The tribe of Dan was the head of this group of tribes, and their ensign was an eagle. The northern tribes depicted the essence of destiny. While the Promised Land of Canaan was the destiny of the Israelites who came out of Egypt, destiny is when we come into our inheritance in Christ. This is a unique burden of Dan, Asher and Naphtali, where a believers we must attain the image and likeness of Christ. "For whom He foreknew, He also predestined to be conformed to the image of His Son, that He might be the firstborn among many brethren" Romans 8:29. Jesus came to model for us the measure and stature of our predestination. No one should be confused about their destiny, rather we should all look up to the standard Jesus set while here on earth as our goal of destiny. As we endeavor to be Christlike, we shall ultimately receive our inheritance in Christ.

The eagle, which is the ensign of the northern tribes, exhibits distinct qualities compared to other birds. "Why do you say, O Jacob, and speak, O Israel: "My way is hidden from the Lord, and my just claim is passed over by my God"? Have you not known? Have you not heard? The everlasting God, the Lord, the Creator of the ends of the earth, neither faints nor is weary. His understanding is unsearchable. He gives power to the weak, and to those who have no might He increases strength. Even the youths shall faint and be weary, and the young men shall utterly fall, but those who wait on the Lord shall renew their strength; they shall mount up with wings like eagles, they shall run and not be weary, They shall walk and not faint" Isaiah 40:27-31. Unlike other birds who utilize their wings in flight from one point to another, the eagle does not depend on its ability to fly. Rather, it waits for a wind blowing in its desired direction and yields its wings to soar upon the wind. This way, it achieves higher elevations with greater speeds in flight compared with other birds. Jesus Christ invoked this characteristic to explain the salvation experience to Nicodemus the pharisee. "Do not marvel that I said to you, 'You must be born again.' The wind blows where it wishes, and you hear the sound of it, but cannot tell where it comes from and where it goes. So is everyone who is born of the Spirit" John 3:7&8.

Furthermore, the eagle grooms its eaglets in a profound way. "As an eagle stirs up its nest, hovers over its young, spreading out its wings, taking them up, carrying them on its wings, So the Lord alone led him, and there was no foreign god with him" Deuteronomy 32:11&12. The eagle builds a nest on high elevations for the eaglet. When it is time to train the eaglet for their unique manner of flight, the eagle releases the eaglet from a high point so that it drops towards the earth. The eaglet would wonder why it has been subjected to this scary exercise and will scream for help until the eagle swoops down to catch it before it falls. The eagle will repeat this exercise until the eaglet does exactly how the eagle soars upon the wings of the wind. This is how God led Israel through the wilderness until they reached the Promised Land.

Chapter Ten

The Tribe of

Dan

"And Bilhah conceived and bore Jacob a son. Then Rachel said, "God has judged my case; and He has also heard my voice and given me a son." Therefore she called his name Dan" Genesis 30:5&6. Dan is ascribed a name that means 'judge' or 'justice'. He is the legal tribe that is in charge of spiritual justice. Jacob blesses this tribe in line with this name. "Dan shall judge his people as one of the tribes of Israel. Dan shall be a serpent by the way, a viper by the path, that bites the horse's heels so that its rider shall fall backward. I have waited for your salvation, O Lord!" Genesis 49:16-18. According to this blessing, Dan is an advocate that defeats the prosecutor in a legal case. Dan is blessed with wisdom for the justice of redemption. This blessing plays out in the dramatic scenario that seals Israel's release from the bondage of Egypt. "So they took their journey from Succoth and camped in Etham at the edge of the wilderness. And the Lord went before them by day in a pillar of cloud to lead the way, and by night in a pillar of fire to give them light, so as to go by day and night. He did not take away the pillar of cloud by day or the pillar of fire by night from before the people" Exodus 13:20-22.

"Now the Lord spoke to Moses, saying: "Speak to the children of Israel, that they turn and camp before Pi Hahiroth, between Migdol and the sea, opposite Baal Zephon; you shall camp before it by the sea. For Pharaoh will say of the children of Israel, 'They are bewildered by the land; the wilderness has closed them in.' Then I will harden Pharaoh's heart, so that he will pursue them; and I will gain honor over Pharaoh and over all his army, that the Egyptians may know that I am the Lord." And they did so. Now it was told the king of Egypt that the people had fled, and the heart of Pharaoh and his servants was turned against the people; and they said, "Why have we done this, that we have let Israel go from serving us?" So he made ready his chariot and took his people with him. Also, he took six hundred choice chariots, and all the chariots of Egypt with captains over every one of them. And the Lord hardened the heart of Pharaoh king of Egypt, and he pursued the children of Israel; and the children of Israel went out with boldness. So the Egyptians pursued them, all the horses and chariots of Pharaoh, his horsemen and his army, and overtook them camping by the sea beside Pi Hahiroth, before Baal Zephon. And when Pharaoh drew near, the children of Israel lifted their eyes, and behold, the Egyptians marched after them. So they were very afraid, and the children of Israel cried out to the Lord. Then they said to Moses, "Because there were no graves in Egypt, have you taken us away to die in the wilderness? Why have you so dealt with us, to bring us up out of Egypt? Is this not the word that we told you in Egypt, saying, 'Let us alone that we may serve the Egyptians'? For it would have been better for us to serve the Egyptians than that we should die in the wilderness." And Moses said to the people, "Do not be afraid. Stand still, and see the salvation of the Lord, which He will accomplish for you today. For the Egyptians whom you see today, you shall see again no more forever. The Lord will fight for you, and you shall hold your peace." And the Lord said to Moses, "Why do you cry to Me? Tell the children of Israel to go forward. But lift up your rod, and stretch out your hand over the sea and divide it. And the children of Israel shall go on dry ground through the midst of the sea. And I indeed will harden the hearts of the Egyptians, and they shall follow them. So I will gain honor over Pharaoh and over all his army, his chariots, and his horsemen. Then the Egyptians shall know that I am the Lord, when I have gained honor for Myself over Pharaoh, his chariots, and his horsemen." And the Angel of God, who went before the camp of Israel, moved and went behind them; and the pillar of cloud went from before them and stood behind them. So it came between the camp of the Egyptians and the camp of Israel. Thus it was a cloud and darkness to the one, and it gave light by night to the other, so that the one did not come near the other all that night. Then Moses stretched out his hand over the sea; and the Lord caused the sea to go back by a strong east wind all that night, and made the sea into dry land, and the waters were divided. So the children of Israel went into the midst of the sea on the dry ground, and the waters were a wall to them on their right hand and on their left. And the Egyptians pursued and went after

116

them into the midst of the sea, all Pharaoh's horses, his chariots, and his horsemen. Now it came to pass, in the morning watch, that the Lord looked down upon the army of the Egyptians through the pillar of fire and cloud, and He troubled the army of the Egyptians. And He took off their chariot wheels, so that they drove them with difficulty; and the Egyptians said, "Let us flee from the face of Israel, for the Lord fights for them against the Egyptians." Then the Lord said to Moses, "Stretch out your hand over the sea, that the waters may come back upon the Egyptians, on their chariots, and on their horsemen." And Moses stretched out his hand over the sea; and when the morning appeared, the sea returned to its full depth, while the Egyptians were fleeing into it. So the Lord overthrew the Egyptians in the midst of the sea. Then the waters returned and covered the chariots, the horsemen, and all the army of Pharaoh that came into the sea after them. Not so much as one of them remained. But the children of Israel had walked on dry land in the midst of the sea, and the waters were a wall to them on their right hand and on their left. So the Lord saved Israel that day out of the hand of the Egyptians, and Israel saw the Egyptians dead on the seashore. Thus Israel saw the great work which the Lord had done in Egypt; so the people feared the Lord, and believed the Lord and His servant Moses" Exodus 14:1-31.

The destruction of Pharaoh's army in the Red Sea completed the deliverance of Israel from the bondage of Egypt. For the construction of the tabernacle of Moses, Aholiab from the tribe of Dan was enlisted alongside Bezaleel from Judah. "And I, indeed I, have appointed with him Aholiab the son of Ahisamach, of the tribe of

Dan; and I have put wisdom in the hearts of all the gifted artisans, that they may make all that I have commanded you" Exodus 31:6. This elaborate tabernacle was a model of the heavenly tabernacle that was revealed to Moses. It was the throne room of God where royal judgment was adjudicated. While Bezaleel from the tribe of Judah was inherently endowed to appreciate the royalty it entailed, Aholiab from the tribe of Dan could fathom the justice aspects of the tabernacle. Dan enshrines the Old Dispensation Era concept of the Nazarite Consecration.

"Then the Lord spoke to Moses, saying, "Speak to the children of Israel, and say to them: 'When either a man or woman consecrates an offering to take the vow of a Nazirite, to separate himself to the Lord, he shall separate himself from wine and similar drink; he shall drink neither vinegar made from wine nor vinegar made from similar drink; neither shall he drink any grape juice, nor eat fresh grapes or raisins. All the days of his separation he shall eat nothing that is produced by the grapevine, from seed to skin. 'All the days of the vow of his separation no razor shall come upon his head; until the days are fulfilled for which he separated himself to the Lord, he shall be holy. Then he shall let the locks of the hair of his head grow. All the days that he separates himself to the Lord he shall not go near a dead body" Numbers 6:1-6. The Nazarite consecration entailed abstinence from wine, shaving one's hair and contact with the dead. Those who observed this consecration positioned themselves to be used of God to accomplish unusual divine assignments.

Samson is an example of a Danite who was used of God to bring deliverance to Israel from Philistine oppression.

"Again, the children of Israel did evil in the sight of the Lord, and the Lord delivered them into the hand of the Philistines for forty years. Now there was a certain man from Zorah, of the family of the Danites, whose name was Manoah; and his wife was barren and had no children. And the Angel of the Lord appeared to the woman and said to her, "Indeed now, you are barren and have borne no children, but you shall conceive and bear a son. Now therefore, please be careful not to drink wine or similar drink, and not to eat anything unclean. For behold, you shall conceive and bear a son. And no razor shall come upon his head, for the child shall be a Nazirite to God from the womb; and he shall begin to deliver Israel out of the hand of the Philistines." So the woman came and told her husband, saying, "A Man of God came to me, and His countenance was like the countenance of the Angel of God, very awesome; but I did not ask Him where He was from, and He did not tell me His name. And He said to me, 'Behold, you shall conceive and bear a son. Now drink no wine or similar drink, nor eat anything unclean, for the child shall be a Nazirite to God from the womb to the day of his death.'" Then Manoah prayed to the Lord, and said, "O my Lord, please let the Man of God whom You sent come to us again and teach us what we shall do for the child who will be born" Judges 13:1-8.

When Samson observed the Nazarite consecration, he was divinely empowered as a one-man army to defeat the Philistines. He was only subdued by the enemy when he became careless with this consecration. However, when he was restored with his consecration, his power returned, and he destroyed the Philistines.

Notable examples of those who were divinely used to accomplish great feats in the scriptures include Samuel the prophet who was used of God to institute the monarchy of Israel as well as John the Baptist, forerunner of our Lord Jesus Christ. Our Lord Jesus Christ grew up in Nazareth which was a community of those who observed the Nazarite consecration. "Now when Herod was dead, behold, an angel of the Lord appeared in a dream to Joseph in Egypt, saying, "Arise, take the young Child and His mother, and go to the land of Israel, for those who sought the young Child's life are dead." Then he arose, took the young Child and His mother, and came into the land of Israel. But when he heard that Archelaus was reigning over Judea instead of his father Herod, he was afraid to go there. And being warned by God in a dream, he turned aside into the region of Galilee. And he came and dwelt in a city called Nazareth, that it might be fulfilled which was spoken by the prophets, "He shall be called a Nazarene" Matthew 2:19-23. From this scripture, it is obvious that Jesus observed the Nazarite consecration that earned him the identity 'Jesus Christ of Nazareth'.

Dan is a divine advocate but is not legalistic. He deals with bloodline contentions and advocates to end curse mandates. "Then Jesus entered and passed through Jericho. Now behold, there was a man named Zacchaeus who was a chief tax collector, and he was rich. And he sought to see who Jesus was, but could not because of the crowd, for he was of short stature. So he ran ahead and climbed up into a sycamore tree to see Him, for He was going to pass that way. And when Jesus came to the place, He looked up and saw him, and said to him, "Zacchaeus, make haste and come down, for today I must stay at your house." So he made haste and came down, and received Him joyfully. But when they saw it, they all complained, saying, "He has gone to be a guest with a man who is a sinner." Then Zacchaeus stood and said to the Lord, "Look, Lord, I give half of my goods to the poor; and if I have taken anything from anyone by false accusation, I restore fourfold." And Jesus said to him, "Today salvation has come to this house, because he also is a son of Abraham; for the Son of Man has come to seek and to save that which was lost" Luke 19:1-10. At the time of this narrative, the Romans had colonized Israel and commissioned certain people as tax collectors. In the same way people panic today when they receive an unexpected mail from the tax authorities, people hated the tax collectors in Israel. Zacchaeus was one of such tax collectors and sought to encounter Jesus. When Jesus reached out to Zacchaeus, there was an overwhelming opposition from the crowd. This resistance is what takes place in the spiritual realm when there are bloodline contentions and curse mandates against a person or a family. Zacchaeus invoked the premise of restitution to deal with these accusations and Jesus acknowledged this as Zacchaeus' salvation!

Persistent violations of divine principles are the cause of chronic infirmities and demonic oppression "If we say that we have no sin, we deceive ourselves, and the truth is not in us. If we confess our sins, He is faithful and just to forgive us our sins and to cleanse us from all unrighteousness. If we say that we have not sinned, we make Him a liar, and His word is not in us" 1 John 1:8-10. "My little children, these things I write to you, so that you may not sin. And if anyone sins, we have an Advocate with the Father, Jesus Christ the righteous. And He Himself is the propitiation for our sins, and not for ours only but also for the whole world" 1 John 2:1-2.

Heaven's court room scenario that convenes every year on the Day of Atonement did not end with the advent of the New Covenant. The changes are that atonement is not a function of the high priest of the Levitical order nor by the blood of animal sacrifices. The following revelation to the prophet Zechariah signified how atonement would be adjudicated in the New Testament Era. "Then he showed me Joshua the high priest standing before the Angel of the Lord, and Satan standing at his right hand to oppose him. And the Lord said to Satan, "The Lord rebuke you, Satan! The Lord who has chosen Jerusalem rebuke you! Is this not a brand plucked from the fire?" Now Joshua was clothed with filthy garments, and was standing before the Angel. Then He answered and spoke to those who stood before Him, saying, "Take away the filthy garments from him." And to him He said, "See, I have removed your iniquity from you, and I will clothe you with rich robes." And I said, "Let them put a clean turban on his head." So they put a clean turban on his head, and they put the clothes on him. And the Angel of the Lord stood by. Then the Angel of the Lord admonished Joshua, saying, "Thus says the Lord of hosts: 'If you will walk in My ways, and if you will keep My command, then you shall also judge My house, and likewise have charge of My courts; I will give you places to walk among these who stand here. 'Hear, O Joshua, the high priest, you and your companions who sit before you, for they are a wondrous sign; for behold, I am bringing forth My Servant the BRANCH. For behold, the stone that I have laid before Joshua: upon the stone are seven eyes. Behold, I will engrave its inscription,' Says the Lord of hosts, 'and I will remove the iniquity of that land in one day" Zechariah 3:1-9.

Satan has always been a prosecutor and continues to this day in that capacity at heaven's court of justice. "So the great dragon was cast out, that serpent of old, called the Devil and Satan, who deceives the whole world; he was cast to the earth, and his angels were cast out with him. Then I heard a loud voice saying in heaven, "Now salvation, and strength, and the kingdom of our God, and the power of His Christ have come, for the accuser of our brethren, who accused them before our God day and night, has been cast down. And they overcame him by the blood of the Lamb and by the word of their testimony, and they did not love their lives to the death" Revelations 12:9-11. Despite his continuing mission to prosecute us based on bloodline transgressions and curse mandates, Jesus Christ went to the cross to lay the path for our victory and redemption. 'And they overcame him by the blood of the Lamb and by the word of their testimony'. Dan is the Israelite tribe that contends for bloodline inheritance.

Harness

Chapter Eleven

The Tribe of

Asher

"And Leah's maid Zilpah bore Jacob a second son. Then Leah said, "I am happy, for the daughters will call me blessed." So she called his name Asher" Genesis 30:12&13. The name Asher means 'to be blessed'. Jacob ratifies this name with a function core to our existence as humans. "Bread from Asher shall be rich, and he shall yield royal dainties" Genesis 49:20. Food is a necessity of our human existence. Asher would become the source of quality food that sustains human life. "Then God blessed them, and God said to them, "Be fruitful and multiply; fill the earth and subdue it; have dominion over the fish of the sea, over the birds of the air, and over every living thing that moves on the earth" Genesis 1:28. Asher models our blessings of divine sustenance. Most of the sustainability principles taught in the scriptures were based on agriculture. All other vocations are offshoots of agriculture, so we learn preservation of inheritance through agricultural principles. The way in which farmers were supposed to cultivate seed sheds light on the right way of investment. Furthermore, God scheduled sustainability visitations to coincide with the agricultural calendar. This way they could acknowledge His role in fostering their prosperity. "And the Lord spoke to Moses, saying, "Speak to the children of Israel, and say to them: 'The feasts of the Lord, which you shall proclaim to be holy convocations, these are My feasts" Leviticus 23:1&2.

The Sabbath was a rest from work scheduled for the seventh day of the week and it symbolized faith in God. "Six days shall work be done, but the seventh day is a Sabbath of solemn rest, a holy convocation. You shall do no work on it; it is the Sabbath of the Lord in all your dwellings" Leviticus 23:3. Contrary to the common notion that it was initiated by the Mosaic covenant, the Sabbath was an integral part of the creation framework. However, God did not enforce it until Israel was in the wilderness enroute to the Promised Land. "Therefore, since a promise remains of entering His rest, let us fear lest any of you seem to have come short of it. For indeed the gospel was preached to us as well as to them; but the word which they heard did not profit them, not being mixed with faith in those who heard it. For we who have believed do enter that rest, as He has said: "So I swore in My wrath, they shall not enter My rest,'" although the works were finished from the foundation of the world. For He has spoken in a certain place of the seventh day in this way: "And God rested on the seventh day from all His works"; and again in this place: "They shall not enter My rest." Since therefore it remains that some must enter it, and those to whom it was first preached did not enter because of disobedience, again He designates a certain day, saying in David, "Today," after such a long time, as it has been said: "Today, if you will hear His voice, Do not harden your hearts" Hebrews 4:1-7. The significance of the Sabbath is clearly the disposition of faith in the heart. "So then faith comes by hearing, and hearing by the word of God" Romans 19:17. This faith is contingent of a personal relationship with God where we submit to his dealings with us and trust in His promises.

The Passover and Unleavened Bread was a feast that symbolized the cross of our Lord Jesus Christ. "'These are the feasts of the Lord, holy convocations which you shall proclaim at their appointed times. On the fourteenth day of the first month at twilight is the Lord's Passover. And on the fifteenth day of the same month is the Feast of Unleavened Bread to the Lord; seven days you must eat unleavened bread. On the first day you shall have a holy convocation; you shall do no customary work on it. But you shall offer an offering made by fire to the Lord for seven days. The seventh day shall be a holy convocation; you shall do no customary work on it'" Leviticus 23:4-8. This feast was first observed at the eve of the departure of the Israelites from the bondage of Egypt. The king of Egypt had resisted every attempt by Moses to secure Israel's release, but then this feast was the final straw that broke the camel's back. At midnight God dispatched a destruction angel to execute all the firstborn of the Egyptians who had not observed the Passover, so their doorposts were not marked with blood. The essence of this blood that preserved the firstborns of the Israelites and secured their release from the bondage of Egypt, is how the blood of Jesus Christ redeems us today. "In Him we have redemption through His blood, the forgiveness of sins, according to the riches of His grace" Ephesians 1:7. The Passover and Unleavened Bread is the lifestyle to which we are called as believers in Christ. "When He had called the people to Himself, with His disciples also, He said to them, "Whoever desires to come after Me, let him deny himself, and take up his cross, and follow Me. For whoever desires to save his life will lose it, but whoever loses his life for My sake and the gospel's will save it" Mark 8:34&35.

The Feast of Firstfruits was symbolic of the resurrection of Jesus Christ from the dead. "And the Lord spoke to Moses, saying, "Speak to the children of Israel, and say to them: 'When you come into the land which I give to you, and reap its harvest, then you shall bring a sheaf of the firstfruits of your harvest to the priest. He shall wave the sheaf before the Lord, to be accepted on your behalf; on the day after the Sabbath the priest shall wave it. And you shall offer on that day, when you wave the sheaf, a male lamb of the first year, without blemish, as a burnt offering to the Lord. Its grain offering shall be two-tenths of an ephah of fine flour mixed with oil, an offering made by fire to the Lord, for a sweet aroma; and its drink offering shall be of wine, one-fourth of a hin. You shall eat neither bread nor parched grain nor fresh grain until the same day that you have brought an offering to your God; it shall be a statute forever throughout your generations in all your dwellings" Leviticus 23:9-14. Immediately after Moses secured their release from the bondage of Egypt, God instituted the feast of firstfruits. "And it shall be, when the

Lord brings you into the land of the Canaanites, as He swore to you and your fathers, and gives it to you, that you shall set apart to the Lord all that open the womb, that is, every firstborn that comes from an animal which you have; the males shall be the Lord's. But every firstborn of a donkey you shall redeem with a lamb; and if you will not redeem it, then you shall break its neck. And all the firstborn of man among your sons you shall redeem. So it shall be, when your son asks you in time to come, saying, 'What is this?' that you shall say to him, 'By strength of hand the Lord brought us out of Egypt, out of the house of bondage. And it came to pass, when Pharaoh was stubborn about letting us go, that the Lord killed all the firstborn in the land of Egypt, both the firstborn of man and the firstborn of beast. Therefore I sacrifice to the Lord all males that open the womb, but all the firstborn of my sons I redeem.' It shall be as a sign on your hand and as frontlets between your eyes, for by strength of hand the Lord brought us out of Egypt" Exodus 13:11-16. Owing to the death of the firstborn of the Egyptians which triggered the release of the Israelites from bondage, firstfruits was instituted to preserve the spiritual dominance of the Israelites. This practice will invoke a supernatural sign on their hands and eyes by which they will accomplish great things and have dominion always. The timing of firstfruits coincided with the beginning of harvest, so they were to bring sheaves of their first harvest as an offering to God as well as their firstborn sons and livestock. In the New Testament Era, Jesus Christ who is our Passover Lamb that was crucified at the cross is also our Resurrected Lord. "But now Christ is risen from the dead, and has become the firstfruits of those who have fallen asleep. For since by man came death, by Man also came the resurrection of the dead. For as in Adam all die, even so in Christ all shall be made alive" 1 Corinthians 15:20-22. "So also is the resurrection of the dead. The body is sown in corruption, it is raised in incorruption. It is sown in dishonor, it is raised in glory. It is sown in weakness, it is raised in power. It is sown a natural body, it is raised a spiritual body. There is a natural body, and there is a spiritual body. And so it is written, "The first man Adam became a living being." The last Adam became a life-giving spirit. However, the spiritual is not first, but the natural, and afterward the spiritual. The first man was of the earth, made of dust; the second Man is the Lord from heaven. As was the man of dust, so also are those who are made of dust; and as is the heavenly Man, so also are those who are heavenly. And as we have borne the image of the man of dust, we shall also bear the image of the heavenly Man" 1 Corinthians 15:42-49. Jesus Christ who assigns us our cross as disciples also fosters our resurrection in four ways. First, we die to corruption, and we are raised incorruptible. Secondly, we die to weakness, and we are raised in power. Thirdly, we die to the natural and we are raised to become spiritual. Fourthly, we die to dishonor, and we are raised with glory.

The Feast of Pentecost symbolizes the birth of the New Testament Church. "'And you shall count for yourselves from the day after the Sabbath, from the day that you brought the sheaf of the wave offering: seven Sabbaths shall be completed. Count fifty days to the day after the seventh Sabbath; then you shall offer a new grain offering to the Lord. You shall bring from your dwellings two wave loaves of two-tenths of an ephah. They shall be of fine flour; they shall be baked with leaven. They are the firstfruits to the Lord. And you shall offer with the bread seven lambs of the first year, without blemish, one young bull, and two rams. They shall be as a burnt offering to the Lord, with their grain offering and their drink offerings, an offering made by fire for a sweet aroma to the Lord. Then you shall sacrifice one kid of the goats as a sin offering, and two male lambs of the first year as a sacrifice of a peace offering. The priest shall wave them with the bread of the firstfruits as a wave offering before the Lord, with the two lambs. They shall be holy to the Lord for the priest. And you shall proclaim on the same day that it is a holy convocation to you. You shall do no customary work on it. It shall be a statute forever in all your dwellings throughout your generations" 'When you reap the harvest of your land, you shall not wholly reap the corners of your field when you reap, nor shall you gather any gleaning from your harvest. You shall leave them for the poor and for the stranger: I am the Lord your God'" Leviticus 23:15-22. Fifty days after the feast of firstfruits, the Israelites celebrated the feast of weeks also known as Pentecost. At this time, they had reaped their harvests and estimated their tithes, so they brought them to the house of God together with the prescribed offerings. It was on such occasion after the resurrection and ascension of Jesus Christ that the Church was born. "When the Day of Pentecost had fully come, they were all with one accord in one place. And suddenly there came a sound from heaven, as of a rushing mighty wind, and it filled the whole house where they were sitting. Then there appeared to them divided tongues, as of fire, and one sat upon each of them. And they were all filled with the Holy Spirit and began to speak with other tongues, as the Spirit gave them utterance. And there were dwelling in Jerusalem Jews, devout men, from every nation under heaven. And when this sound occurred, the multitude came together, and were confused, because everyone heard them speak in his own language. Then they were all amazed and marveled, saying to one another, "Look, are not all these who speak Galileans? And how is it that we hear, each in our own language in which we were born? Parthians and Medes and Elamites, those dwelling in Mesopotamia, Judea and Cappadocia, Pontus and Asia, Phrygia and Pamphylia, Egypt and the parts of Libya adjoining Cyrene, visitors from Rome, both Jews and proselytes, Cretans and Arabs, we hear them speaking in our own tongues the wonderful works of God." So they were all amazed and perplexed, saying to one another, "Whatever could this mean?" Others mocking said, "They are full of new wine." But Peter, standing up with the eleven, raised his voice and said to them, "Men of Judea and all who dwell in Jerusalem, let this be known to you, and heed my words. For these are not drunk, as you suppose, since it is only the third hour of the day. But this is what was spoken by the prophet Joel: 'And it shall come to pass in the last days, says God, that I will pour out of My Spirit on all flesh; your sons and your daughters shall prophesy, your young men shall see visions, your old men shall dream dreams. And on My menservants and on My maidservants I will pour out My Spirit in those days; And they shall prophesy. I will show wonders in heaven above And signs in the earth beneath: Blood and fire and vapor of smoke. The sun shall be turned into darkness, and the moon into blood, before the coming of the great and awesome day of the Lord. And it shall come to pass That whoever calls on the name of the Lord shall be saved'" Acts 2:1-21. Prior to this manifestation, Jesus had instructed the disciples to tarry in Jerusalem for this encounter where they will be endued with power from heaven. This manifestation of the outpouring of the Holy Spirit on the disciples, marked the birth of the Church of our Lord Jesus Christ.

The Feast of Trumpets symbolizes divine order in the Church. "Then the Lord spoke to Moses, saying, "Speak to the children of Israel, saying: 'In the seventh month, on the first day of the month, you shall have a sabbath-rest, a memorial of blowing of trumpets, a holy convocation. You shall do no customary work on it; and you shall offer an offering made by fire to the Lord'" Leviticus 23:23-25. Commemorated with the blowing of trumpets, it was a call to divine order where God's people came into alignment with angels. Two silver trumpets were made at the instruction of God for various prompts such as when the Israelites were to gather at the tabernacle, or when the leaders were being summoned, or when they were to advance in their journeyings or when there was war or during their feasts. The apostle Paul invokes this significance to quell any attitude that suggests that God entertains disorderliness in the Church. "But now, brethren, if I come to you speaking with tongues, what shall I profit you unless I speak to you either by revelation, by knowledge, by prophesying, or by teaching? Even things without life, whether flute or harp, when they make a sound, unless they make a distinction in the sounds, how will it be known what is piped or played? For if the trumpet makes an uncertain sound, who will prepare for battle?" 1 Corinthians 14:6-8. Though God has endowed us with supernatural gifts which may sound chaotic in manifestation, God is not the author of confusion, so we are expected to conduct ourselves with decency and order.

The Day of Atonement symbolizes divine justice. "And the Lord spoke to Moses, saying: "Also the tenth day of this seventh month shall be the Day of Atonement. It shall be a holy convocation for you; you shall afflict your souls, and offer an offering made by fire to the Lord. And you shall do no work on that same day, for it is the Day of Atonement, to make atonement for you before the Lord your God. For any person who is not afflicted in soul on that same day shall be cut off from his people. And any person who does any work on that same day, that person I will destroy from among his people. you shall do no manner of work; it shall be a statute forever throughout your generations in all your dwellings. It shall be to you a sabbath of solemn rest, and you shall afflict your souls; on the ninth day of the month at evening, from evening to evening, you shall celebrate your sabbath" Leviticus 23:26-32. This feast was the heavenly court room scenario where Satan is the prosecutor, Jesus Christ is our Advocate and God Almighty is Judge of all. On this day, Satan brings up a litany of accusations against people to seek judgment against them. The believer who observed this day with fasting and brokenness, identified with Jesus Christ as their Advocate. This way the blood of Jesus terminates curse mandates that the kingdom of darkness may be litigating against the believer. "For if the blood of bulls and goats and the ashes of a heifer, sprinkling the unclean, sanctifies for the purifying of the flesh, how much more shall the blood of Christ, who through the eternal Spirit offered Himself without spot to God, cleanse your conscience from dead works to serve the living God? And for this reason, He is the Mediator of the new covenant, by means of death, for the redemption of the transgressions under the first covenant, that those who are called may receive the promise of the eternal inheritance" Hebrews 9:13-15.

The Feast of Tabernacles symbolized divine promises. "Then the Lord spoke to Moses, saying, "Speak to the children of Israel, saying: 'The fifteenth day of this seventh month shall be the Feast of Tabernacles for seven days to the Lord. On the first day there shall be a holy convocation. You shall do no customary work on it. For seven days you shall offer an offering made by fire to the Lord. On the eighth day you shall have a holy convocation, and you shall offer an offering made by fire to the Lord. It is a sacred assembly, and you shall do no customary work on it. 'These are the feasts of the Lord which you shall proclaim to be holy convocations, to offer an offering made by fire to the Lord, a burnt offering and a grain offering, a sacrifice and drink offerings, everything on its day, besides the Sabbaths of the Lord, besides your gifts, besides all your vows, and besides all your freewill offerings which you give to the Lord. 'Also, on the fifteenth day of the seventh month, when you have gathered in the fruit of the land, you shall keep the feast of the Lord for seven days; on the first day there shall be a sabbath-rest, and on the eighth day a sabbath-rest. And you shall take for yourselves on the first day the fruit of beautiful trees, branches of palm trees, the boughs of leafy trees, and willows of the brook; and you shall rejoice before the Lord your God for seven days. You shall keep it as a feast to the Lord for seven days in the year. It shall be a statute forever in your generations. You shall celebrate it in the seventh month. You shall dwell in booths for seven days. All who are native Israelites shall dwell in booths, that your generations may know that I made the children of Israel dwell in booths when I brought them out of the land of Egypt: I am the Lord your God'" Leviticus 23:33-43. On this occasion of the feast of tabernacles the Israelites erected booths with the branches of the various kinds of trees that were made in the Garden of Eden to represent man's destiny. It was to remind them of how God took them through the wilderness and ultimately fulfilled the promise of blessing them with the Promised Land. "In Him also we have obtained an inheritance, being predestined according to the purpose of Him who works all things according to the counsel of His will, that we who first trusted in Christ should be to the praise of His glory. In Him you also trusted, after you heard the word of truth, the gospel of your salvation; in whom also, having believed, you were sealed with the Holy Spirit of promise, who is the guarantee of our inheritance until the redemption of the purchased possession, to the praise of His glory" Ephesians 2:11-14. In Christ we are given the promise of an inheritance, and the endowment of the Holy Spirit is the token guaranteeing this inheritance.

The seventh year Sabbath was a release from debt (Deuteronomy 15). Also, the fiftieth year was the Jubilee Sabbath that fostered restoration from disenfranchisement (Leviticus 25). These divine visits were for preservation of inheritance. Asher aligns his life and work with divine principles and visitations to sustain human life.

Chapter Twelve

The Tribe of

Naphtali

"And Rachel's maid Bilhah conceived again and bore Jacob a second son. Then Rachel said, "With great wrestling I have wrestled with my sister, and indeed I have prevailed." So she called his name Naphtali" Genesis 30:7-8. Rachel assigned her maid Bilhah to Jacob a second time and she conceived a son who she named Naphtali. A psychological warfare had been raging in the household of Jacob between Rachel and Leah. They traded words to intimidate each other as would be expected of bitter rivals sharing the same space. Rachel expresses her sentiment of victory with this second son by her auspices for Jacob. Jacob ratified this name by the blessing he imparted upon this son. "Naphtali is a deer let loose; he uses beautiful words" Genesis 49:21. Naphtali is blessed to be a communicator who fosters restoration of inheritance by winning the war of words. He inherently knows how to inform, motivate and engage.

As an **informant**, Naphtali furnishes with knowledge to overcome ignorance. For this reason, this tribe was chosen alongside with the tribe of Zebulun to broadcast the identity of the Messiah Jesus Christ. "And leaving Nazareth, He came and dwelt in Capernaum, which is by the sea, in the regions of Zebulun and Naphtali, that it might be fulfilled which was spoken by Isaiah the prophet, saying: "The land of Zebulun and the land of Naphtali, by the way of the sea, beyond the Jordan, Galilee of the Gentiles: The people who sat in darkness have seen a great light, and upon those who sat in the region and shadow of death Light has dawned." From that time Jesus began to preach and to say, "Repent, for the kingdom of heaven is at hand" Matthew 4:13-17. While Zebulun was endowed to supernaturally identify Jesus Christ, Naphtali was blessed to spread this information across Israel. For this reason, Jesus chose Capernaum in the region of Zebulun and Naphtali to establish His ministry headquarters. Operating from here, the ministry of Jesus Christ was publicized by the blessings on the tribe of Naphtali.

Motivation is where the right words based on legitimate references are spoken at the right time to inspire righteousness. Jesus often used parables to motivate His audience. "And the disciples came and said to Him, "Why do You speak to them in parables?" He answered and said to them, "Because it has been given to you to know the mysteries of the kingdom of heaven, but to them it has not been given. For whoever has, to him more will be given, and he will have abundance; but whoever does not have, even what he has will be taken away from him. Therefore, I speak to them in parables, because seeing they do not see, and hearing they do not hear, nor do they understand. And in them the prophecy of Isaiah is fulfilled, which says: 'Hearing you will hear and shall not understand and seeing you will see and not perceive; for the hearts of this people have grown dull. Their ears are hard of hearing, and their eyes they have closed, lest they should see with their eyes and hear with their ears, lest they should understand with their hearts and turn, so that I should heal them.' But blessed are your eyes for they see, and your ears for they hear; for assuredly, I say to you that many prophets and righteous men desired to see what you see, and did not see it, and to hear what you hear, and did not hear it" Matthew 13:10-17. The Israelites were suffering from a condition of dullness in their spiritual senses, for which reason it was difficult to reach their hearts directly with spiritual truths. It was necessary to use common life scenarios which they could relate, to convey to them spiritual truths.

Engage - Engage is where the enemy wages psychological warfare using words intended to trigger fear and discouragement to weaken our morale, but we respond by declaring our faith in divine mandates. There were all sorts of arguments taking place in Israel concerning the identity and legitimacy of Jesus Christ. Knowing this, Jesus decided to engage His disciples accordingly, to dispel the rumors. "When Jesus came into the region of Caesarea Philippi, He asked His disciples, saying, "Who do men say that I, the Son of Man, am?" So they said, "Some say John the Baptist, some Elijah, and others Jeremiah or one of the prophets." He said to them, "But who do you say that I am?" Simon Peter answered and said, "You are the Christ, the Son of the living God." Jesus answered and said to him, "Blessed are you, Simon Bar-Jonah, for flesh and blood has not revealed this to you, but My Father who is in heaven. And I also say to you that you are Peter, and on this rock, I will build My church, and the gates of Hades shall not prevail against it. And I will give you the keys of the kingdom of heaven, and whatever you bind on earth will be bound in heaven, and whatever you loose on earth will be loosed in heaven." Then He commanded His disciples that they should tell no one that He was Jesus the Christ" Matthew 16:13-20. Jesus asked the disciples whatever they had gathered from public opinion and then He requires their personal conviction. Jesus ascertains that the conviction of Peter was divinely inspired, and it was upon this premise of revelation that the Church would be established.

PART FIVE:

The Central Tribe

Chapter Thirteen

The Tribe of

Levi

"She conceived again and bore a son, and said, "Now this time my husband will become attached to me, because I have borne him three sons." Therefore, his name was called Levi" Genesis 29:34. Levi is the third son Leah conceived for Jacob. During this period, Leah was going through the turmoil of emotional frustration owing to Jacob's failure to demonstrate her anticipated endearment. The essence of the name Levi is her detachment from Jacob. This impacts Levi's character as a young man and is manifested in his actions with Simeon concerning the massacre of Shechem's people.

Prior to his death, Jacob said this concerning these two brothers. "Simeon and Levi are brothers; Instruments of cruelty are in their dwelling place. Let not my soul enter their council; Let not my honor be united to their assembly; For in their anger they slew a man, And in their self-will they hamstrung an ox. Cursed be their anger, for it is fierce; And their wrath, for it is cruel! I will divide them in Jacob and scatter them in Israel" Genesis 49:5-7. The life story of Levi took a dramatic turn towards the end of Israel's bondage in Egypt. "And a man of the house of Levi went and took as wife a daughter of Levi. So the woman conceived and bore a son. And when she saw that he was a beautiful child, she hid him three months. But when she could no longer hide him, she took an ark of bulrushes for him, daubed it with asphalt and pitch, put the child in it, and laid it in the reeds by the river's bank. And his sister stood afar off, to know what would be done to him. Then the daughter of Pharaoh came down to bathe at the river. And her maidens walked along the riverside; and when she saw the ark among the reeds, she sent her maid to get it. And when she opened it, she saw the child, and behold, the baby wept. So she had compassion on him, and said, "This is one of the Hebrews' children." Then his sister said to Pharaoh's daughter, "Shall I go and call a nurse for you from the Hebrew women, that she may nurse the child for you?" And Pharaoh's daughter said to her, "Go." So the maiden went and called the child's mother. Then Pharaoh's daughter said to her, "Take this child away and nurse him for me, and I will give you your wages." So the woman took the child and nursed him. And the child grew, and she brought him to Pharaoh's daughter, and he became her son. So she called his name Moses, saying, "Because I drew him out of the water" Exodus 2:1-10. Moses is born at a time when the Pharaoh of Egypt had enacted a decree that any male born Israelite should be thrown into the river. The Egyptians were weary of the Israelites who had increased in number and were very prosperous. Their fear was that the Israelites could start a rebellion or support an enemy to usurp the dominance of Egypt. However, when Moses was born, his mother Jochebed was convicted in her heart that Moses was a special child, and so she decided to obey the king's order in such a way as to preserve the life of Moses. Moses was discovered by the daughter of Pharaoh who paid Jochebed to nurse Moses. By this arrangement, she was able to reveal to Moses his true identity.

Now an adult, Moses encountered an Egyptian bullying an Israelite, so he killed him and concealed this Egyptian in the sand. On another occasion he saw two Israelites fighting and when he attempted to resolve their issue, they rebuked him. Moses realized that the Israelite he spared from the bullying Egyptian had spread the information, so he fled to Midian. It is at Midian that Moses encounters God for the first time while caring for the sheep of Jethro his father-in-law. God gave Moses the mission to secure the deliverance of the Israelites from the bondage of Egypt. Through various signs and plagues, God demonstrated His power through Moses and eventually the Israelites came out of Egypt and went through the wilderness enroute to the Promised Land.

At some point in the wilderness, God summoned Moses to come up the mountain for the ten commandments. While Moses was tarrying in the presence of God for forty days and nights, the Israelites got impatient with his absence. "Now when the people saw that Moses delayed coming down from the mountain, the people gathered together to Aaron, and said to him, "Come, make us gods that shall go before us; for as for this Moses, the man who brought us up out of the land of Egypt, we do not know what has become of him." And Aaron said to them, "Break off the golden earrings which are in the ears of your wives, your sons, and your daughters, and bring them to me." So all the people broke off the golden earrings which were in their ears, and brought them to Aaron. And he received the gold from their hand, and he fashioned it with an engraving tool, and made a molded calf. Then they said, "This is your god, O Israel, that brought you out of the land of Egypt!" So when Aaron saw it, he built an altar before it. And Aaron made a proclamation and said, "Tomorrow is a feast to the Lord." Then they rose early on the next day, offered burnt offerings, and brought peace offerings; and the people sat down to eat and drink, and rose up to play. And the Lord said to Moses, "Go, get down! For your people whom you brought out of the land of Egypt have corrupted themselves. They have turned aside quickly out of the way which I commanded them. They have made themselves a molded calf, and worshiped it and sacrificed to it, and said, 'This is your god, O Israel, that brought you out of the land of Egypt!'" And the Lord said to Moses, "I have seen this people, and indeed it is a stiff-necked people! Now therefore, let Me alone, that My wrath may burn hot against them and I may consume them. And I will make of you a great nation." Then Moses pleaded with the Lord his God, and said: "Lord, why does Your wrath burn hot against Your people whom You have brought out of the land of Egypt with great power and with a mighty hand? Why should the Egyptians speak, and say, 'He brought them out to harm them, to kill them in the mountains, and to consume them from the face of the earth'? Turn from Your fierce wrath, and relent from this harm to Your people. Remember Abraham, Isaac, and Israel, Your servants, to whom You swore by Your own self, and said to them, 'I will multiply your descendants as the stars of heaven; and all this land that I have spoken of I give to your descendants, and they shall inherit it forever.'" So the Lord relented from the harm which He said He would do to His people. And Moses turned and went down from the mountain, and the two tablets of the Testimony were in his hand. The tablets were written on both sides; on the one side and on the other they were written. Now the tablets were the work of God, and the writing was the writing of God engraved on the tablets. And when Joshua heard the noise of the people as they shouted, he said to Moses, "There is a noise of war in the camp." But he said: "It is not the noise of the shout of victory, nor the noise of the cry of defeat, but the sound of singing I hear." So it was, as soon as he came near the camp, that he saw the calf and the dancing. So Moses' anger became hot, and he cast the tablets out of his hands and broke them at the foot of the mountain. Then he took the calf which they had made, burned it in the fire, and ground it to powder; and he scattered it on the water and made the children of Israel drink it. And Moses said to Aaron, "What did this people do to you that you have brought so great a sin upon them?" So Aaron said, "Do not let the anger of my lord become hot. You know the people, that they are set on evil. For they said to me, 'Make us gods that shall go before us; as for this Moses, the man who brought us out of the land of Egypt, we do not know what has become of him.' And I said to them, 'Whoever has any gold, let them break it off.' So they gave it to me, and I cast it into the fire, and this calf came out." Now when Moses saw that the people were unrestrained (for Aaron had not restrained them, to their shame among their enemies), then Moses stood in the entrance of the camp, and said, "Whoever is on the Lord's side, come to me!" And all the sons of Levi gathered themselves together to him. And he said to them, "Thus says the Lord God of Israel: 'Let every man put his sword on his side, and go in and out from entrance to entrance throughout the camp, and let every man kill his brother, every man his companion, and every man his neighbor.'" So the sons of Levi did according to the word of Moses. And about three thousand men of the people fell that day" Exodus 32:1-28.

When Moses commanded a killing in the camp to avert the wrath of God, it was only the Levites who acted accordingly. They instinctively rose up to the occasion and turned their curse into the blessing of becoming the custodians of the tabernacle. Moses confers this blessing on the Levites, "And of Levi he said: "Let Your Thummim and Your Urim be with Your holy one, Whom You tested at Massah, and with whom You contended at the waters of Meribah, who says of his father and mother, 'I have not seen them'; nor did he acknowledge his brothers, or know his own children; for they have observed Your word and kept Your covenant. They shall teach Jacob Your judgments, and Israel Your law. They shall put incense before You, And a whole burnt sacrifice on Your altar. Bless his substance, Lord, and accept the work of his hands; strike the loins of those who rise against him, and of those who hate him, that they rise not again" Deuteronomy 33:8-11. The Levites became the priests of the Mosaic covenant and occupied a position central to all Israel. "But you shall appoint the Levites over the tabernacle of the Testimony, over all its furnishings, and over all things that belong to it; they shall carry the tabernacle and all its furnishings; they shall attend to it and camp around the tabernacle. And when the tabernacle is to go forward, the Levites shall take it down; and when the tabernacle is to be set up, the Levites shall set it up. The outsider who comes near shall be put to death. The children of Israel shall pitch their tents, everyone by his own camp, everyone by his own standard, according to their armies; but the Levites shall camp around the tabernacle of the Testimony, that there may be no wrath on the congregation of the children of Israel; and the Levites shall keep charge of the tabernacle of the Testimony." Thus the children of Israel did; according to all that the Lord commanded Moses, so they did" Numbers 1:50-54.

God's vision for Israel was that they would all serve as priests. "And Moses went up to God, and the Lord called to him from the mountain, saying, "Thus you shall say to the house of Jacob, and tell the children of Israel: 'You have seen what I did to the Egyptians, and how I bore you on eagles' wings and brought you to Myself. Now therefore, if you will indeed obey My voice and keep My covenant, then you shall be a special treasure to Me above all people; for all the earth is Mine. And you shall be to Me a kingdom of priests and a holy nation.' These are the words which you shall speak to the children of Israel" Exodus 19:3-6. The apostle Peter quotes from this scripture to unveil how this divine vision manifests with us in the New Testament era. "But you are a chosen generation, a royal priesthood, a holy nation, His own special people, that you may proclaim the praises of Him who called you out of darkness into His marvelous light; who once were not a people but are now the people of God, who had not obtained mercy but now have obtained mercy" 1 Peter 2:9. Royal priests speak to how we all belong to various tribes with a unique prophetic gate as well as our mandate to serve as priests. The Levites were the custodians and served as ministers at the tabernacle of Moses. "Do you not know that you are the temple of God and that the Spirit of God dwells in you? 17 If anyone defiles the temple of God, God will destroy him. For the temple of God is holy, which temple you are" 1 Corinthians 3:16&17. Today in the New Testament era, we are the tabernacle as well as the priests. To understand how we are the tabernacle, it is important to study the objects of worship in the tabernacle that was revealed to Moses. Interestingly, they provide insights of how we can serve as competent royal priests.

Chapter Fourteen

The

Priestly Armor

"Now take Aaron your brother, and his sons with him, from among the children of Israel, that he may minister to Me as priest, Aaron and Aaron's sons: Nadab, Abihu, Eleazar, and Ithamar. And you shall make holy garments for Aaron your brother, for glory and for beauty. So you shall speak to all who are gifted artisans, whom I have filled with the spirit of wisdom, that they may make Aaron's garments, to consecrate him, that he may minister to Me as priest. And these are the garments which they shall make: a breastplate, an ephod, a robe, a skillfully woven tunic, a turban, and a sash. So they shall make holy garments for Aaron your brother and his sons, that he may minister to Me as priest" Exodus 28:1-4. "And you shall make for them linen trousers to cover their nakedness; they shall reach from the waist to the thighs. They shall be on Aaron and on his sons when they come into the tabernacle of meeting, or when they come near the altar to minister in the holy place, that they do not incur iniquity and die. It shall be a statute forever to him and his descendants after him" Exodus 28:42&43.

"Finally, my brethren, be strong in the Lord and in the power of His might. Put on the whole armor of God, that you may be able to stand against the wiles of the devil. For we do not wrestle against flesh and blood, but against principalities, against powers, against the rulers of the darkness of this age, against spiritual hosts of wickedness in the heavenly places. Therefore take up the whole armor of God, that you may be able to withstand in the evil day, and having done all, to stand. Stand therefore, having girded your waist with truth, having put on the breastplate of righteousness, and having shod your feet with the preparation of the gospel of peace; above all, taking the shield of faith with which you will be able to quench all the fiery darts of the wicked one. And take the helmet of salvation, and the sword of the Spirit, which is the word of God; praying always with all prayer and supplication in the Spirit, being watchful to this end with all perseverance and supplication for all the saints" Ephesians 6:10-18.

"Who shall separate us from the love of Christ? Shall tribulation, or distress, or persecution, or famine, or nakedness, or peril, or sword? As it is written: "For Your sake we are killed all day long; We are accounted as sheep for the slaughter." Yet in all these things we are more than conquerors through Him who loved us. For I am persuaded that neither death nor life, nor angels nor principalities nor powers, nor things present nor things to come, nor height nor depth, nor any other created thing, shall be able to separate us from the love of God which is in Christ Jesus our Lord" Romans 8:35-39.

The priestly armor corresponded with the objects of fellowship in the tabernacle, as well as the harness of four family groups by which the twelve tribes were organized to camp around the tabernacle. To understand the priestly armor, we shall mix and match the regalia of the Old Dispensation Priest, with the New Dispensation armor of God. The four ways by which the priest was mantled, were the armor of light, blood, oil and glory. These four armors were designed to mitigate against the frameworks by which the kingdom of darkness execute their evil schemes. The four-dimensional operations of the kingdom of darkness are Existence, Elements, Territory and Time.

Armor of Light

Seducing spirits of the kingdom of darkness assign themselves to inspire lustfulness to terminate the light of the believer. "The night is far spent; the day is at hand. Therefore, let us cast off the works of darkness, and let us put on the armor of light" Romans 13:12. The sash of the priest is the equivalent of the 'belt of truth' by which the believer must be armed. As the name implies, it is the commitment to truth. Jesus Christ said, "I am the way, the truth, and the life. No one comes to the Father except through Me" John 14:6. People often use the word 'fact' interchangeably with 'truth'. However, facts are different from truths. Facts are physical manifestations, while truths may exist in the spiritual realm awaiting physical manifestation. The scriptures are fundamental truths that serve as a reference point for ascertaining whatever constitutes darkness. The sash or belt of truth is core to the armor of light. The armor of light is designed to resist the 'existence framework', where Seducing spirits collaborate with humans who dabble in witchcraft to perpetuate lust among humans. To overcome these forces, the believer is expected to be devout and walk in divine truth. In this way, we become sanctified by the truth and mantled with the armor of light.

Armor of Blood

The linen breeches of the priest served as the equivalent of the sandals of preparedness to preach the gospel of peace. Preaching the gospel is our witness of the life, death and resurrection of our Lord Jesus Christ. It is how we bring the grace of Christ's redemption to the lost as well as our victory over demonic powers. The 'elements framework' is where demonic powers collaborate with human authorities to disrupt nature. These forces execute curse mandates by orchestrating infirmities in humans, addictions and destructive occurrences. To overcome these forces, the priest was expected to serve as an intercessor at the altar of sacrifice. This is where members of the tribe of Levi volunteered to serve in the offering of animal blood sacrifices. Owing to their work with blood, they were mantled with the armor of blood in the same way as the preaching of the gospel.

Armor of Oil

The tunic or coat of the priest served as the equivalent of prayer in the armor of the believer. Tending the lampstand at the Holy Place in the tabernacle was an important function of the priests. Oil which is significant of the anointing of the Holy Spirit was the fuel for the light of the lampstand. Furthermore, there was a special anointing by which the priest was consecrated for ministry. "Moreover, the Lord spoke to Moses, saying: "Also take for yourself quality spices, five hundred shekels of liquid myrrh, half as much sweet-smelling cinnamon (two hundred and fifty shekels), two hundred and fifty shekels of sweet-smelling cane, five hundred shekels of cassia, according to the shekel of the sanctuary, and a hin of olive oil. And you shall make from these a holy anointing oil, an ointment compounded according to the art of the perfumer. It shall be a holy anointing oil" Exodus 30:22-25. "And you shall anoint Aaron and his sons, and consecrate them, that they may minister to Me as priests" Exodus 30:30.

The four spices of the special anointing oil for the priests were Cassia, Myrrh, Calamus and Cinnamon. Cassia was introduced to a wilderness to stimulate forestation, and it is how the anointed priest was equipped to change the barren landscape of his assigned territory. Myrrh was used to eliminate inherent odors and preserve the dead. This signified the impact of the anointed priest, to deal with all that may have been done over several years to frustrate the divine purpose of people. Calamus is a psychoactive spice component of the anointing of the priest, that stimulates the creativity potentials of people. Cinnamon is a flavor and taste spice component of the priest's anointing, that stimulates equity in people. The 'territory framework' is where Demonic Principalities collaborate with human rulers to introduce barren culture, that directs the worship of communities to the devil. It takes the ministry of an anointed priest to overcome these forces of the territory framework.

Armor of Glory

The breastplate, ephod, turban and robe were four priestly attires that matched the breastplate of righteousness, the shield of faith, the helmet of salvation and the sword of the spirit respectively in the armor of the believer. The 'time framework' is where Satan orchestrates famine which is significant of economic hardships. Statistics show that one percent of the world controls most of the riches of the world, and the rest struggle for survival. Satan controls the systems by which our world functions to perpetuate the poverty people experience today. It requires the ministry of an anointed high priest to overcome his diabolical schemes. Wearing the breastplate, the High Priest was equipped to make destiny-based decisions for everyone in Israel. The anointed high priest was called, commissioned and compassionate. Mantled with the ephod of his calling, the anointed high priest was poised to always offer true and proper worship to counteract delays orchestrated by Satan. Wearing the turban of his commission, the anointed high priest had a specific divine assignment to disrupt ambitious satanic detours. Mantled with the robe of his compassion, the anointed high priest empathized with those who struggled with the difficult issues of life.

Daily Armor Prayer

Lord Jesus, I beseech you to mantle me with the Armor of Light, that is the belt of truth. Grant me the grace to walk humbly before you with a good and pure conscience.

Lord Jesus, I beseech you to mantle me with Armor of Blood, that is the sandals of preparedness to preach the gospel of peace. Grant me the grace to be a witness of the life, death and resurrection of our Lord Jesus Christ.

Lord Jesus, I beseech you to mantle me with the Armor of Oil, that is the priestly coat. Grant me the grace to pray all manner of prayers, supplications and thanksgivings that are required of me. Spice my anointing with Cassia, that is the grace to turn every wilderness in my space into a forest. Spice me with Myrrh, that is the grace to turn every instance of death in my space into life. Spice me with Calamus, that is the grace to foster creativity in my space. Spice me with Cinnamon, that is the grace to foster equity in my space in Jesus name.

Lord Jesus, I beseech you to mantle me with the Armor of Glory.

Mantle me with the breastplate of righteousness. Grant me the grace to appropriate your Word for every challenge and opportunity, as well as the grace to be a faithful steward of resources.

Mantle me Lord Jesus with the shield of faith, that is the ephod for worshipping you in spirit and in truth. Grant me Frankincense, that is the grace to worship you with inspired sanctification. Grant me Onycha, that is the grace to worship you with inspired intercession. Grant me Stacte, that is the grace to worship you with inspired adoration. Grant me Galbanum, that is the grace to worship you with the inspired fat of offerings.

Mantle me Lord Jesus with the helmet of salvation, that is the turban of holiness. Grant me Fine Linen, that is the grace to cast down arguments and foster restitution in my space. Grant me Scarlet, the grace to cast down every high thing and ambitious goal that exalts itself above the knowledge of God, and foster redemption in my space. Grant me Blue, the grace to take captive every thought and subject it to the obedience of Christ, and foster release in my space. Grant me Purple, the grace to punish every disobedience while I walk in obedience and foster restoration in my space.

Mantle me Lord Jesus with the priestly robe and equip my heart with the Urim and Thummim, that is the grace to exercise the prerogative of mercy, and manifest your goodness everywhere in Jesus name. Amen!

Harness

SECTION TWO

Kingdom Economics

In this section, I intend to unveil how the model of the kingdom of Christ differs from the kingdoms of the world. Every system by which the world functions, whether as government structures, economies, or technology, mimic divine systems either in a true or perverted way. Where the model is pure it liberates and empowers people to engage their potential for the benefit of all. However, when a model is perverted, it suppresses and exploits many people.

A typical example is what history teaches us of the democratic system of government that is widely adopted across the world today. It started as monarchies where all the power of governance was vested with the ruling king or queen. If the ruler happened to be a good or wicked person, then it reflected on how their subjects benefited or suffered from their reign. Super kings who had conquered various territories had to deploy governors to take charge of them. The Roman Emperors governed their vast empires with Senators who constituted the legislative arm of government. Through much blood shedding the French Revolution adopted universal suffrage to calm down an overly oppressed populace. The United States at its inception formally adopted the fine-tuned democracy that entails an executive, legislature and judiciary. It is interesting that while the world experimented over several years and evolved with a government system that seems fair to all, Isaiah the prophet tells in scripture, "For the Lord is our judge, the Lord is our lawgiver, the Lord is our king; he will save us" Isaiah 33:22. The model that evolved over several years entailing much oppression and suffering could have been known simply by seeking the mind of God in the scriptures. Jesus Christ came to introduce us to the gospel of the kingdom. "Now after that John was put in prison, Jesus came into Galilee, preaching the gospel of the kingdom of God, And saying, the time is fulfilled, and the kingdom of God is at hand: repent ye, and believe the gospel" Mark 1:14&15. Though the gospel of the kingdom was the theme of Christ's message that resounds throughout the scriptures, some of us have doctored this message into the gospel of our Church denomination. "Having a form of godliness but denying the power thereof: from such turn away" 2 Timothy 3:15. By ignoring the fulness of truths that unleash the kingdom of Christ, Christians are not excluded from the exploitation and sufferings in our world.

The mission statement of our Lord Jesus Christ is enshrined in His first recorded sermon: "And He was handed the book of the prophet Isaiah. And when He had opened the book, He found the place where it was written, "The Spirit of the Lord is upon Me, because He has anointed Me to preach the gospel to the poor. He has sent Me to heal the brokenhearted, to proclaim liberty to the captives and recovery of sight to the blind, to set at liberty those who are oppressed; To proclaim the acceptable year of the Lord" Luke 4:17-19. The fullness of this statement includes the following taken from Isaiah 61:2b-4, "…And the day of vengeance of our God; To comfort all who mourn, to console those who mourn in Zion, to give them beauty for ashes, the oil of joy for mourning, the garment of praise for the spirit of heaviness; that they may be called trees of righteousness, the planting of the Lord, that He may be glorified. And they shall rebuild the ancient ruins, they shall raise up the former devastations, and they shall repair the waste cities, the desolations of many generations."

The mission of our Lord Jesus Christ was to unveil the kingdom model which replaces the imperfect as well as perverseness of worldly systems that suppress and exploit people. One word that summarizes the goal of a worldly system is 'money' which is the focus of economics. However Jesus teaches us that: "No one can serve two masters; for either he will hate the one and love the other, or else he will be loyal to the one and despise the other. You cannot serve God and mammon" Matthew 6:24. Mammon is used here to mean money. Jesus taught that it was impossible to equate God the owner and ruler of the universe with money. Money is the substance of riches which all belong to God the creator of all things. While worldly systems place money at the forefront of all human endeavoring, the kingdom of Christ places the wellbeing of humans as core.

Economics is a social science that focuses on the production, distribution and consumption of goods and services. This discipline analyses how we make decisions concerning the realities of scarcity and choice. It is obvious that as humans we have unlimited wants and yet our resources are often limited. Historically, the world has been shaped by five economic systems, and countries choose their preference. First is Primitivism where individuals or communities produced their necessities. Second is Feudalism where landowners leased property to peasants who cultivated it and paid the lords. Third is Capitalism where entrepreneurs organized capital to set up various kinds of businesses for profit. Fourth is

Socialism where cooperative communities set up enterprises for their common benefit and not necessarily for profit. Finally, Communism is where the government establishes the enterprises that exist within a country. For several years, nations have been inclined to their choice among these five systems which has also shaped their global alliances.

While there are merits that can be attributed to each of these systems, so far none of them have exclusively demonstrated their efficacy in resolving overwhelmingly man's issues of scarcity and choice. The issue of poverty in our world continues to escalate with some groups benefiting to the detriment of others. Could it be that primitivism, feudalism, capitalism, socialism and communism are all a progressive nuance to the ultimate system that resolves scarcity and choice?

Jesus Christ came to model the original image and likeness of God for which man was created to restore our pursuit of divine destiny and glory. As we traverse this section of the book, it is my hope that we shall find our place in the kingdom economy as was originally intended.

Chapter Fifteen

Intuitiveness

"You shall not sow your vineyard with different kinds of seed, lest the yield of the seed which you have sown, and the fruit of your vineyard be defiled" Deuteronomy 22:9

In my second year of high school, we lived in a multi-purpose three-story building. My family occupied the entire third floor while a publishing company occupied the ground floor. The publisher was a distinguished gentleman who was single at the time and so would often spend the night at work. In the late afternoons when he would often come out of the office for a breeze of fresh air while reading the daily newspapers, I would approach him for a chat. In those days the newspaper vendors would brandish the daily publications to those driving in traffic as well as from door to door. As a young student I would notice the headlines on my way to school. At that early age, I was totally disinterested in news on politics, crime, sports and so on, with an exception for headlines concerning the economy. Whenever I noticed an economic news headline in the morning, I would hang out in front of the building waiting for the publisher to come out. I would engage him in conversation in which I often quizzed him about the rationale for government policies and projects. Around this same period, I began to envisage a future in which I would become an economist, so this became my career focus until I attained master's level Business Analyst.

To be Intuitive is the ability to know something that is hidden from our natural sense of contact, without the need for conscious reasoning. The western tribes of Israel that consist of Ephraim, Manasseh and Benjamin are responsible for excellence progress. While Ephraim represents skill, Manasseh signifies transformation and Benjamin depicts initiative. The Rulers and Chief Executives of this world emulate models of the kingdom of darkness in how they operate, however the Lord Jesus Christ has not called us for any mission that is generic in nature. 'Excellence progress' entails us being fashioned primarily into tools for building a kingdom like no other. "For we are His workmanship, created in Christ Jesus for good works, which God prepared beforehand that we should walk in them" Ephesians 2:10. To build the throne of the eternal kingdom, the Lord Jesus Christ works in us through the scriptures so we can develop inherent skills, and transforms us through trials for kingdom initiatives. Ephraim's skills go beyond head knowledge. "For though by this time you ought to be teachers, you need someone to teach you again the first principles of the oracles of God; and you have come to need milk and not solid food. For everyone who partakes only of milk is unskilled in the word of righteousness, for he is a babe. But solid food belongs to those who are of full age, that is, those who by reason of use have their senses exercised to discern both good and evil" Hebrews 5:12-14. Skill entails exercise of what one is taught until we become conversant with its application in real life scenarios. Whatever we are taught in any vocation is an accumulation of knowledge and practice experiences over several generations. However, without knowledge of the scriptures, all that we are taught in secular training of any profession will always lack the degree of excellence that our Lord Jesus Christ intends for us to attain. "All Scripture is given by inspiration of God, and is profitable for doctrine, for reproof, for correction, for instruction in righteousness, that the man of God may be complete, thoroughly equipped for every good work" 2 Timothy 3:16&17. Each one of us ought to become highly acquainted with divine truth to the extent that we can detect any secular premise that does not conform.

Manasseh's transformation entails trials. "For You, O God, have tested us; You have refined us as silver is refined. You brought us into the net; You laid affliction on our backs. You have caused men to ride over our heads; We went through fire and through water; But You brought us out to a wealthy place" Psalms 66:10-12. Through adversities that come our way, we are purged of all the impurities that impair our sense of intuition. "The words of the Lord are pure words, like silver tried in a furnace of earth, purified seven times" Psalms 12:6. Through fire we are forged by God to become one with knowledge. "Listen, O coastlands, to Me, and take heed, you peoples from afar! The Lord has called Me from the womb; from the matrix of My mother He has made mention of My name. And He has made My mouth like a sharp sword; in the shadow of His hand He has hidden me, and made me a polished shaft; in His quiver He has hidden Me" Isaiah 49:1&2. This scripture tells of how we are crafted to become intuitively high precision weapons. Like a warrior whose weapon is customized to fit his unique disposition, He hides us in His quiver.

The initiative of Benjamin is to identify with a cause. "Drink water from your own cistern and running water from your own well. Should your fountains be dispersed abroad, streams of water in the streets? Let them be only your own, and not for strangers with you. Let your fountain be blessed, and rejoice with the wife of your youth. As a loving deer and a graceful doe, let her breasts satisfy you at all times; and always be enraptured with her love. For why should you, my son, be enraptured by an immoral woman, and be embraced in the arms of a seductress?" Proverbs 5:15-20. There is a fountain of legitimate passion resident in everyone. It is triggered and comes to light whenever the pure water of God flows over our soul. At some point every human being becomes aware of their passion and while some incline their life pursuits to synch with it, many often discard it when they consider lucrative trends and become opportunistic. Those who pursue their passion relentlessly often attain great heights in that arena.

Intuition is our supernatural sense of contact, based on a good conscience by the sanctification of divine truths. Sanctification was the function of the brazen laver which was the first object of fellowship in the tabernacle. Then the Lord spoke to Moses, saying, "You shall also make a laver of bronze, with its base also of bronze, for washing. You shall put it between the tabernacle of meeting and the altar. And you shall put water in it, for Aaron and his sons shall wash their hands and their feet in water from it. When they go into the tabernacle of meeting, or when they come near the altar to minister, to burn an offering made by fire to the Lord, they shall wash with water, lest they die. So they shall wash their hands and their feet, lest they die. And it shall be a statute forever to them to him and his descendants throughout their generations" Exodus 30:17-21. The brazen laver was a basin made from highly polished brass that gave a mirror reflection of whoever stood in its view. This basin was filled with water so that those who came to the Tabernacle could wash their hands and feet. The mirror reflection from the laver allowed people to see how their works and ways conflicted with God. With the water which signified God's word, they washed their hands and feet until their works and ways conformed to God's requirements. "Husbands, love your wives, just as Christ also loved the church and gave Himself for her, that He might sanctify and cleanse her with the washing of water by the word, that He might present her to Himself a glorious church, not having spot or wrinkle or any such thing, but that she should be holy and without blemish" Ephesians 5:25-27. Spots, wrinkles and blemishes are the impact of sin on the human body. They impair our spiritual sense of touch and isolate us from such access to God. In the Old Dispensation era, this was a condition commonly known as leprosy. A leper was forbidden from fellowship in the tabernacle unless they became cleansed of this condition. This was the condition of Naaman the Syrian general until he was supernaturally cleansed by God's word through Elisha the prophet. Elisha gave instructions through his servant Gehazi for Naaman's healing but Naaman felt disrespected by this as well as the directive to go and wash seven times in the river Jordan. It is obvious that Naaman was arrogant and had no spiritual values which was likely the root for his condition of leprosy. His own servants appealed to him to get rid of the arrogance and submit to God's word which when he did, he was healed. Dipping in water seven times cleansed Naaman of leprosy and this is significant of how God's word is intended to cleanse us of the spots, wrinkles and blemishes that impair our intuitiveness. When Naaman was healed, he requested that two mule loads of Israelite earth be given to him so it could become the platform upon which to worship the God of Israel. This request signified that he was abandoning the idolatry that was practiced by his native Syrians to maintain intuitive contact with the Almighty God. (2 Kings 5)

God's word plays a role in how the human mind is designed to make us intuitive. The conscience is the first faculty of the mind that serves as the brazen laver of the human temple. The conscience behaves like a water filter and separates good and right from bad and wrong. This way the conscience distinguishes whatever information we encounter so we can determine if it is acceptable or not. Interestingly, we are born with an empty conscience and are vested with the responsibility of developing it. There are four types of conscience identified in the scriptures. First is a Good and Pure conscience, which is one that is knowledgeable and upholds divine truths as well as the skills of one's vocation. A Weak Conscience is where a person has little knowledge of divine truths as well as not being skillful vocationally. A Defiled Conscience is where a person chooses to fill their minds with falsehoods and so they pivot themselves to what is convenient. A Conscience Seared with Hot Iron is where a person constantly elects to do the wrong thing even though they know what is right.

A good and pure conscience is the bedrock of a functional intuition. "You shall not sow your vineyard with different kinds of seed, lest the yield of the seed which you have sown, and the fruit of your vineyard be defiled" Deuteronomy 22:9. Seed is the idea for which a mission is initiated, while fruit is the impact of the mission. Usually, the legitimate idea for a mission inspires the entrepreneurial mind to mobilize the resources for pursuit. Others who are intrigued by this idea identify with this cause as executives or as silent partners. Jesus put it this way, "Again, the kingdom of heaven is like treasure hidden in a field, which a man found and hid; and for joy over it he goes and sells all that he has and buys that field. "Again, the kingdom of heaven is like a merchant seeking beautiful pearls, who, when he had found one pearl of great price, went and sold all that he had and bought it" Matthew 13:44-46. Here, the pearl of great price is the idea, while the field of treasure is the core concept that drives the mission. Cultivating a parcel of land with different kinds of seeds may not seem wrong to today's farmers because our agricultural science proves that there are benefits to intercropping. However, our science often focuses on the benefits of a research subject that may be blindsided to consequences, yet unknown to humans. This is not a new spectacle where research that was lauded as a scientific breakthrough ended up being discarded later when further research unveiled the adverse consequences of what was initially touted as effective. One of the fundamental premises of science is knowledge of the properties of an element or substance. Such knowledge guides how you utilize or combine it with other substances so that catastrophic consequences can be averted. Even where you procure a manufactured product, it is incumbent upon the manufacturer to provide a manual that furnishes one with guidance. If one does not abide by the guidance of the manufacturer and there are adverse consequences, then no warranty on the product can be claimed. In our instance of the scripture, the product is land that is to be cultivated with crops, and the creator of this land is God Almighty. His Word furnishes us with the properties of land such that it must not be intercropped or else its produce would be defiled. Land is significant of the human heart that must not be tasked with any other mission except what it was divinely intended to accomplish. An enterprise that shifts focus for the sole intention of making more money gets defiled. Defilement is to lose the intuitive sense or the temperature of one's core mission. In the same way that a high temperature of a person gives concern to a medical doctor to administer treatment to a patient, a mission can be overheated and must be addressed. The lack of intuitiveness is what spurs business leaders to shift focus rather than to indulge it when the external signs indicate an overheating in performance.

The common philosophy of most enterprises is to make lots of money and so whatever inclination makes this possible is considered a good business decision. Several years ago, I was involved in the marble business working in partnership with a friend. One of the contracts I secured for the company involved tiling the floors of the offices in a mega facility. The owners of the project wanted express execution of the marble tiling contract, but then the Plaster-of-Paris style ceiling was not yet executed. We were tasked to help find a contractor to execute the ceiling contract and my partner insisted that we take on that contract. Though I knew better, I succumbed to the rationale of a 'business decision' as is known commonly. We hired skilled workers to execute the project, but then the lines of the ceiling when finished were not perfectly straight. The workers did all that was possible and yet this could not be rectified. I resorted to seeking God prayerfully to ascertain why this was happening and He showed me that a serpent had affixed itself to the ceiling. This meant that because we had strayed away from our core mission, we had opened the door for the enemy to invade our workspace. Though the client was satisfied with our execution of the marbling contract, the ceiling task ruined our reputation. The problem here was that we had no sense of intuitiveness with the ceiling task so we could not supervise the execution effectively.

It is interesting how science classifies land as an unliving thing and yet throughout the scripture land is spoken of as living thing. Foremost, God speaks to land and it responds, "Then God said, "Let the waters under the heavens be gathered together into one place, and let the dry land appear"; and it was so" Genesis 1:9. Furthermore, land makes decisions concerning its inhabitants, "You shall therefore keep My statutes and My judgments, and shall not commit any of these abominations, either any of your own nation or any stranger who dwells among you, for all these abominations the men of the land have done, who were before you, and thus the land is defiled, lest the land vomit you out also when you defile it, as it vomited out the nations that were before you" Leviticus 18:26-28. When the Israelites violated the seventh year sabbaths and were in default, the land vomited them out and they ended up in Babylonian captivity for seventy years so the land could enjoy its due rest.

A command of God transcends whatever we know or may ever get to know as humans, and so it is important to accept His word as a standard for our endeavors. Rejecting a divine command fosters a dysfunctional conscience and breaks the circuit of our intuitiveness with God the creator and maker of the universe. Since economics is the center of gravity for all industries, developing skill in a vocation without the essence of a good and pure conscience is the short-circuiting that paralyses our quest to foster economic prosperity for all.

Certain industries such as education, manufacturing, oil-mining and retail require a pooling of highly intuitive minds that are inclined to the same goal. They thrive on the integrity of knowledge that is passed on generationally and so the economic concept of Socialism that indulges those with a cooperative mindset is best suited for such endeavors.

Harness

Chapter Sixteen

Instinctiveness

"You shall not plow with an ox and a donkey together"
Deuteronomy 22:10

I became committed to the Lord Jesus Christ as a student in college. My zeal to know God was strong and I studied books authored by renown bible teacher Derek Prince who has now gone to be with the Lord. One day I was walking the hallway on campus reading his book on 'Obedience to the Holy Spirit' when I first heard the Holy Spirit say, "go into the lecture hall and lay down". It was an odd instruction but then I had been learning about Him, so I obeyed. The moment I lay down on the pew-like chair, I fell in a trance seeing myself talking with a friend named Peter at a car workshop in our neighborhood. He proposed to me that we enter business together where he would oversee marketing and I offered to be the administrator. On my way to church the following day, I decided to pass by Peter's house to check on him. I rang the bell to his apartment and when he came out, he said, "Hey Ken, I have been looking for you." He took me in his car, and we went to the same auto workshop I saw in my vision. There he proposed that we start a business and offered to be the marketer. As I agreed and offered to be the administrator, I immediately remembered the vision of the previous day. This is how we entered a business venture as partners and secured a major distributorship for salt.

To be instinctive is to have inherent virtues and vices not thought about, planned, or learned. The apostle Paul makes reference to this trait, "When I call to remembrance the genuine faith that is in you, which dwelt first in your grandmother Lois and your mother Eunice, and I am persuaded is in you also" 2 Timothy 1:5. Ancestral virtues travel the bloodline of family relatives, so they usually have common traits. The Israelite tribes of Dan, Asher and Naphtali were positioned at the northern coordinate of the tabernacle and were significant of inheritance progress. Inheritance entails whatever is passed on to us from our ancestors. While the tribe of Dan signifies justice, Asher depicts blessings and Naphtali represents communication.

Dan is the Israelite tribe that tackles bloodline issues of **justice and injustice**. Virtues in the blood often trigger justice while vices in the blood are the root of injustice for members of a family. The burden of exercising the virtues that foster justice as well as dealing with the vices responsible for injustice is distributed to members of a family by divine design. Every family ought to leverage their virtues of favor and justice to unravel the vices of their disfavor of injustice. Often, we find family members embroiled in the unnecessary burden of quarrelling and in competition with one another. The kingdom of darkness distracts members of a family unit from their core burden of tackling bloodline injustices so they may not unleash the fullness of their virtues and justice.

Asher is the Israelite tribe with a burden for our fellowship with God at the appointed times to invoke blessings that neutralize curses. While virtues trigger blessings, vices manifest like a curse. To nurture divine blessings to overcome curses, God scheduled divine visitations that tallied with agriculture which is man's primary occupation. Passover which signifies death on the cross coincided with sowing seeds. First-fruits that signified resurrection coincided with the first crops of the field. Pentecost, which signified the birth of the Church coincided with the fullness of harvest. Trumpets which signified divine order coincided with victory through alignment. Atonement signified the peace of God which Israel sought at the heavenly court of divine justice. Tabernacles which signified divine destiny coincided with Israel celebrating the promises of God. The divine prescriptions for these appointed times of fellowship with God is how we are empowered to overcome curses and manifest blessings.

Naphtali enshrines communication narratives about a family that can either invoke or expel good. Familiar spirits whisper to those with whom they are inclined to know about the injustices of a bloodline. Usually those involved in the occult or seek mediums become aware of these injustices and dispense evil accordingly. In primitive times, those who received such information from familiar spirits would pass it on to rumor mongers who often spread it in the community. It is terrible where everyone in a community is aware of vices or injustices that plague your family except for yourself. The consequence is that the people who often character assassinate you do not share good opportunities with you. What changes the narrative concerning us is when we start to preach the gospel of Jesus Christ in our community. Our witness of His life, death and resurrection breaks the impact of the false narrative concerning our lives. Souls get saved and the network of evil reports concerning us is disrupted.

The weight of virtues versus our vices impacts our instinctiveness. Instinctiveness is related to the emotions of the human soul. It is the faculty of the mind by which we relate to the environment. When our virtues outweigh our vices, we often manifest stable emotions and vice versa. Any aspect of our human character over which we totally possess control indicates we have a stable emotion. We can demonstrate virtues such as love, kindness, self-control, patience, joy to any degree that we consider appropriate. "If anyone comes to Me and does not hate his father and mother, wife and children, brothers and sisters, yes, and his own life also, he cannot be My disciple" Luke 14:26. "Be angry, and do not sin", do not let the sun go down on your wrath" Ephesians 4:26. Assuming occasion warrants, we may also exhibit vices like anger and hate in a measured way.

However, any condition where one exhibits extreme behaviors, addictions and is unable to control lusts is considered as unstable emotions. Lust is like eggs that are inherited ancestrally and so they reside in the bloodline. "Let no one say when he is tempted, "I am tempted by

God"; for God cannot be tempted by evil, nor does He Himself tempt anyone. But each one is tempted when he is drawn away by his own desires and enticed. Then, when desire has conceived, it gives birth to sin; and sin, when it is full-grown, brings forth death" James 1:13-15. Eggs of lust are usually formed whenever we violate our conscience and persist with depravities. These depravities turn into eggs of lust which are bloodline vices. Evil spirits are able recognize which eggs of lust reside in a bloodline and can conceive them to birth sin. Usually, a person who possesses such eggs of lust are powerless to resist the enticement of spirits of lust. Many people have been incarcerated in prisons throughout the world for crimes resulting from eggs of lust in the bloodline. Certain addictive behaviors that underline common dysfunctions of society as well as chronic infirmities are also bloodline related. "For consider Him who endured such hostility from sinners against Himself, lest you become weary and discouraged in your souls. You have not yet resisted to bloodshed, striving against sin. And you have forgotten the exhortation which speaks to you as to sons: "My son, do not despise the chastening of the Lord, nor be discouraged when you are rebuked by Him; For whom the Lord loves He chastens, and scourges every son whom He receives." If you endure chastening, God deals with you as with sons; for what son is there whom a father does not chasten? But if you are without chastening, of which all have become partakers, then you are illegitimate and not sons. Furthermore, we have had human fathers who corrected us, and we paid them respect. Shall we not much more readily be in subjection to the Father of spirits and live? For they indeed for a few days chastened us as seemed best to them, but He for our profit, that we may be partakers of His holiness. Now no chastening seems to be joyful for the present, but painful; nevertheless, afterward it yields the peaceable fruit of righteousness to those who have been trained by it. Therefore strengthen the hands which hang down, and the feeble knees, and make straight paths for your feet, so that what is lame may not be dislocated, but rather be healed" Hebrews 12:3-13. Here, we are told of how we engage chastening to bring repeated offenders to observe discipline. However, there is a chastening that is divinely orchestrated and designed to deal with addictions, chronic infirmities and demonic oppression. Such chastening is prescribed for the devout believer through the voice of the blood of Jesus. "But you have come to Mount Zion and to the city of the living God, the heavenly Jerusalem, to an innumerable company of angels, to the general assembly and church of the firstborn who are registered in heaven, to God the Judge of all, to the spirits of just men made perfect, to Jesus the Mediator of the new covenant, and to the blood of sprinkling that speaks better things than that of Abel" Hebrews 12:22-24. Through the blood of Jesus Christ that was offered on the old-rugged cross, there is a path of redemption for the bloodline of every family.

Instinctiveness is supernatural discernment fostered by the path of consecration that the blood of the Cross of Jesus Christ lays out for us. The Old Dispensation Era model of the cross of our Lord Jesus Christ was the altar of sacrifice in the tabernacle of Moses. "He made the altar of burnt offering of acacia wood; five cubits was its length and five cubits its width, it was square, and its height was three cubits. He made its horns on its four corners; the horns were of one piece with it. And he overlaid it with bronze. He made all the utensils for the altar: the pans, the shovels, the basins, the forks, and the firepans; all its utensils he made of bronze. And he made a grate of bronze network for the altar, under its rim, midway from the bottom. He cast four rings for the four corners of the bronze grating, as holders for the poles. And he made the poles of acacia wood and overlaid them with bronze. Then he put the poles into the rings on the sides of the altar, with which to bear it. He made the altar hollow with boards" Exodus 38:1-7. The altar of sacrifice was where animal blood sacrifices were offered. It was constructed with acacia also known as shittim wood which was a high-quality wood that did not easily rot, signifying God's word. This was overlaid with bronze metal that signifies trials. Whereas in the Old Dispensation era, animal sacrifices were offered for sin, the altar of sacrifice is significant today of the cross of our Lord Jesus Christ. Jesus Christ who is the Word of God is also the Lamb of God that was slain for our sins. Jesus Christ taught us the concept of the cross, "When He had called the people to Himself, with His disciples also, He said to them, "Whoever desires to come after Me, let him deny himself, and take up his cross, and follow Me. For whoever desires to save his life will lose it, but whoever loses his life for My sake and the gospel's will save it. For what will it profit a man if he gains the whole world, and loses his own soul? Or what will a man give in exchange for his soul?" Mark 8:34-37. The cross is the place of consecration. Consecration is to be dedicated to God by sacrifice and all believers are expected to live a life of sacrifice. Jesus Christ lays out a cross for each of us to carry and this becomes our path of consecration. It entails abstinence that is dictated by the blood of sprinkling so we can overcome ancestral bloodline issues. Hebrews 12:24 says we have come "to Jesus the Mediator of the new covenant, and to the blood of sprinkling that speaks better things than that of Abel."

When an animal sacrifice is offered on the altar, it oozes out a scent that is inhaled by God. "Then Noah built an altar to the Lord, and took of every clean animal and of every clean bird, and offered burnt offerings on the altar. And the Lord smelled a soothing aroma. Then the Lord said in His heart, "I will never again curse the ground for man's sake, although the imagination of man's heart is evil from his youth; nor will I again destroy every living thing as I have done" Genesis 8:20&21. When God inhaled the smell of Noah's sacrifice, He made a significant decision that reversed a curse. The sacrifice of a consecrated life offers up a sweet-smelling odor to God. Apostle Paul teaches in 2 Corinthians 2:14-17, "Now thanks be to God who always leads us in triumph in Christ, and through us diffuses the fragrance of His knowledge in every place. For we are to God the fragrance of Christ among those who are being saved and among those who are perishing. To the one we are the aroma of death leading to death, and to the other the aroma of life leading to life. And who is sufficient for these things? For we are not, as so many, peddling the word of God; but as of sincerity, but as from God, we speak in the sight of God in Christ." The scent of our sacrifice is the standard for our discernment. In the same way a person who constantly smells bad would not be able to distinguish a foul odor in another, the degree of our discernment is contingent on how well we smell with God. Discernment is our spiritual sense of smell by which we distinguish legitimate virtues from vices.

During the journey of Israel in the wilderness towards the Promised Land, God showed Moses the tabernacle in heaven and mandated him to build the same for Israel. However, the Israelites lacked the skills to construct such an elaborate and sophisticated design. In Egypt, the Israelites were 'hewers of wood and drawers of water'. They were subjected to the menial labor required by the Egyptian craftsmen who implemented the projects of the Pharaoh. "Then the Lord spoke to Moses, saying: "See, I have called by name Bezalel the son of Uri, the son of Hur, of the tribe of Judah. And I have filled him with the Spirit of God, in wisdom, in understanding, in knowledge, and in all manner of workmanship, to design artistic works, to work in gold, in silver, in bronze, in cutting jewels for setting, in carving wood, and to work in all manner of workmanship. "And I, indeed I, have appointed with him Aholiab the son of Ahisamach, of the tribe of Dan; and I have put wisdom in the hearts of all the gifted artisans, that they may make all that I have commanded you: the tabernacle of meeting, the ark of the Testimony and the mercy seat that is on it, and all the furniture of the tabernacle, the table and its utensils, the pure gold lampstand with all its utensils, the altar of incense, the altar of burnt offering with all its utensils, and the laver and its base, the garments of ministry, the holy garments for Aaron the priest and the garments of his sons, to minister as priests, and the anointing oil and sweet incense for the holy place. According to all that I have commanded you they shall do" Exodus 31:1-11. Royalty and Justice were the two-fold fundamental purpose of God for the tabernacle. Bezaleel and Aholiab were called of God to implement the design of this tabernacle owing to their family origins. Bezaleel was the son of Uri, the son of Hur, of the tribe of Judah. He was from the tribe blessed with royalty. "Judah, you are he whom your brothers shall praise; Your hand shall be on the neck of your enemies; Your father's children shall bow down before you. Judah is a lion's whelp; From the prey, my son, you have gone up. He bows down, he lies down as a lion; And as a lion, who shall rouse him? The scepter shall not depart from Judah, nor a lawgiver from between his feet, until Shiloh comes; And to Him shall be the obedience of the people. Binding his donkey to the vine, and his donkey's colt to the choice vine, He washed his garments in wine, and his clothes in the blood of grapes. His eyes are darker than wine, and his teeth whiter than milk" Genesis 49:8-12. The blessing on the tribe of Judah was a prophetic revelation to Jacob. This blessing was inherent in Bezaleel so he could fathom the royal design of the tabernacle and would not be comfortable compromising it. Similarly, Aholiab was chosen from the tribe of Dan. "Dan shall judge his people as one of the tribes of Israel. Dan shall be a serpent by the way, a viper by the path, that bites the horse's heels so that its rider shall fall backward. I have waited for your salvation, O Lord!" Genesis 49:16-18. Jacob blessed Dan to administer justice. This blessing was inherent in Aholiab as a virtue for which reason he would not compromise the essence of justice in the execution of the design of the tabernacle. When the tabernacle was completed according to the divine design, God's glory came down and filled it so that Israel continued to experience His goodness through fellowship.

One of our dysfunctions in society today is rooted in how we assign people for tasks which require discernment. Certain assignments of our corporate endeavors require people who belong to specific families that are divinely mandated. "You shall not plow with an ox and a donkey together" Deuteronomy 22:10. Though the ox and donkey may look alike in stature, they have a completely different bone disposition. Yoking both to execute the task of plowing a field will place one in a disadvantaged position. This command of the scriptures speaks to how we establish teams for a given task. Oftentimes our quest is to assemble those with qualities that are visibly coherent with our objectives and yet inherent burdens are vastly ignored. It is for this reason that assuming we take a sum of all formal missions of governments, corporations, non-profits, educational institutions and individuals across the world, then chronic issues like poverty, premature death, homelessness, joblessness and so on should have waned significantly. Organizations that report the global state of affairs such as the World Health Organization, World Food Program, and World Bank among others all predict crisis of magnanimous proportions as the future for our world.

Our world is never plagued with the lack of great ideas rather it is the misplacement of potential. Every day new missions are established with the quest to solve human problems, but then most only aggravate our condition with their endless appetite for more profit. Corporate entities lower standards, twist policies and manipulate the unsuspecting to make more money. Many corporate leaders are simply burdenless for the plight of humanity and so we are altogether bankrupt in our health, nutrition, finances, education, entertainment, politics, technology as well as all other sectors. A burdenless society is the recipe for self-destruction. Prior to the captivity of Israel by the

Babylonians and the destruction of Jerusalem, the Prophet Ezekiel received this word from God, "Then He called out in my hearing with a loud voice, saying, "Let those who have charge over the city draw near, each with a deadly weapon in his hand." And suddenly six men came from the direction of the upper gate, which faces north, each with his battle-ax in his hand. One man among them was clothed with linen and had a writer's inkhorn at his side. They went in and stood beside the bronze altar. Now the glory of the God of Israel had gone up from the cherub, where it had been, to the threshold of the temple. And He called to the man clothed with linen, who had the writer's inkhorn at his side; and the Lord said to him, "Go through the midst of the city, through the midst of Jerusalem, and put a mark on the foreheads of the men who sigh and cry over all the abominations that are done within it." To the others He said in my hearing, "Go after him through the city and kill; do not let your eye spare, nor have any pity. Utterly slay old and young men, maidens and little children and women; but do not come near anyone on whom is the mark; and begin at My sanctuary." So they began with the elders who were before the temple. Then He said to them, "Defile the temple, and fill the courts with the slain. Go out!" And they went out and killed in the city" Ezekiel 9:1-7.

Notice that among the six who were sent to destroy the people was one who had an inkhorn. With this, he marked the foreheads of all those who had developed a burden for the sins of the land. These are those whose hearts cry for the evil that is practiced in society and are seeking divine intervention. Such are those who will be spared the wrath of divine judgment. Those who get complacent, emulating evil, wicked and corrupt practices in the land will not be spared the wrath of God's judgment on society.

Many entities hire brilliant lawyers with the mandate to craft policies commonly known as 'fine print' that mostly exonerate their oppressive tactics while providing very little or no recourse for customers. Enterprises that would survive unusual circumstances that may plague our world will have to identify with a legitimate burden of society and engage those who are genetically poised to adjudicate such injustices. Such entities ought to pursue a reversal of exploitative objectives. This will define their value proposition for marketing and public relations narrative.

Primitivism is the economic concept that involves a burden of adjudication of bloodline issues that is best suited for industries such as legal, agriculture-food and media-publishing.

Chapter Seventeen

Perceptiveness

"The spirit of a man is the lamp of the Lord,
Searching all the inner depths of his heart" Proverbs
20:27

It was in the morning before office hours, and I was at my desk in the office of the business I started with Peter, my friend. I desired to serve at Church as a Sunday School teacher so I usually came in early so I could spend some time in the scriptures. On this occasion while studying the scriptures, I heard the Holy Spirit say, "Pastor Walley." I was frightened, thinking this was a mistake of identity and so I quickly moved over to the guest chair of my desk and continued studying. Suddenly whatever I read turned into a supernatural revelation. The scriptures jumped at me such that they became visual manifestations. Then the Holy Spirit spoke again, "Pastor Walley, don't you see how simple I have made my word to you?" Now I knew it was not an identity mistake but that was my call to serve as a priest alongside my call to business. God scheduled my pastoral training, so I left the business that I started with Peter. One day during my pastoral development, the Lord wanted to teach me His presence, so He prompted a friend named Karl and his wife to invite me to attend a service at the local Church where they were members. When we arrived at the Church premises, I noticed a fleet of the best luxury vehicles. The auditorium was lush with high-grade carpeting that made you feel as though you were in the living room of a very rich person. Though the auditorium was large, there were beautiful chandeliers hanging from the ceiling for every section. The seats were very comfortable and made you feel at home. There was prayer at the beginning of the service and when praise and worship started, the sound from the public address system and musical instruments seemed as though one was playing studio recorded music from a compact disk player. It was all so perfect and impressive. However, as I settled in from being wowed by all the physical features of this Church, I began to feel an unease in my spirit. I tried to plug into the praise, but I struggled. For the first time as a Christian, I experienced contrast. Though the praise was gospel music that touted God's goodness, His presence was absent. At some point during the worship, the wife of the pastor of the Church took over and led a brief part of the worship to bring this session to an end. For this brief period when the pastor's wife led worship, I felt the presence of God ushered into the auditorium but as soon as she handed over to her husband who was the pastor, the unease in my spirit resumed. The pastor of the Church was charismatic and ministered to people with the gifts of the Holy Spirit at work through Him, and yet I felt an unease all through his ministering. After the service I was invited to have lunch with my friend Karl and his wife at their home. They asked my opinion of their Church, and I narrated my impressions of their gorgeous Church facility, but also my unease with the absence of God's presence except when the wife of the pastor ministered during worship. It was as though I had dropped a bombshell as their demeanor changed from smiles to uneasiness. Then Karl's wife, who had been a member of this Church from the beginning, began to narrate the history of the Church. The wife of the pastor was the one who God called to start the Church at which time the husband was not saved. However, he became saved and endowed with the gifts of the Holy Spirit. He was a successful businessman with rich friends that he brought into the Church and so he exerted the culturally skewed male dominance over the ministry.

Perceptiveness is to engage values and inherent virtues in observation and processing of facts. It is our supernatural envisioning of the strategic way to implement a goal. Reuben, Simeon and Gad are the Israelite tribes responsible for administrative progress. The essence of administrative progress is how Israel distributes the bounty of major breakthroughs of the kingdom. Reuben enshrines the science of creativity and innovation, Simeon embodies compassion for universal sustenance, while Gad fosters the security and defense of a new space.

A compelling modern-day example of how Reuben was designed to be creative and innovative intellectually was the mission of Evangelist Oral Roberts to establish a university. 'The Oral Roberts University was founded by Evangelist Oral Roberts because of his obedience to God's mandate to build a university on God's authority and the Holy Spirit. God's commission to Oral Roberts was to 'Raise up your students to hear My voice, to go where My light is dim, where My voice is heard small, and My healing power is not known, even to the uttermost bounds of the earth. Their work will exceed yours, and in this I am well pleased'. Roberts placed special importance on the Prayer Tower, even though the concept of a building specifically dedicated to prayer at the center of the campus caused considerable tension.... The university built the City of Faith Medical and Research Center hospital in 1981 and started the Oral Roberts University School of Medicine in 1978'. Oral Roberts had been used of God to bring supernatural healing to his generation on a significant scale. Yet God mandated that he establish an institution of academic research for medicine as well as other disciplines of science and the arts. All the disciplines of science and philosophy involve the observation of the works of God to determine their properties and potential applications. To foster these abilities in humans, everyone has an intellect which is a faculty of the mind. According to the unique prophetic blessing on each of the twelve tribes that determined their vocations, everyone's intellect is designed to work in a unique way that matches their prophetic inclination.

The compassion of Simeon for universal sustenance is first unveiled in how Israel experienced supernatural providence in the wilderness. "So it was that quail came up at evening and covered the camp, and in the morning the dew lay all around the camp. And when the layer of dew lifted, there, on the surface of the wilderness, was a small round substance, as fine as frost on the ground. So when the children of Israel saw it, they said to one another, "What is it?" For they did not know what it was. And Moses said to them, "This is the bread which the Lord has given you to eat. This is the thing which the Lord has commanded: 'Let every man gather it according to each one's need, one omer for each person, according to the number of persons; let every man take for those who are in his tent.' Then the children of Israel did so and gathered, some more, some less. So when they measured it by omers, he who gathered much had nothing left over, and he who gathered little had no lack. Every man had gathered according to each one's need. And Moses said, "Let no one leave any of it till morning." Notwithstanding they did not heed Moses. But some of them left part of it until morning, and it bred worms and stank. And Moses was angry with them. So they gathered it every morning, every man according to his need. And when the sun became hot, it melted. And so it was, on the sixth day, that they gathered twice as much bread, two omers for each one. And all the rulers of the congregation came and told Moses. Then he said to them, "This is what the Lord has said: 'Tomorrow is a Sabbath rest, a holy Sabbath to the Lord. Bake what you will bake today, and boil what you will boil; and lay up for yourselves all that remains, to be kept until morning.' So they laid it up till morning, as Moses commanded; and it did not stink, nor were there any worms in it. Then Moses said, "Eat that today, for today is a Sabbath to the Lord; today you will not find it in the field. Six days you shall gather it, but on the seventh day, the Sabbath, there will be none" Exodus 16:13-26. This model for supernatural sustenance was invoked by the apostle Paul for the Christians in Corinth, "I speak not by commandment, but I am testing the sincerity of your love by the diligence of others. For you know the grace of our Lord Jesus Christ, that though He was rich, yet for your sakes He became poor, that you through His poverty might become rich. And in this I give advice: It is to your advantage not only to be doing what you began and were desiring to do a year ago; but now you also must complete the doing of it; that as there was a readiness to desire it, so there also may be a completion out of what you have. For if there is first a willing mind, it is accepted according to what one has, and not according to what he does not have. For I do not mean that others should be eased and you burdened; but by an equality, that now at this time your abundance may supply their lack, that their abundance also may supply your lack, that there may be equality. As it is written, "He who gathered much had nothing left over, and he who gathered little had no lack" 2 Corinthians 8:8-15. At the onset of the New Testament Church, this commonality concept was introduced to tackle lack among the new believers. "Now the multitude of those who believed were of one heart and one soul; neither did anyone say that any of the things he possessed was his own, but they had all things in common. And with great power the apostles gave witness to the resurrection of the Lord Jesus. And great grace was upon them all. Nor was there anyone among them who lacked; for all who were possessors of lands or houses sold them, and brought the proceeds of the things that were sold, and laid them at the apostles' feet; and they distributed to each as anyone had need. And Joses, who was also named Barnabas by the apostles (which is translated Son of Encouragement), a Levite of the country of Cyprus, having land, sold it, and brought the money and laid it at the apostles' feet" Acts 4:32-37. Here, the believers availed resources to tackle the needs of each other, so no one lacked. Basic and investment necessities were mitigated this way, through the pooling of resources. Using the five loaves and two fishes that was the lunch of a young boy availed as seed, Jesus invoked a supernatural process by which thousands of people were fed with twelve baskets full as leftovers. The providence of God is the seed that must be subjected to its due process for multiplication to meet our needs. Without applying the due process for each kind of seed, we resort to barren methods with adverse consequences.

The concern of Gad is the security and defense of any new space where we are blessed with advancement. Corporate blessings are unleashed on God's people whenever they have complied with the requisite divine premises. However, some believers get crafty in their ways to covert more than their fair share. An instance was prior to the death of King David when the throne of Israel was promised to his son Solomon. "Then Adonijah the son of Haggith exalted himself, saying, "I will be king"; and he prepared for himself chariots and horsemen, and fifty men to run before him. (And his father had not rebuked him at any time by saying, "Why have you done so?" He was also very good-looking. His mother had borne him after Absalom.) Then he conferred with Joab the son of Zeruiah and with Abiathar the priest, and they followed and helped Adonijah. But Zadok the priest, Benaiah the son of Jehoiada, Nathan the prophet, Shimei, Rei, and the mighty men who belonged to David were not with Adonijah. And Adonijah sacrificed sheep and oxen and fattened cattle by the stone of Zoheleth, which is by En Rogel; he also invited all his brothers, the king's sons, and all the men of Judah, the king's servants. But he did not invite Nathan the prophet, Benaiah, the mighty men, or Solomon his brother" 1 Kings 1:5-10. Notice that Adonijah had the looks of a distinguished personality of one fit to be king. He surrounded himself with members of his father's government who were discontented with the king. Adonijah's intention was to usurp the throne and establish himself as king of Israel. Using manipulative tactics, he organized a feast for his coronation but did not invite those who were loyal to King David. Nathan the prophet got wind of Adonijah's plot and notified the king, so the coup was foiled, and Solomon was installed as king of Israel. Today, we see the same manipulative tactics at work with crafty believers who are often impatient with God's plan for their lives, and devise schemes to defraud other believers. Some believers also avail themselves to the schemes of secular enterprises that engage their services as employees or agents to exploit God's people. Gad calls out those who opt for shortcuts that are not compliant with divine prescriptions.

Perception is a role of the intellect, which is the faculty of the mind for thoughts or reasoning. Here, we process information based on conscience values, emotional virtues, and facts. Intellect is the eye of the mind where we rationalize information, indulge sentiments, analyze optimism and weigh the arguments of pessimism. We must engage a functional intellect alongside the anointing of the Holy Spirit, to develop comprehensive perception. Spiritually, the lampstand of the tabernacle of Moses was the fellowship object that aided perception. "And you shall command the children of Israel that they bring you pure oil of pressed olives for the light, to cause the lamp to burn continually. In the tabernacle of meeting, outside the veil which is before the Testimony, Aaron and his sons shall tend it from evening until morning before the Lord. It shall be a statute forever to their generations on behalf of the children of Israel" Exodus 27:20-21. The Lampstand, also known as Candlestick, was the only source of light in the Holy Place which was enclosed with curtains. Olive oil fueled the seven-branched lampstand. This lamp was tendered constantly to ensure there was light in the Holy Place, and it signified prayer. "Pray without ceasing, in everything give thanks; for this is the will of God in Christ Jesus for you. Do not quench the Spirit. Do not despise prophecies. Test all things; hold fast what is good" 1 Thessalonians 5:17-21. Prayer is our communion with God and He answers us when we persist. He shows us what is taking place in the spiritual realm of which we must be aware. The seven lights of the lampstand unveil the seven Spirits of the Lord. "The Spirit of the Lord shall rest upon Him, The Spirit of wisdom and understanding, The Spirit of counsel and might, The Spirit of knowledge and of the fear of the Lord" Isaiah 11:2. The Spirit of Knowledge is usually the first way God answers us when we seek Him concerning an issue that entails process. What is revealed here may be coded and entail divine symbols. To grasp such revelation, we pray for the Spirit of Understanding. The third is the Spirit of Wisdom, that is how the Holy Spirit micro-manages our role in the process of this revelation. Assuming we are compliant with His leading, our path leads us out of the cycle of circumstances by which the kingdom of darkness held us captive. They notice we are breaking out and launch attacks to hinder us. Here the Spirit of the Lord inspires us with testimonies of the scriptures showing instances of past deliverance. At this point we may become so discouraged by the obstructions of the kingdom of darkness that we often want to quit serving God. The Spirit of the Fear of the Lord inspires us with reverence so we can continue our spiritual serving in God's house. As we persevere with divine inspiration, the Spirit of Counsel manifests by showing us people who we should consult for our breakthrough. Assuming we are diligent and heed their counsel, the Spirit of Might kicks in to manifest our breakthrough. "For this reason I bow my knees to the Father of our Lord Jesus Christ, from whom the whole family in heaven and earth is named, that He would grant you, according to the riches of His glory, to be strengthened with might through His Spirit in the inner man, that Christ may dwell in your hearts through faith; that you, being rooted and grounded in love, may be able to comprehend with all the saints what is the width and length and depth and heigh, to know the love of Christ which passes knowledge; that you may be filled with all the fullness of God. Now to Him who is able to do exceedingly abundantly above all that we ask or think, according to the power that works in us" Ephesians 3:14-20. The oil that fueled the lampstand was prayer. Prayer for a breakthrough process triggers the anointing in us. Like an olive seed that is first broken out of the fruit, crushed and pressed to produce oil, brokenness, contrition and pressure unleashes our anointing. Through the perseverance of seeking the seven Spirits of God, we are furnished with the anointing of the Holy Spirit to supernaturally enhance our intellect.

Our academic institutions have set standards that define who is intelligent or otherwise. One such is the intelligent quotient (IQ) by which people are measured. 'An intelligence quotient (IQ) is a total score derived from a set of standardized tests or subtests designed to assess human intelligence. Originally, IQ was a score obtained by dividing a person's mental age score, obtained by administering an intelligence test, by the person's chronological age, both expressed in terms of years and months. The resulting fraction (quotient) was multiplied by 100 to obtain the IQ score' (Quote is Courtesy of Wikipedia). Using this standard as well as others, academic institutions admit students, test and grade them. Many people are often disqualified and fail tests that gauge their intellectual capability unfairly. Some of such people who were disqualified or thrown out of academic institutions are responsible for the significant inventions responsible for the progress our world has experienced. Unfortunately, most employers are trapped in the same mindset of hiring only those certified by the famous academic institutions. While some of those not hired get discouraged about their potential and get relegated to menial occupations, others persistently carve their own path and are responsible for the industry disruptions that has fostered significant progress of society. Furthermore, the practice of engaging only those who fit into the box of an intelligence quotient eliminates so many who could have otherwise contributed to the progress of our world. A significant crisis of our world today is how we are disposing of those who we have characterized as unintelligent. An analogy that describes this is a crude oil refinery that uses the process of fractional distillation to capture only petrol for vehicles, and lets off the byproducts of diesel, kerosine and natural gas as waste. The challenge in disposing of the so-called waste in a proper way may become so expensive that it makes the refining of petrol an unprofitable venture. Another unintended consequence is that we assign those we consider as intellectuals to serve in areas that require high intuitiveness and instinctiveness. Such substitution of intellectual functions for highly intuitive and instinctive requirements are responsible for the failures and bankruptcies that are so prevalent with enterprises manned by certified and experienced professionals.

A tragedy of our world is that many Christians pray for God to give them bread while unbelievers devise crafty ways to grab the resources of the world and multiply them through ungodly methods. However, when God opens the heaven to provide rain that triggers abundance of bread, within the bread is the seed of future sustenance. I believe that when God gave Oral Roberts the anointing to heal the sick, it was the seed to pave the way for research in medicine and other disciplines for which his university embarked. Some of the crisis the university went through, underscore the lack of harness in the body of Christ. In addition to pursuing great visionary projects that reflect our potential, the essence of accountability structures within our harness cannot be overemphasized.

Health-Medical, Chemicals-Science, Automotive, Engineering, Technology, Business Services, Security-Defense are among the industries that require intellectual prowess but then the extrication of God from their methods is a fundamental flaw.

Chapter Eighteen

Resoluteness

"Therefore, my beloved, as you have always obeyed, not
as in my presence only, but now much more in my
absence, work out your own salvation with fear and
trembling; for it is God who works in you both to will and
to do for His good pleasure" Philippians 2:12&13

In my third year of high school till I completed, I spent the
summer holidays working with my mom at her wholesale
business. My elder brothers Benny and Fred engaged in
the crude oil business and here I also served as an
assistant. In my last year of high school, I partnered with
Benny to open a food processing plant. When I finished
high school, I began my own business in fashion
accessories and video tapes. These were my business
experiences until I was admitted to college where the Lord
gave me the business in which I partnered with Peter.
After a while I was divinely directed, to leave the business

for training to become a pastor. At one point, the Lord instructed that I start a fellowship which eventually grew into a Church. I was serving as a fulltime pastor and forgot completely about my first mandate for business. One day when I went to seek the Lord about the ministry, He reminded me that I was not called to be a conventional pastor but bi-vocational and my message was Christian finance. I decided to seek Him further for insights of this unique message, and He taught me the principles of finance from the scriptures. It was around this time that He opened the doors for me to be engaged in the marble business, and so my experience in business was boosted and I became rich with the application of divine principles. The Lord mandated me to convene seminars for Christians on this subject, so I embarked on this mission and flourished. During one of these seminars, the Lord gave me a vision of the world engulfed in a crisis of economic decline. In the vision he declared vividly that the solution was to engage "Economic Segmentation". Though I was a student of economics, I had not heard of this concept, so I searched fruitlessly for the topic. However, the sense of the phrase led me to weigh the concept of industry clustering which has its roots in kingdom prophetic gates and apostolic foundations.

To be resolute is to engage godly values, inherent virtues, the anointing and endowment to tackle objectives according to covenant relationships. It is the faithful stewardship of time and our resources, that is a function of human will. Judah, Zebulun and Issachar were the Israelite tribes responsible for competitive progress which entails how we take new territories. The essence of our royalty is the blessing upon Judah while Zebulun enshrines the endowments of the Holy Spirit and Issachar is the embodiment of time.

Judah is a revelatory king, worshipper and warrior. The essence of being revelatory is the quest to avoid human errors in judgment. "It is the glory of God to conceal a thing: but the honor of kings is to search out a matter" Proverbs 25:2. Judah seeks God for insight into the complex issues of the world, and worship is how he encounters God who unveils the path for progress. "But the hour is coming, and now is, when the true worshipers will worship the Father in spirit and truth; for the Father is seeking such to worship Him" John 4:23. The revelation from worship becomes the mandate by which Judah engages the owners of a space in warfare. "Shall the prey be taken from the mighty, Or the captives of the righteous be delivered? But thus says the Lord: "Even the captives of the mighty shall be taken away, And the prey of the terrible be delivered; For I will contend with him who contends with you, And I will save your children" Isaiah 49:24&25.

Zebulun enshrines the manifestation of the gifts of the Holy Spirit. In the absence of all the gadgets and Global Positioning System (GPS) by which mariners navigate the seas today, Zebulun was the tribe that could traverse the open seas by paying attention to the constellations. "There are diversities of gifts, but the same Spirit. There are differences of ministries, but the same Lord. And there are diversities of activities, but it is the same God who works all in all. But the manifestation of the Spirit is given to each one for the profit of all: for to one is given the word of wisdom through the Spirit, to another the word of knowledge through the same Spirit, to another faith by the same Spirit, to another gifts of healings by the same Spirit, to another the working of miracles, to another prophecy, to another discerning of spirits, to another different kinds of tongues, to another the interpretation of tongues. But one and the same Spirit works all these things, distributing to each one individually as He wills" 1 Corinthians 12:4-11. Through the spiritual gifts we can participate in our designated measure of the omniscience, omnipresence and omnipotence of God.

Issachar starts out as a good steward of Chronos time and evolves to master Kairos time. "Of the sons of Issachar who had understanding of the times, to know what Israel ought to do, their chiefs were two hundred; and all their brethren were at their command" 1 Chronicles 12:32. Often we are able to know God's plans for our lives but then the timing for various objectives becomes elusive. Kairos is that unique ability to match revelation with divine timing.

Royal authority is what you allow or disallow based on your values, virtues, anointing and relationships. It is your 'voice' as a king and the table of showbread in the tabernacle of Moses was the object of fellowship that furnished God's people with this authority. "You shall also make a table of acacia wood; two cubits shall be its length, a cubit its width, and a cubit and a half its height. And you shall overlay it with pure gold, and make a molding of gold all around. You shall make for it a frame of a handbreadth all around, and you shall make a gold molding for the frame all around. And you shall make for it four rings of gold, and put the rings on the four corners that are at its four legs. The rings shall be close to the frame, as holders for the poles to bear the table. And you shall make the poles of acacia wood, and overlay them with gold, that the table may be carried with them. You shall make its dishes, its pans, its pitchers, and its bowls for pouring. You shall make them of pure gold. And you shall set the showbread on the table before Me always" Exodus 25:23-30. The table of showbread was constructed with acacia wood and overlaid with pure gold. The top of the table was molded into a crown to depict royalty. Each week, twelve loaves of bread that were freshly baked were placed on this table. This table signified royal providence for the tribes of Israel. "And Jesus said to them, "I am the bread of life. He who comes to Me shall never hunger, and he who believes in Me shall never thirst" John 6:35. Jesus said of Himself to be the provision of God for our sustenance. Justification is what is divinely assigned to us based on our faith. "Now the just shall live by faith; But if anyone draws back, My soul has no pleasure in him" Hebrews 10:38. Every week we attend Church to receive a message from our Lord Jesus Christ through His servants. This message is supposed to inform our faith and guide how we confront our challenges and manage our opportunities.

The way by which Joseph administered Egypt during his tenure as Prime Minister is a model for the stewardship of kingdom resources. Prior to this, Joseph was imprisoned because Potiphar's wife had falsely accused him of attempting to rape her. He was placed in a dungeon, which is an underground prison where two of Pharaoh's servants, a butler and a baker were also held. They both had dreams in one night and Joseph helped interpret their dreams. The baker dreamt that he was carrying three baskets, and the birds of the air ate them. Since it was not divinely designed that he should serve animals, this dream meant that the baker's destiny was death in three days. However, the butler's dream was that he served the Pharaoh with three cups. This meant a restoration of purpose and came to pass in three days. Joseph did not interpret dreams by using a dream book standard. His relationship with God was the key. This will play out two years later when the Pharaoh had a dream and there was no magician, dream interpreter or wise man in Egypt who could interpret it. The butler who was restored, remembered the ministry of Joseph to him and recommended Joseph to the Pharaoh. The Pharaoh ordered Joseph to be brought out of prison immediately, to help interpret his dreams. In the presence of Pharaoh, a very confident Joseph declares that his ability to interpret dreams stems from his relationship with God. He made it clear to the Pharaoh that the interpretation of the dream would be an answer from God. "Then Pharaoh said to Joseph: "Behold, in my dream I stood on the bank of the river. Suddenly, seven cows came up out of the river, fine looking and fat; and they fed in the meadow. Then behold, seven other cows came up after them, poor and very ugly and gaunt, such ugliness as I have never seen in all the land of Egypt. And the gaunt and ugly cows ate up the first seven, the fat cows. When they had eaten them up, no one would have known that they had eaten them, for they were just as ugly as at the beginning. So I awoke. Also, I saw in my dream, and suddenly seven heads came up on one stalk, full and good. Then behold, seven heads, withered, thin, and blighted by the east wind, sprang up after them. And the thin heads devoured the seven good heads. So I told this to the magicians; but there was no one who could explain it to me". Then Joseph said to Pharaoh, "The dreams of Pharaoh are one; God has shown Pharaoh what He is about to do: The seven good cows are seven years, and the seven good heads are seven years; the dreams are one. And the seven thin and ugly cows which came up after them are seven years, and the seven empty heads blighted by the east wind are seven years of famine. This is the thing which I have spoken to Pharaoh. God has shown Pharaoh what He is about to do. Indeed, seven years of great plenty will come throughout all the land of Egypt; but after them seven years of famine will arise, and all the plenty will be forgotten in the land of Egypt; and the famine will deplete the land. So the plenty will not be known in the land because of the famine following, for it will be very severe. And the dream was repeated to Pharaoh twice because the thing is established by God, and God will shortly bring it to pass. "Now therefore, let Pharaoh select a discerning and wise man, and set him over the land of Egypt. Let Pharaoh do this, and let him appoint officers over the land, to collect one-fifth of the produce of the land of Egypt in the seven plentiful years. And let them gather all the food of those good years that are coming, and store up grain under the authority of Pharaoh, and let them keep food in the cities. Then that food shall be as a reserve for the land for the seven years of famine which shall be in the land of Egypt that the land may not perish during the famine." So the advice was good in the eyes of Pharaoh and in the eyes of all his servants. And Pharaoh said to his servants, "Can we find such a one as this, a man in whom is the Spirit of God?" Genesis 41:17-38. No magician or wise man in the service of Pharaoh could interpret the dream. It was beyond their prognostications and did not fit into the context of their dream books. This dream was God's global economic agenda. It was God's plan to elevate Joseph to the place of world leadership and Joseph had been preparing for this moment all his life.

There was to be seven years of plenty to be followed by seven years of lack. Joseph's remedy for the adverse consequence of the revelation was to procure one-fifth of the corn in the first seven years to take care of the later years. This insight into the dream and the wisdom for ameliorating the challenge was totally new to the Pharaoh, his counselors and officials. The interpretation of Joseph totally defied the wisdom of the Egyptian system. Their economy was not structured to fourteen-year cycles. Furthermore one-fifth was not a significant figure in their prognostication. Mathematically, if the people lived on 80% in the first seven years, it would have been impossible to sustain Egypt for the later seven years with only 20%.

The Pharaoh realized that the solutions Joseph brought forth were as peculiar in nature as the dream itself. An entity he was not aware of had convicted him with a dream that none of the subjects in his kingdom could understand. If Joseph's interpretation made accurate sense, then his solutions were equally credible. Since the dream was decoded by Joseph, it was evidence of his relationship with the entity that furnished Pharaoh with the dream. The Pharaoh is particularly concerned that the consequences of doing nothing about this dream could diminish his kingdom considerably. Though Joseph was not an Egyptian by descent and obviously not a member of the royal family, the Pharaoh is left with no other options. Joseph was the perfect choice for this job and so the rape charge was immediately dropped. Pharaoh appointed Joseph to the position of Prime Minister and gave him the signet ring. This level of authority entrusted to Joseph was such that nothing significant was to be done in Egypt without the approval of Joseph. "Pharaoh also said to Joseph, "I am Pharaoh, and without your consent no man may lift his hand or foot in all the land of Egypt." This meant that Joseph was given the authority to alter the entire system of Egypt so that their economy could be sustained in this fourteen-year economic cycle.

A Time of Abundance

King Solomon taught that there are twenty-eight distinctions of time for which we ought to pay attention. "To everything there is a season, a time for every purpose under heaven: A time to be born, and a time to die; A time to plant, and a time to pluck what is planted; A time to kill, and a time to heal; A time to break down, and a time to build up; A time to weep, and a time to laugh; A time to mourn, and a time to dance; A time to cast away stones, and a time to gather stones; A time to embrace, and a time to refrain from embracing; A time to gain, and a time to lose; A time to keep, and a time to throw away; A time to tear, and a time to sew; A time to keep silence, and a time to speak; A time to love, and a time to hate; A time of war, and a time of peace. What profit has the worker from that in which he labors? I have seen the God-given task with which the sons of men are to be occupied. He has made everything beautiful in its time. Also, He has put eternity in their hearts, except that no one can find out the work that God does from beginning" Ecclesiastes 3:1-11. Though sunrise and sunset within a twenty-four period was generally considered as a day, the Israelites knew that the purpose of a day could go way beyond. Although secular traditions considered time only as Chronos, that is 'a succession of moments measured by length', the Israelites understood that time was a Kairos, that is, a divine function. Every day has a function determined by God. A day does not end until man fulfils his assignment from God and brings proper closure to it. Time presents itself either as a challenge or opportunity. When we are confronted with a negative circumstance in life, we stand up to the challenge and confront it until there is evidence of positive change. We must identify what opportunities each time presents and make the best of it. For instance, weeping, which is significant of intense prayer, does not end until we have reason to laugh; mourning which is relevant of fasting does not end until we have the reason to dance, warfare continues until victory becomes imminent and we have peace. If we are sensitive to time, we rise to every challenge and turn it around for our good.

Joseph understood the dynamics of time, and its stewardship. Seven years of abundant harvests followed by seven years of gruesome famine will complete this fourteen-year cycle. Whenever God orchestrates time change that results in a famine, the righteous are exempted. Various scriptural instances confirm that God preserves the righteous, so they do not experience the adverse consequences of a famine. 2 Kings 8:1-6 records one instance of deliverance from a famine, "Then Elisha spoke to the woman whose son he had restored to life, saying, "Arise and go, you and your household, and stay wherever you can; for the LORD has called for a famine, and furthermore, it will come upon the land for seven years." So the woman arose and did according to the saying of the man of God, and she went with her household and dwelt in the land of the Philistines seven years. It came to pass, at the end of seven years that the woman returned from the land of the Philistines; and she went to make an appeal to the king for her house and for her land. Then the king talked with Gehazi, the servant of the man of God, saying, "Tell me, please, all the great things Elisha has done." Now it happened, as he was telling the king how he had restored the dead to life, that there was the woman whose son he had restored to life, appealing to the king for her house and for her land. And Gehazi said, "My lord, O king, this is the woman, and this is her son whom Elisha restored to life." And when the king asked the woman, she told him. So the king appointed a certain officer for her, saying, "Restore all that was hers, and all the proceeds of the field from the day that she left the land until now."

Another instance is recorded in the book of Acts 11:27-30, "And in these days prophets came from Jerusalem to Antioch. Then one of them, named Agabus, stood up and showed by the Spirit that there was going to be a great famine throughout all the world, which also happened in the days of Claudius Caesar. Then the disciples, each according to his ability, determined to send relief to the brethren dwelling in Judea. This they also did and sent it to the elders by the hands of Barnabas and Saul." Famine is significant of economic recession or depression. Rainfall is God's revelation that teaches us how to invest our life, time and resources. God's goodness facilitates our minds with wisdom that make us economically successful. Whenever God is not acknowledged in any society or sphere of human existence, the judgment of famine becomes inevitable at some point. Only the just are blessed with the revelation to escape such famine.

One-fifth

Exchange is the basis of mutual coexistence underlining both human and divine experiences. A close look at the ecosystem gives a great picture of interdependence that stems from exchange. Wherever rainfall and sunshine are consistent, there is a tendency for a forest to develop. On a day when the sun gets very hot, there is a great chance that there will be rainfall later in this forest. Sunshine causes the trees to emit increased moisture into the atmosphere. The moisture forms rain clouds which ultimately return to the earth as rainfall. Deserts hardly receive rainfall, and this reality is the reason why environmentalists encourage the planting of trees to alter weather patterns in such areas. Essentially the principle here is that the earth must give back to the heavens to continue the cycle of interdependence that results in the proper functioning of the ecosystem. Tithing is the essence of acknowledging divine providence to sustain the relationship between us and God. "…for He makes His sun rise on the evil and on the good, and sends rain on the just and on the unjust…" Matthew 5:45. The sunshine and rainfall we experience are evidence of the provision of God to facilitate our prosperity. When we give tithes and offerings to God's priests, we reciprocate His blessings, and the cycle of prosperity is sustained.

As early as the era of Adam, the scripture tells of Cain and Abel offering up sacrifices to God. Abel's sacrifice was first, fat and flock which fulfilled the exact requirement of the tithe and was accepted by God. Abraham the patriarch gave ten percent of all his goods to Melchizedek the priest as tithe, so it is obvious that the principle of tithing was instituted by God from the beginning. Tithing is an acknowledgement of divine providence and serves as thanksgiving to God. Joseph's strategy of buying up twenty percent of the produce during the seven years of harvest to sustain the seven-year famine is derived from the principle of restitution. Ten percent in the scriptures is associated with the tithe while the various prescribed offerings add up to a further ten percent. The sum of twenty percent is the figure for restitution when we default from tithing. Often, famine is heaven's way of telling the earth, it is in default. The righteous who give ten percent tithes and respond to divine conviction by giving offerings, fulfill the twenty percent restitution that sustains the provision of rainfall and sunshine from above. To reward the righteous for their giving, God blesses them with the wealth of the wicked. "A good man leaves an inheritance for his children's children, but a sinner's wealth is stored up for the righteous" Proverbs 13:22. The just receives an inheritance of sustained blessings of providence that continues to affect several generations after them.

Joseph's Investment

With the prevailing economic boom predicted for Egypt, corn was probably sold at one dollar for a hundred-kilogram bag. Joseph bought so much corn and had to build huge silos for storage. Since no one prior to that time had any reason to store corn for seven years, one of Joseph's stewardships was to develop technology to preserve the corn. For seven years, Joseph used money from the Pharaoh's treasury to procure corn. It is surprising that though everyone in Egypt must have heard about the Pharaoh's dream and the interpretation for which Joseph had been promoted, no one was interested in engaging in this strategic investment. The obvious reason was that they did not have a relationship with the God of Joseph, who requires restitution from His servants to sustain economic prosperity. The Egyptians kept spending their harvests as usual in anticipation of the next year's harvest. Considering that the famine Joseph anticipated was seven years away, it was a reality that their minds could not grasp. As far as they were concerned, Joseph was the biggest joke around town. Just imagine how they felt when Joseph gave them money for corn that was in so much abundance! They probably laughed at Joseph secretly. If you consider the nature of an agricultural community where everyone experienced bumper harvests, no one would be interested in buying corn. It was the commonest commodity around. The supply was so high that there was practically no demand for it.

There is a dichotomy about former and latter rain revelations that distinguished Joseph's approach to corn investment. When the unbeliever is experiencing a harvest, the believer usually is in seedtime and vice versa. The former rain teaches us how to invest our life, time and resources while the blessings we get at the time of the latter rain are wheat, wine and oil. The Prophet Joel wrote this about the rains in Joel 2:23-24, "Be glad then, you children of Zion, And rejoice in the LORD your God; For He has given you the former rain moderately, And He will cause the rain to come down for you, The former rain, and the latter rain in the first month. The threshing floors shall be full of wheat, and the vats shall overflow with new wine and oil." Joseph's investment was patterned after the former and latter rain. The harvest of oil is the yield from the investment of life, while wine is the yield from the investment of time, and wheat is the yield from the investment of financial resources. How we invest our life, time and resources determines the oil, wine and wheat we accrue as harvest.

Life/Oil: The value of our life begins to appreciate through the development of our God given potentials. Our level of education, information and practical experience in the arena of divine potential determines our oil yield. Joseph developed the value of his life to the degree that he could administer the highest office in Egypt next to the Pharaoh. Typically, we would say that through the training from his father Jacob and the positive attitude he developed despite the challenges he encountered, Joseph increased in the anointing. To further understand the significance of the anointing in relation to wealth we would invoke the parable Jesus Christ taught about the unjust steward. In the parable of the unjust steward, when he was given notice of job termination he negotiated with the clients who had outstanding balances. "So he called every one of his master's debtors to him, and said to the first, 'How much do you owe my master?' And he said, 'A hundred measures of oil.' So he said to him, 'Take your bill, and sit down quickly and write fifty.' Then he said to another, 'And how much do you owe?' So he said, 'A hundred measures of wheat.' And he said to him, 'Take your bill, and write eighty.' So the master commended the unjust steward because he had dealt shrewdly" Luke 16:5-8. The client who owed oil represents those people who God brings our way so we can help with our gifts and potentials.

The oil is significant of our endowments by which we are expected to "love our neighbor as ourselves." This is an unreserved commitment to help those who need our talents to progress in life. Mathematically, the investment of our oil in others must measure up to fifty percent. The unjust steward underwrote the debt of the oil customer by fifty percent. Significantly it means that he offered free service of his divine potential to this customer.

Resources/Wheat: From the parable of the unjust steward, we know that the client who owed a hundred measures of wheat received a discount of twenty percent. This is significant of the unjust steward invoking the principle of restitution. We are expected to give ten percent tithes and offerings that altogether add up to twenty percent restitution. This is how we position ourselves to earn the blessing of wealth transfer from the wicked. Harnessing our material resources to invest in the direction of our divine conviction determines how much we get as dividends. With the value of corn at an all-time low during the first seven years, Joseph bought large quantities up to twenty percent of the total corn harvest of Egypt.

Time/Wine: Sunshine and rainfall are divine provisions that God makes accessible to all on the face of the earth. It is the inspiration to do the right thing at the right time. "He waters the mountains from his upper chambers; the earth is satisfied by the fruit of his work. He makes grass grow for the cattle, and plants for man to cultivate, bringing forth food from the earth: wine that gladdens the heart of man, oil to make his face shine, and bread that sustains his heart" Psalm 105:13-15. We enjoy emotional fulfillment, peace and prosperity because He blesses us with the potential to succeed in our endeavors. Knowing what to do at the right time when there is heavenly support is fundamental to sustainable success. It is because of insight of the fourteen-year stewardship of wealth that Joseph built silos for long term food storage to preserve the lives of the Egyptians.

Gold Money

Joseph understood the dynamics of money in such a way that the Egyptians did not. "Now there was no bread in all the land; for the famine was very severe, so that the land of Egypt and the land of Canaan languished because of the famine. And Joseph gathered up all the money that was found in the land of Egypt and in the land of Canaan, for the grain which they bought; and Joseph brought the money into Pharaoh's house" Genesis 47:13&14. After the seven years of abundance, all the money of the known world economy was gravitating towards Joseph, because he had their survival commodity in his hands. The corn had become more valuable than money.

Money is a medium of exchange, a measure and store of value, as well as a standard for deferred payments. Previously, people would have to find those who needed what they had to do an exchange. As a medium of exchange, money facilitates complex transactions without the inconvenience of trading by barter. It is an effective way of quantifying the value of products and services. Money measures itself as an independent standard relative to anything. From goodwill to alimony, it serves well as a measure of value. We retain value by converting perishable items into money. Great goals can be broken up into achievable units of money and payment deferred over time. Huge debts can also be spread out and accomplished within the framework of time.

Most people are ignorant about the dynamics of money, so they lose money as quickly as they make it. It is a frustrating experience when you work so hard to make money, only to find yourself broke again in the vicious cycle of lack and abundance. Often, what certain advisors recommend as wealth building plans only tend to be pyramid schemes that crash on unsuspecting investors.

First Law of Money – 'Everyone Can Make Money'

Turn on a television set and you will find a teenager acting either in a drama series, movie or commercial. Look through the pages of a magazine and you will probably find an advert featuring a baby model. As young as these people may be, they earn a lot of money for their work. Every service you provide that is useful for someone will generate money. Every product that benefits people will also generate income. Making money is not contingent on us having jobs, nor is it based on someone helping us. God blesses all of us with the privilege to make wealth. Our lives, time and resources are given to us by God to generate wealth. Most often the reason we seem never to get enough is because we are paying attention to how others are making money and because we cannot get it the same way, we become frustrated.

Like every other Egyptian, Joseph had life, time and access to material resources, however the difference was what Joseph knew about money. After seven years of abundance was over, the famine started. Every farmer who anticipated the former rain was disappointed. They failed to pay attention to the revelation about a seven-year famine that Joseph had previously informed them. Now these farmers required food supplies to sustain their families and livestock and so this was the beginning of Joseph's harvest. As we have established earlier, the former rain and latter rain cycles of the just and unjust are opposite. "When the righteous are in authority, the people rejoice: but when the wicked bear rule, the people mourn" Proverbs 29:2. At a time when most people especially the wicked prosper with ease, righteous people endure a lot of hardships associated with 'sowing in tears'. Harvest time for the wicked is seed time for the righteous and vice versa.

When the famine begun, the Egyptians came to Joseph to procure food. Though Joseph had bought the corn from them at perhaps one dollar for a hundred-kilogram bag, he now sold it for probably a hundred dollars per bag. At this point, they were using large sums of money to buy food just to satisfy their hungry stomachs. Money from the Egyptians was now gravitating to Joseph, not as an investment but for their survival. Within one year, money failed in the land of Egypt. The reason for which all the money of the Egyptians ended up with Joseph, was because he understood money better. Joseph helped them make money in the first seven years only to redirect all their money back to him.

Joseph was the only one who clearly understood why God gave the people so much corn for the first seven years. Once Joseph was given the mandate by Pharaoh, he began to buy up corn at a very low rate. Though at this onset, corn was in abundance, Joseph knew by revelation that the corn was going to be scarce after seven years. When the world is experiencing success and there is a general sense of economic boom, God usually convicts us to invest in areas that may not align with popular investment trends. When the Egyptians were experiencing a bumper harvest and procuring consumer goods, that was when Joseph was investing. Joseph used Pharaoh's money for corn until the seven years of abundance ended and the famine started.

Levels of Money

Most people can only relate to a good job or a great business opportunity as God's way of blessing them to prosper financially. Rather, God prospers us by inspiring us on how to add value to our life, time and financial resources. The former rain revelation is the privilege of knowing exactly how to strategically harness our life, time and material resources. Without the component of the former rain revelation, what we have is an ordinary life, blindness to time and the lowest form of money. Though everyone can make money, we have various levels of money. Jesus taught a parable in Matthew 13:45&46, "Again, the kingdom of heaven is like a merchant seeking beautiful pearls, who, when he had found one pearl of great price, went and sold all that he had and bought it." This man was on the lookout for higher money and when he found such an investment opportunity, he liquidated all his assets to make the strategic investment. In economics the value of a nation's currency is directly linked to its productivity, exports, imports and fiscal policies. The value of the United States dollar is not the same as the Canadian dollar or British pound. How you invest your life, time and resources determines the value of your money. There is lower money and higher money. Money may appreciate from the lowest form all the way to the seventh dimension. Your money level is determined by the value of your life, judgment of time and how you spend your resources. Jesus taught that investment mindedness is a kingdom attribute. Through the development of our spiritual senses, we add value to our life, time and resources until we reach the seventh dimension. Furthermore, we must endeavor to progressively trade our life, time and resources from one level to another. Those who do not fully understand wealth ignorantly trade higher money for lower money and end up losing it. Prior to the 2009 global recession, a renowned German businessman who had genuine wealth from inheritance related investments, bought stocks of other enterprises by way of strategic diversification. With the downturn of the economy and crash of several stocks, he lost so much money that even those banks that previously favored him refused to lend him money for his core business and he ended up committing suicide. The mistake here is what I call a blind investment, which is, trading higher money for lower money. Through fellowship with God, Joseph had developed the value of his life to the level of competence that he understood the important dynamics of time and stewardship. With this spiritual backdrop, Joseph invested in corn at the cheapest possible price and seven years later, all the money in Egypt and the world at large began to gravitate towards him.

When Joseph bought the corn from the Egyptians, he exchanged a medium for a commodity. Joseph traded his money for corn which was of little value at the time because of the abundant supply. The money the Egyptians received was more valuable to them than the corn. At the time Joseph understood that there was going to be a time change, which would automatically switch the dynamics and make corn a more valuable commodity than the current monetary value. This dynamic that distinguished Joseph from the Egyptians is called revelation. The value of his life, time and resources were significantly raised to the seventh dimension.

The Second Law of Money – Money Is Controlled Spiritually

Not long ago, actual gold coins were in circulation as money. For security reasons people deposited their gold coins with goldsmiths and later to banks and accepted receipts as title to the gold. These receipts that gave the bearer the right to their gold were eventually used in multiple transactions such that people often did not go to the bank to withdraw the gold. The banks began to lend out the gold to others who paid interest. Realizing how rich these banks had become by lending out these gold deposits at high interests, governments decided to become players in the world of money. Each government formed a central bank to regulate the activities of banks and exert some form of control on the money supply. To finance some of their operations, governments began to borrow money from the Central bank. Excessive lending to the government placed the banks in a position where if depositors decided to withdraw actual gold with their receipts there would not be enough gold to make the receipts good. The government decided to pull a fast one on depositors. They changed the laws governing money and printed new receipts that did not give bearers access to actual gold. In the United States of America these new receipts were marked as 'Federal Reserve Note'. By a stroke of a pen, people were denied access to their gold deposits and even the receipts no longer belonged to them. They call it legislation enacted by elected representatives of the people. Today, you do not own fiduciary notes issued by any government even though you earned it. In some nations, additional laws have been passed to ensure that there is a limit to how much cash you can have on you at any point in time. Also, any money found on you may be confiscated by officials of the government, so long as they issue you a form to sign off your forfeiture.

Anyone who can put into place laws that govern the use of money controls the money supply. Local banks have rules that govern their transactions with clients. For certain deposit accounts, they have laws as to how much of your money you can withdraw within a certain framework of time. Another rule with most banks is that when you issue a check to an individual, they may only cash the check from your account for a fee unless they agree to open an account with the same bank. When banks issue out loans to customers, they reserve the right to change interest rates and other conditions at any time and without prior notice to the customer. Knowing what power they leverage in the flow of money, financial institutions regularly craft new policies that manipulate the flow of money to their own advantage.

Huge corporations have tapped into this practice and would grant a customer significant discount, if only they would subscribe to use the company credit card as a means of payment for goods and services. They understand that a credit card issued to you would garner loyalty in patronage. You are their target market, they have your full contact information and so they can string you to make purchases at random. Furthermore, they know that if you default on payment, they make more profit by charging you interest. Also, another scheme certain organizations have developed to control money flow is often labeled as 'network marketing'. Here people are offered an opportunity to partner with owners of the organization and can determine their position in the chain of profit sharing by the number of clients they sign up. Whichever way you look at it, the underlining strategy of these schemes are intended to control the direction of the flow of money.

Money responds to any system that is well crafted to attract it. From one level to another, money will continue to gravitate towards the most superior system set in place for it. "Will you set your eyes on that which is not? For riches certainly make themselves wings; they fly away like an eagle toward heaven" Proverbs 23:5. A superior system acts like a magnet that sucks up money from lower systems. Some cultures of people have been able to establish riches because they understand money flow and have set up a tradition to control it. In such a system members of the clan buy from one another and spread opportunities only among themselves. The primary characteristic of such a system is that less money flows out as compared with inflows. Some of these cultures have managed to pass on the tradition of functioning within the framework of the system for generations. Though this tradition may not be taught as a formal instruction, everyone in that culture naturally patronizes the system.

Most people are content when their needs are met and have enough surpluses to lavish on their desires. So long as they continue to make money, they do not pay attention to the future from a divine perspective. They fellowship with God only when it is convenient, like on Christmas Eve, New Years Eve, Easter, on their beds of affliction or in deep trouble and cannot find a human solution. Most people do not realize that fellowship with God is linked to economic prosperity. They even criticize ministers of the gospel who teach financial prosperity, and sometimes classify them as crooks. The scriptures point us to the divine way for achieving true prosperity.

When you add time to your money, it either puts you in a deficit or profit. Time is the revelation of what God expects of us at every point. This revelation is what sends our money up to the seventh dimension. Our burden is to seek revelation of how to harness resources to make wealth. Higher money attracts lower money. Higher money is the money of the future. Higher money is what is positioned spiritually. The reason we should position ourselves to attain higher money is because higher money takes care of tomorrow.

The big players in the world of finance understand that legislation can always stimulate or change the direction of money flow. They own financial institutions which are subject to certain government regulations that sometimes limit their liberty to establish certain crafty rules for customers. By hiring the services of lobbyists, they constantly influence politicians to legislate laws that increase their freedom to control the money flow. Think of this cycle, where you get hired to work for a big retail or entertainment corporation. Those who own the majority shares in this corporation where you work also own the majority shares of the commercial bank where you are a customer. Since the majority shareholders serve on the board of directors, they are the real owners of the corporation. When you receive your salary slip, it only tells you how much has been deposited into your bank account. You rarely go and cash out all the money. You write a check to the mortgage company and mail it. You also issue a check for your car loan, insurance premium, gas, telephone, cable and credit card bill. Guess what, the same owners of the corporation where you work also own the mortgage company, insurance company, Gas Company, Telephone and Cable Company as well as the bank where you are a customer. So that the money you were paid as salary never left the bank. The only amount of money that you may classify as yours is what you took out of the ATM machine. In fact, that money is not yours since it is marked 'FEDERAL RESERVE NOTE'. With their understanding of the dynamics of money flow, these big players in the world of finance own all the money in circulation. They also understand that the government of a state is not the government officials who receive a paycheck for their work, but rather anybody who can manipulate the authorities.

Unfortunately, many Christians are naïve about these dynamics of money flow. This is the reason why wealth transfer from the wicked to the just is only a cliché that has not become a reality for most believers. The level of poverty in the Church is worse than with unbelievers. We fail to leverage our large population as the framework for a system that attracts money flow and for the preservation of wealth. Worst of all, the big players in the world of finance have identified us as a formidable market and have set in place a system to redirect our riches towards them. They have set up so called 'Faith Divisions' in most major corporations to specifically target the Christian religious market. These divisions study our psyche and spending patterns to effectively plunder us. One such strategy is that they sign contracts with popular ministers of the gospel to publish and sell their books, literature and music. We call it a testimony on the pulpit to have a major corporation sign a deal with our ministers to publish their products. Of course, it would garner in some royalties, but the question is 'how much, and who are the beneficiaries of the bigger chunk of the profits involved?' Christians buy these products and yet the money flows to secular corporations. They pay a little fraction of the money as royalty check which is deposited into the account of the minister. As you already know, the money never leaves the account, so they keep turning it around to generate interest by issuing out loans. Christians borrow consumer loans from these banks and remain in debt and poverty.

To break this cycle, we must not just be interested in making money but pay careful attention to where our money is headed. Just as a business that spends more than it earns ends up in a loss, our revenue must exceed expenditure to become profitable. It is not how much money we save in the bank that increases our wealth, but rather it is how we invest and spend our resources. A chunk of the money we spend to procure our needs must head back to us. Essentially, we must spend money with those who are willing to spend on us, and save money with those who will invest in us. We must belong to a system that retains our money so we can always have access to it. This is the only framework by which we can reverse the current trend that robs believers and stream the riches of the wicked towards us. Obviously, a system that is diligently crafted upon divine principles and revelation is the ultimate of all other systems. Such a system takes money to the seventh dimension and retains it as wealth for the just.

During the reign of Ahab king of Israel who was married to Jezebel, there was unrighteousness and persecution of the prophets of God. Elijah the prophet proclaimed a famine on the land and the heavens withheld the rains. Significantly today, we would say there was an economic recession. However, the word of the Lord came to Elijah, "Get away from here and turn eastward, and hide by the Brook Cherith, which flows into the Jordan. And it will be that you shall drink from the brook, and I have commanded the ravens to feed you there" 1 Kings 17:3&4. Supernatural sustenance was the divine plan for Elijah during that time of recession. Ravens are known to be selfish by nature, and if you imagine how little one raven could carry from one point to another, then you realize that it was nothing short of a miracle how several ravens would feed a man. Elijah received a revelation from God as to the specific place where ravens had been commanded to feed him. The scripture continues, "So he went and did according to the word of the LORD, for he went and stayed by the Brook Cherith, which flows into the Jordan. The ravens brought him bread and meat in the morning, and bread and meat in the evening; and he drank from the brook" verse 5-6. At the exact place where Elijah was instructed to position himself, the ravens obeyed divine instruction to provide for his sustenance morning and evening, so that he was exonerated from the effects of the famine. After a while the brook dried up and the ravens stopped bringing the supplies of food. Elijah sought God and received another instruction, "Arise, go to Zarephath, which belongs to Sidon, and dwell there. See, I have commanded a widow there to provide for you." So he arose and went to Zarephath. And when he came to the gate of the city, indeed a widow was there gathering sticks. And he called to her and said, "Please bring me a little water in a cup, that I may drink." And as she was going to get it, he called to her and said, "Please bring me a morsel of bread in your hand." So she said, "As the LORD your God lives, I do not have bread, only a handful of flour in a bin, and a little oil in a jar; and see, I am gathering a couple of sticks that I may go in and prepare it for myself and my son, that we may eat it, and die." And Elijah said to her, "Do not fear; go and do as you have said, but make me a small cake from it first, and bring it to me; and afterward make some for yourself and your son. For thus says the LORD God of Israel: 'The bin of flour shall not be used up, nor shall the jar of oil run dry, until the day the LORD sends rain on the earth." So she went away and did according to the word of Elijah; and she and he and her household ate for many days. The bin of flour was not used up, nor did the jar of oil run dry, according to the word of the LORD which He spoke by Elijah" verse 9-15. When the brook Cherith dried up and the ravens did not show up with food supply for Elijah, we would probably have thought that it was time for him to begin to figure out ways and means to survive the famine. The responsibility for our sustenance regardless of the economic environment we may find ourselves in is entirely divine, and so we must resort to seeking the Lord for divine direction. Most often our providence is linked to a challenge, like in the instance of Elijah where God had commanded a widow to sustain him. When Elijah got to Zarephath, the widow who was to provide for him was poor, and she was about to gather sticks to prepare a last meal for herself and her son. It is obvious that God wanted to meet this widow's need for sustenance, so He interrupted the food supply by the ravens to reposition Elijah to orchestrate a miraculous supply of food for the widow. In these two instances we recognize that God is not limited in power to supply our needs. He commanded birds to feed Elijah consistently and when He needed Elijah to become a channel of supply, He blessed the last meal of a poor widow not to run out. We realize here that it is our obedience to divine instruction that empowers God's creation to respond supernaturally to our needs.

Third Law of Money – I Am Either a Servant of God or Mammon

Two spirits assign themselves to money depending on who owns it and how it is acquired. One is the Spirit of God, and the other spirit originates from the devil. "No servant can serve two masters; for either he will hate the one and love the other, or else he will be loyal to the one and despise the other. You cannot serve God and mammon" Luke 16:13. Whose servant we are is determined by our goal or philosophy for work and building up wealth. If your only goal for work is to make money, then you automatically show yourself as a servant of Mammon. Mammon is a spirit that is contrary to God. When we work for mammon, our motivation is to make as much money as possible using any means necessary. However, when we work to serve God, our goal is an inheritance in Christ. As Christians, we are called to work in the service of God regardless of where we work or who hires us. The apostle Paul teaches in Colossians 3:22-25, "Servants, obey in all things your masters according to the flesh; not with eye-service, as men-pleasers; but in singleness of heart, fearing God; And whatsoever ye do, do it heartily, as to the Lord, and not unto men; Knowing that of the Lord ye shall receive the reward of the inheritance: for ye serve the Lord Christ. But he that doeth wrong shall receive for the wrong which he hath done: and there is no respect of persons." In the same way a pastor ministers to those in spiritual need, we are all called to minister in the vocation of our divine purpose to bless others. As opposed to those who work for money, our work starts from the heart. Whether as a plumber, electrician, nurse or teacher, we function within the framework of divine principles and revelation to impact people at work. Though we may receive a salary for our services, we do not draw our fulfillment from it and rather we depend on receiving an inheritance from God as reward. An inheritance from God comes as the blessing of wealth. The Spirit of the blessing of wealth assigns itself to those who engage divine principles in the process of acquiring wealth. Often, it might seem as though our righteous efforts only deplete our material resources. However, every act of righteousness in the process of work or in our financial endeavors earns us credit toward our inheritance. "In Him also we have obtained an inheritance, being predestined according to the purpose of

Him who works all things according to the counsel of His will" Ephesians 1:11. Our inheritance is a promise from God as the reward for pursuit of divine purpose. For instance, the believer whose divine purpose is to be a medical doctor may inherit an already established hospital or probably acquire very cheaply a building suitable for medical practice or phenomenal opportunities in the medical world. Every time we align our work to fulfill divine principles angels manifest to orchestrate the blessing of wealth.

When Potiphar bought Joseph as a slave, he did not realize that he had just coveted the spirit of the blessing of wealth. There was a manifestation of phenomenal increase which may have prompted him to investigate. He found out that the spirit of the blessing of wealth was upon Joseph, so he promoted him as steward of his entire estate. Another instance in the scriptures is Jacob who worked for his uncle Laban for fourteen years as dowry for Leah and Rachel. At one point Jacob decided to leave to start his own animal husbandry but Laban made him an offer. "And Laban said unto him, I pray thee, if I have found favor in thine eyes, tarry: for I have learned by experience that the LORD hath blessed me for thy sake. And he said, Appoint me thy wages, and I will give it. And he said unto him, Thou knowest how I have served thee, and how thy cattle was with me. For it was little which thou hadst before I came, and it is now increased unto a multitude; and the LORD hath blessed thee since my coming: and now when shall I provide for mine own house also? And he said, What shall I give thee? And Jacob said, Thou shalt not give me any thing: if thou wilt do this thing for me, I will again feed and keep thy flock. I will pass through all thy flock to day, removing from thence all the speckled and spotted cattle, and all the brown cattle among the sheep, and the spotted and speckled among the goats: and of such shall be my hire. So shall my righteousness answer for me in time to come, when it shall come for my hire before thy face: every one that is not speckled and spotted among the goats, and brown among the sheep, that shall be counted stolen with me. And Laban said, Behold, I would it might be according to thy word. ...And the man increased exceedingly, and had much cattle, and maidservants, and menservants, and camels, and asses" Genesis 30:27-43. Jacob had learnt how to take care of sheep from his father Isaac who had also learnt from Abraham who was taught by God. By applying these divine principles Jacob invoked the Spirit of the blessing of wealth on the sheep of Laban and so there was phenomenal increase. When Laban saw the trend of increase, he went and consulted with the diviners, and they confirmed that Jacob was endowed with the Spirit of blessing of wealth. This is why Laban was willing to enter into a profit-sharing agreement with Jacob. By applying divine principles to our work, every believer can invoke the Spirit of the blessing of wealth and leverage bargaining power in any endeavor.

Working with the singular mindset of acquiring riches invokes the spirit of the curse of mammon. Such a mindset has the potential of corrupting our values and consequently our approach to work and business practice. Without the application of scriptural principles in our work and financial endeavors, the tendency is to operate satanic ways. In the same way divine principles invoke angelic ministry, a satanic system automatically invokes the manifestation of demonic spirits. An angel from God provides the Prophet Zechariah with a vision that underscores this truth in Zechariah 5:1-4, "Then I turned and raised my eyes, and saw there a flying scroll. And he said to me, "What do you see?" So I answered, "I see a flying scroll. Its length is twenty cubits and its width ten cubits." Then he said to me, "This is the curse that goes out over the face of the whole earth: 'Every thief shall be expelled,' according to this side of the scroll; and, 'Every perjurer shall be expelled,' according to that side of it." "I will send out the curse," says the LORD of hosts; "It shall enter the house of the thief and the house of the one who swears falsely by My name. It shall remain in the midst of his house and consume it, with its timber and stones." The flying curse identifies with every material substance that is acquired through unjust means. Based on how the owner acquired it, the flying curse either settles down to frustrate the ownership or moves away. Stealing and lying are two vices that underline every satanic way of amassing riches. The spirit of the curse of mammon causes businesses to fail, people lose their jobs and property. This curse breeds poverty, failure and financial frustration wherever it identifies unrighteousness. Essentially, where there are no angels assigned to money or material riches, the curse of mammon establishes itself. In extreme cases the spirit of the curse of mammon may even cause people to become physically ill or handicapped. The scripture records a scenario in 2 Kings 5 where Naaman, captain of the Syrian army came to Elisha to seek healing for leprosy. After Naaman was healed by the supernatural miracle that occurred by dipping himself in the Jordan seven times, Naaman offered Elisha material riches as payment for the healing. Elisha refused to accept the payment and

Naaman went off on his journey back to Syria. Gehazi the servant of Elisha was not pleased that his master had refused the payment from Naaman, so he secretly went after Naaman and lied in order to receive the payment. Elisha perceived supernaturally what had transpired between Gehazi and Naaman. "Then he said to him, "Did not my heart go with you when the man turned back from his chariot to meet you? Is it time to receive money and to receive clothing, olive groves and vineyards, sheep and oxen, male and female servants? Therefore, the leprosy of Naaman shall cling to you and your descendants forever." And he went out from his presence leprous, as white as snow" 2 Kings 26&27. Gehazi would have inherited the anointing of Elisha, but his heart was set on the wrong reward. The spirit of the curse of mammon came upon him. He inherited the leprosy of Naaman for practicing deception. Worst of all the curse of leprosy became an ancestral curse on the descendants of Gehazi.

Money must never become the motivation for work because any material achievement that is accrued cannot be sustained. "Labor not to be rich: cease from thine own wisdom" Proverbs 23:4. The only resources that we can sustain as legacy from generation to generation are those things that qualify as inheritance.

The Fourth Law of Money – The Love of Money is the Root of all Evil

Love is a disposition of the soul that determines our associations and attraction to people, places and things. Often our disposition of love is poorly managed through wrong choices that leave us victims of circumstances that we could never have imagined. The apostle Paul admonishes us in 1 Timothy 6:3-10, "But godliness with contentment is great gain. For we brought nothing into this world, and it is certain we can carry nothing out. And having food and raiment let us be therewith content. But they that will be rich fall into temptation and a snare, and into many foolish and hurtful lusts, which drown men in destruction and perdition. For the love of money is the root of all evil: which while some coveted after, they have erred from the faith, and pierced themselves through with many sorrows. But thou, O man of God, flee these things; and follow after righteousness, godliness, faith, love, patience, meekness." Our primary need for money is to meet the basic needs of life. The moment our soul gets wrapped around money, the manifestation of vices such as fighting, greed, self-centeredness, deception and a whole host of them become inevitable. A strong emotional attachment to money invokes negative vices to become preeminent in one's life. A strong attachment to money breeds constant contention between friends, partners and family members. There is usually peace between friends and family until there is a money issue. Those who love money may sometimes kill for it or even break up with their spouse in marriage for the sake of money.

A significant spiritual breakthrough that qualifies a believer for promotion to manage abundance is an emotional detachment from riches. God trains us in the place of lack as well as abundance to ascertain if we would forsake His will. The apostle Paul wrote in Philippians 4:10-13 about his disposition about financial support from the Churches he had established. "But I rejoiced in the Lord greatly that now at last your care for me has flourished again; though you surely did care, but you lacked opportunity. Not that

I speak in regard to need, for I have learned in whatever state I am, to be content: I know how to be abased, and I know how to abound. Everywhere and in all things I have learned both to be full and to be hungry, both to abound and to suffer need. I can do all things through Christ who strengthens me." Paul appreciates support from the Philippians, but he does not expect and depend on this support as a source of sustenance. He had trained himself to be content with divine providence. When there is a supply of abundance, we accomplish those things for which we require much money. But then in the absence of abundant financial resources we still press forward with those accomplishments that require little money to attain.

For those who are in love with money, no amount of money is ever enough. Even when they have an abundance of it, they are still merciless with those who owe them a little sum of money. The love of money creates a restlessness and constant anxiety of the soul. It robs us of our tranquility in Christ and makes our lives miserable. Most people will tell you they are stressed out simply because they do not have a lot of money to spend. Our joy as Christians is not contingent on how much money we have stacked up in the bank, for we can do all things through Christ. God will provide us with whatever we need at any given point in time to advance in our pursuits. If we understand that "God shall supply all our needs according to His riches in glory" then we take joy in the fact that He has already provided what we need now. When you need money to pay off your debts, do not become anxious. Money as a standard for deferred payment means that you can negotiate with your creditors to pay off your debts according to your income. Do not be afraid of the bank or credit collectors. It is just a system put in place by a group of people. Simply call them, tell them you want to spread the payment over a time schedule, and they will not refuse you. As a matter of fact, they would be glad if you called them to renegotiate the debt instead of playing 'hide-and-seek' tactics. The huge project that requires a large sum of money should be broken down into achievable goals. We need to reposition our minds to the degree where we will not allow systems established by men to oppress us. Jesus Christ has set us free and so we are free indeed.

We must not allow the opinion of men to determine our approach to finances. It is important that we appreciate our financial level and never be in competition with others. Also, we should never attempt to impress other people. The current financial system is designed to make us feel that we could have access to everything today and not wait for tomorrow. They make us an offer, and we must close the deal now or lose the deal. We are placed under duress to accept things we do not need and opportunities for which we are not ready. Their agenda is that we should mortgage our future for today's gratification. This is how many people get trapped with unnecessary debt and the consequence of financial frustration.

Constantly assess your needs in the light of your financial capabilities before you make a commitment with anyone. Do not make deals under pressure from a salesman or corporation for they have learned the art of closing a deal. Salesmen understand the psychology of selling and know they must not let you off the hook until you have made a commitment. Your money is so critical to their survival, but instead they make you feel the opposite. Always assure yourself that nothing terrible will occur if you do not make a deal over a want.

Do not go shopping because there is a sale offering great discounts. Go shopping because you have planned to buy some essentials. If a sale coincides with your plans, great! Do not allow the corporate world to string you with a noose to take away your money. The corporate world is constantly devising a way to get us to spend money even when we do not have it. Our homes are full of junk that we do not really need. They were just packaged right to appeal to our sense of need, so we purchased and purchased until we ended up indebted to the neck. The love of money is also the reason we have so many substandard products on the markets. Some of the food and drinks the corporate world sells to us have so many chemicals that are the cause of the various incurable diseases that plague us today. A scriptural instance of the consequences for the love of money is recorded in the book of Numbers. Balak a Moabite king who was afraid of the Israelites sent ambassadors to go and hire Balaam the prophet to come and place a curse upon Israel. When the ambassadors came to him, Balaam was not sure of the mission and so he asked the ambassadors to stay for the night so he could consult God. At night, he received a warning from God not to go on the mission to curse Israel. In the morning, he sent the men to go back to their master Balak. Balak then sent a high caliber delegation with greater rewards as an enticement to Balaam to come and curse Israel. When Balaam saw the rewards, he told the men to stay overnight so he could consult God again and by morning he felt the okay to go with the delegation of

Balak to curse Israel. On the way, while riding his donkey he met a resistance and instead of paying attention he continued to smite the donkey for refusing to move. Eventually the donkey spoke to him and rebuked him. "... Balaam the son of Beor, who loved the wages of unrighteousness; but he was rebuked for his iniquity: a dumb donkey speaking with a man's voice restrained the madness of the prophet" 2 Peter 2:15&16. Balaam clearly heard the voice of God the first time, but he was enticed by the rewards of divination offered by Balak, and so he attempted to twist God's will in prayer. In attempting to place a curse upon Israel, God orchestrated a release of prophetic blessings instead. When Balaam realized that he would lose the rewards promised by Balak, he counseled Balak to send their ladies to seduce the Israelite men into fornication. At the opportune time God specifically ordered the Israelites to kill Balaam for his wickedness.

"Do not love the world or anything in the world. If anyone loves the world, the love of the Father is not in him. For everything in the world, the cravings of sinful man, the lust of his eyes and the boasting of what he has and does, comes not from the Father but from the world. The world and its desires pass away, but the man who does the will of God lives forever" 1 John 2:15-17. The word 'love' in this scripture originates from the Greek word 'Agape'. This is God's kind of love. It is the highest kind of love that God expects us to operate in as Christians. This love is not directed at places, material things, money or achievements. It is directed first to God and consequently to human beings. Agape makes us aspire to meet the needs of others. Agape makes us purposeful, channeling our life and resources to fulfill God's agenda for mankind.

Agape does not find fulfillment in financial gratification but rather in fulfilling divine purpose. We are filled with joy not because of how much money is in our bank accounts, or the properties we own or the investments we have or our position at work but rather for impacting others to the glory of God.

The Fifth Law of Money - Money is Convertible from Riches to Wealth

Riches are the physical dimension of our material resources comprising of estates, financial investments and cash, while wealth is the spiritual dimension. Usually when we acquire resources or earn money, it is in the state classified as riches. We may choose to keep them in the state of riches or convert them to wealth. "Cast thy bread upon the waters: for thou shalt find it after many days" Ecclesiastes 11:1. Whenever we earn or receive a resource, it is classified as bread. We may use it to satisfy our needs or wants in whatever way we choose. To guarantee a future harvest, a farmer would set aside some of his present harvests as seed. To cast your bread on the waters is to allocate it as seed. Seed is the broader sense of investment. The waters are a reference to God's word, so the scripture is primarily imploring us to invest in the direction of God's leading. Giving tithes and offerings are specifically required of us according to the scriptures. "Give a portion to seven, and also to eight; for thou knowest not what evil shall be upon the earth" Ecclesiastes 11:2. Seven is reference to the seven-branched candlestick which is the place of the Holy Spirit in the tabernacle. Giving to seven is to be inspired by the Holy Spirit in your giving. Eight is to go beyond the inspiration of the Holy Spirit to help those going through challenges. "If the clouds be full of rain, they empty themselves upon the earth: and if the tree fall toward the south, or toward the north, in the place where the tree falleth, there it shall be" Ecclesiastes 11:3. A tree grows because a seed is sown. The north is the direction of God's throne, and the south is the direction away from it. Whatever is the direction of our investment would determine where our yield comes from. If we invest into those things that we are divinely inspired to pursue, then ultimately our dividends would accrue to us by divine providence. However, if we only invest in the direction that gratifies our intellectual goals then our harvest is subject to physical conditions. Assuming after the farmer has done due diligence to cultivate his soil and sows seeds the right way, but the rain does not water these seeds, there would be no harvest. "As thou knowest not what is the way of the spirit, nor how the bones do grow in the womb of her that is with child: even so thou knowest not the works of God who maketh all" Ecclesiastes 11:5. In the same way, though we may be diligent to invest as smart as we can, the success of any investment is entirely based on divine providence.

The root of any resource determines whether it is holy or not. Our resources are either blessed or cursed. "For if the firstfruit be holy, the lump is also holy: and if the root be holy, so are the branches" Romans 11:16. Tithing is the first 10% of our resources while offerings are divine convictions to give specific sums of money to the Church or other form of spiritual assignment. Tithing and offerings to God are tokens of our thanksgiving and appreciation of God's goodness to us. The moment we give tithes and offerings from money we have received, the remaining balance automatically transitions from riches to wealth. Tithes and offerings are required of us in our covenant relationship with God. We receive the blessings of life, health, peace and prosperity as divine providence in this covenant.

Tithes and offerings are not optional for the believer. It is mandatory that we observe the covenant of tithing. The scriptures say in Malachi 3:6-12, "Will a man rob God? Yet you have robbed Me! But you say, 'In what way have we robbed You?' In tithes and offerings. You are cursed with a curse, for you have robbed Me, even this whole nation. Bring all the tithes into the storehouse, that there may be food in My house, and try Me now in this," Says the LORD of hosts, "if I will not open for you the windows of heaven and pour out for you such blessing that there will not be room enough to receive it. "And I will rebuke the devourer for your sakes, so that he will not destroy the fruit of your ground, nor shall the vine fail to bear fruit for you in the field," says the LORD of hosts; and all nations will call you blessed, for you will be a delightful land," says the LORD of hosts." When we do not honor this part of our covenant relationship with God, we rob Him of what is due to Him. The first consequence is that the hedge of divine protection around our resources is broken. The angels who assign themselves because of the Spirit of the blessing of wealth pull back from guarding what belongs to us when we are in default of tithing and offerings. This opens the door for the spirit of the curse of mammon to come and work havoc in our finances. Secondly, our resources do not transition from riches to wealth. They remain physical and subject to physical conditions. This means that our investments may not receive any divine privileges that stimulate prosperity. In other words, the chances that our investments would prosper, are subject to only natural conditions. Assuming there is any interruption in the conditions that we anticipate for the investment then it fails to thrive. Ultimately, it is only when God's blessing of rain and sunshine visit the earth that we prosper in all our endeavors. Without the blessings of God, a famine could cripple any economy and void our ability to accomplish any plans.

The resource that is not blessed is exposed to Satan. It is our responsibility to convert any money we receive into wealth. Money would always gravitate towards a higher system set in place to attract it. When we pay tithe on our money, it becomes protected by the blood of Jesus. All our resources that remain in the dimension of riches are exposed to the devil. It becomes visible to him, and he inspires people with schemes to rob us of unprotected resources. When Laban was devising to kill Jacob and rob him of his wealth, God revealed this plan to Jacob in a dream and instructed him to take his family and all he had and leave. Jacob was protected because he had made a covenant with God to honor Him with tithes at Bethel.

Joseph prescribed 20% procurement of corn during the seven years of abundance based on the premise of restitution. In this way we sustain the equilibrium of the physical and spiritual realms, and we become heirs of blessings of a substantial inheritance of wealth. When we do not honor the covenant of tithing and offering, the 20" by 10" flying curse gains entrance into our estate and we become the victims of financial frustration. "Then I turned and raised my eyes, and saw there a flying scroll. And he said to me, "What do you see?" So I answered, "I see a flying scroll. Its length is twenty cubits and its width ten cubits." Then he said to me, "This is the curse that goes out over the face of the whole earth: 'Every thief shall be expelled,' according to this side of the scroll; and, 'Every perjurer shall be expelled,' according to that side of it." "I will send out the curse," says the LORD of hosts; "It shall enter the house of the thief and the house of the one who swears falsely by My name. It shall remain in the midst of his house and consume it, with its timber and stones" Zechariah 5:1-4. The flying curse identifies the estate of those who default in tithes and offerings. The first 10% of every income we get belongs to God, and so to hold it back is to steal what belongs to God. In the same way, to make a pledge, to give an offering through conviction and fail to honor it means you lied to God. Both sins invoke the 20" by 10" flying curse that breeds poverty for the thief and perjurer.

The Sixth Law of Money: I must be Generous with Money

Generosity is the key to abundance. Given similar conditions, a farmer who sows his field with many seeds receives a better harvest than one who sows with fewer seeds. Giving to meet the needs of the disadvantaged in society is an investment just like any other regular business. It is a spiritual investment that translates into physical returns. Jesus put it this way, "Blessed are the merciful for they shall obtain mercy" Matthew 5:7. Mercy is to ameliorate the circumstances of others. It goes beyond forgiveness which is a state of the soul pardoning those who do wrong. Mercy, however, is action packed. We go beyond pardon and provide practical help to those in need. In the story of the Good Samaritan, a man travelling from Jerusalem to Jericho was intercepted by robbers who not only stole from him but left him wounded and half dead. The priest and Levite who passed by did not have anything against this man in distress, but they simply did not have bowels of compassion to help ameliorate the man's circumstance. The Good Samaritan saw an opportunity to change this wounded man's situation and administered care. By changing the circumstance of this wounded man, he discharged the virtue of mercy.

When we discharge mercy by providing resources to meet the needs of others, the scripture calls it almsgiving. A classic scenario of a man whose almsgiving invoked heavenly response is recorded in the book of Acts. "There was a certain man in Caesarea called Cornelius, a centurion of the band called the Italian band, A devout man, and one that feared God with all his house, which gave much alms to the people, and prayed to God always. He saw in a vision evidently about the ninth hour of the day an angel of God coming in to him, and saying unto him, Cornelius. And when he looked on him, he was afraid, and said, What is it, Lord? And he said unto him, Thy prayers and thine alms are come up for a memorial before God. And now send men to Joppa, and call for one Simon, whose surname is Peter: He lodges with one Simon a tanner, whose house is by the sea side: he shall tell thee what thou ought to do" Acts 10:1-6. The virtue of generosity through alms giving by Cornelius invoked a divine visitation that opened the doors for Gentiles to receive the baptism of the Holy Spirit. Cornelius and his family became the first non-Israelites to receive this blessing.

Whenever we help those in distress, God sends favor upon our lives. "He that hath pity upon the poor lends unto the LORD; and that which he hath given will he pay him again" Proverbs 19:17. For every act of generosity we do, God considers it a debt He owes us. As a result, He blesses us with supernatural favor that stimulates prosperity in our endeavors. The cycle of wealth generation is like the ecosystem we spoke of earlier. Sunshine is a request from heaven for a release of righteousness from the earth. Plants send forth water through their leaves into the atmosphere and the water forms clouds which in turn releases itself as rainfall to the earth. Forest areas tend to enjoy abundance in rainfall because they harbor greater number of trees with the potential of sending forth much water into the atmosphere. In the same way, a cycle of prosperity is orchestrated through generosity. "There is one who scatters, yet increases more; and there is one who withholds more than is right, but it leads to poverty. The generous soul will be made rich, and he who waters will also be watered himself. The people will curse him who withholds grain, but blessing will be on the head of him who sells it" Proverbs 11:24-26. The more we give to the needy in society the more wealth we generate. Though wealth is spiritual it ultimately translates into financial favor that triggers success in our endeavors.

The Seventh Law of Money – I Must be a Habitual Lender and not a Borrower of Money

Many corporations today have established banking divisions that issue credit to their customers. From auto manufacturing companies to retail businesses, this trend has become a practice for many businesses. Availability of credit guarantees customers have access to funds for procurement, as well as customer loyalty. However, beyond these benefits is the hidden motive of secondary profiteering through interest rates that automatically accrue to the credit given to the customer. Defaulting customers are further charged fees which all together may garner an additional 25 to 50% profit on items sold. In this way, even if a retail business for instance goes out of business, their banking division may remain in business for a very long time by simply collecting interests on credit issued to defaulting customers. This is the reason retail businesses are more willing to issue you a credit card than to sell the wares for which they are in business.

Though business entities have perverted the concept of lending to exploit customers, lending is a divine principle that the believer must adopt to prosper. "The LORD will open to you His good treasure, the heavens, to give the rain to your land in its season, and to bless all the work of your hand. You shall lend to many nations, but you shall not borrow" Deuteronomy 28:12. Lending is a blessing when it is done with the right motive, as opposed to borrowing. There are two kinds of lending, each of which are governed by separate rules.

The first kind of lending is consumer credit to individuals. This credit is directed towards meeting the domestic needs of the borrower. "If you lend money to any of My people who are poor among you, you shall not be like a moneylender to him; you shall not charge him interest" Exodus 22:25. Poor people often borrow money to meet their domestic needs, and for such loans we are not to charge interest. Charging interest on consumer credit amounts to exploiting the poor. The fundamental reason why people borrow to meet domestic needs is because they cannot afford to pay for these needs. If they are made to pay interest on such loans, it permanently robs the poor of the opportunity to get out of poverty.

The second kind of lending is business credit. This kind of credit is targeted towards investment purposes. Business investments are intended to generate profit, so it is not wrong for the lender to participate in the rewards. In the parable of the master who gave talents to his servants Jesus Christ refers to interest from business credit. "But his lord answered and said to him, 'You wicked and lazy servant, you knew that I reap where I have not sown and gather where I have not scattered seed. So, you ought to have deposited my money with the bankers, and at my coming I would have received back my own with interest" Matthew 25:26&27. The master in this parable suggests that the servant who did not want to directly engage in a business, could have deposited the money with the bank who would have loaned it to investors for interest. Lending with interest to business entities that would make profit is not against scriptural principles.

Generally, all lending must not have a hidden agenda. For instance, you realize that a borrower has a property that you desire, so you are willing to extend them credit knowing that when they default you can possess this property. This is called covetousness! "You shall not covet your neighbor's house; you shall not covet your neighbor's wife, nor his male servant, nor his female servant, nor his ox, nor his donkey, nor anything that is your neighbor's" Exodus 20:17. Usually, covetous lenders would request the item that they wish to covet as collateral for the loan.

Whether it is a consumer credit or business credit facility, the motive behind should not be covetousness.

Borrowing is not a blessing, especially when it is consumer credit because it places the borrower at a disadvantage not only financially but spiritually and morally. "The rich rule over the poor, and the borrower is servant to the lender" Proverbs 22:7. A lender has the potential to make the life of a borrower as miserable as possible. In the past borrowers who defaulted in the repayment of loans could eventually end up as slaves of the lender where their debt is offset with labor. Today, rich investors realize how much influence they can wield politically if they control the financial system. Just as much as these investors target their investment in strategic industries, they also invest heavily into the financial institutions. The entire financial system has been hijacked by very rich investors who understand the concept of lenders ruling over borrowers. They employ the services of lobbyists to influence and manipulate legislation to their advantage. To this end, laws are now in place in many nations that encourage borrowing as a way of life.

As opposed to the secular way of lending that results in oppression and exploitation, the scriptural way of lending is structured to empower people. Scriptural lending is governed by the principle of Release. "At the end of every seven years you shall grant a release of debts. And this is the form of the release: Every creditor who has loaned anything to his neighbor shall release it; he shall not require it of his neighbor or his brother, because it is called the LORD's release. Of a foreigner you may require it; but you shall give up your claim to what is owed by your brother, except when there may be no poor among you; for the LORD will greatly bless you in the land which the LORD your God is giving you to possess as an inheritance only if you carefully obey the voice of the LORD your God, to observe with care all these commandments which I command you today. For the LORD your God will bless you just as He promised you; you shall lend to many nations, but you shall not borrow; you shall reign over many nations, but they shall not reign over you" Deuteronomy 15:1-6.

Every seven years all the Israelites were mandated to cancel the debts owed them by other Israelites. It is like the concept of debt cancellation that is practiced by richer nations towards poorer nations. However, with the Israelites this was called the re-lease. Everything we possess is given to us by God. He leases our belongings to us for a period and requires us to manage them until the re-lease. If someone owed you some money, during the release, you re-leased it again. In other words you cancelled the debt. The seventh year, at which time release was practiced, resonates with the seven-branched lampstand in the tabernacle which is synonymous with the work of the Holy Ghost in the life of the believer. Today the principle of re-lease does not tenure after a seven-year pattern but rather under divine inspiration. In essence we execute the re-lease whenever we are prompted by the Holy Ghost to re-lease what is owed to us permanently. Executing the re-lease is evidence of faithful stewardship of God's resources and invokes supernatural favor for prosperity. We are blessed with more resources to continue lending until we become lenders to many nations.

The Eighth Law of Money – I must properly Reward those who work for me

Most business schools would teach you that the fundamental reason a business is established is to make money. As believers, our motives are totally different. We are called to be a blessing. Abraham who is generally described as the father of faith had a calling from God which serves as the basis for all believers. "Now the LORD had said to Abram: "Get out of your country, from your family and from your father's house, to a land that I will show you. I will make you a great nation; I will bless you and make your name great; and you shall be a blessing. I will bless those who bless you, and I will curse him who curses you; and in you all the families of the earth shall be blessed" Genesis 12:1-3. This revelation to Abraham was a covenant that required him to leave his country, his family and father's house to pursue a divine purpose. Abraham would become great if he did so and would become a blessing! No one would be considered blessed unless they get connected to Abraham. Of course, God had Jesus Christ the seed of Abraham in mind when He made that promise. No matter our profession, vocation, business or endeavor, our mission is to be a blessing to people. Money automatically comes to us as a reward for excellence in administering our purpose. Our focus is to be a blessing to those who work for us as well as the recipients of our products and services. When hiring people into your service, there must be a mutual understanding of the salary. Make your employees happy in your service. "You shall not cheat your neighbor, nor rob him. The wages of him who is hired shall not remain with you all night until morning" Leviticus 19:13. It is better to overpay people than to underpay them. Anyone who works within the perimeter of your business or your house must receive blessings for serving you. When they work for you, do not delay payment to them. If you had the power to pay them and you delay it to take care of something that is more important to you, you will lose divine favor. "Come now, you rich, weep and howl for your miseries that are coming upon you! Your riches are corrupted, and your garments are moth-eaten. Your gold and silver are corroded, and their corrosion will be a witness against you and will eat your flesh like fire. You have heaped up treasure in the last days. Indeed the wages of the laborers who mowed your fields, which you kept back by fraud, cry out; and the cries of the reapers have reached the ears of the Lord of Sabaoth. You have lived on the earth in pleasure and luxury; you have fattened your hearts as in a day of slaughter. You have condemned, you have murdered the just; he does not resist you" James 5:1-6.

Money that is due to your human resources as wages that you refuse to give them could invoke the spirit of the curse of mammon. The spirit of the curse of mammon assigns itself to riches that are gained unjustly and destroys it. Corrupted riches, moth-eaten garments, corroded gold and silver are all manifestation of the mammon curse. No matter what we do in secret, there is a referee up in heaven that sees us. If we rob our workers, He judges us with what is due to us. Many corporations often hire skillful lawyers to craft policies that defraud the human resources of the organization. Though they can outwit the judicial system they also have to contend with the Lord of the Harvest. The curse of mammon which is spiritual in nature is assigned to their riches. It may take some years for this manifestation of the curse of mammon, but it surely comes to destroy the riches of the unjust.

One of the strategies that Chief Executive Officers engage in to make their organizations profitable is to lay off workers. A newly employed CEO would want to immediately prove to the Board of Directors which hired him that he is competently turning the company around to achieve profits. By laying off workers, they cut back a significant amount of expenditure which translates into profit. As a result, fewer workers are overloaded with the tasks of those laid off and dare not complain, knowing that they could also easily lose their jobs. They simply work harder to maintain their jobs. Most often, laying off workers is not the root cause of financial difficulties a business may be experiencing. The problem is usually the disparity of income between the management and unskilled labor. In some cases, the wages of one executive could be the sum of wages for one hundred workers. Instead of laying off one hundred workers, they can reduce the wages of ten top executives to accommodate those hundred workers whose livelihood and families depend on their jobs. Such a humane approach may invoke divine favor to turn around the challenges of a business.

The conditions of service in your organization must include health insurance coverage for your employees. "If you see the donkey of one who hates you lying under its burden, and you would refrain from helping it, you shall surely help him with it" Exodus 23:5. If you see your neighbors donkey fall, due to the burden it was carrying, though your neighbor may not be present, you should help that donkey out of the situation. Though this is useful advice on how to treat animals, this principle concerns how we treat employees who get injured on the job. It is unfortunate how many cases are filed in courts each year about employers who refuse to do their due diligence to help workers who get injured on the job.

The Ninth Law of Money – I must be Honest and Fair with People

North America, which used to be the hub of large-scale manufacturing and consequent prosperity has now turned into one giant mall of uncertainty. In the last three decades, instead of building new factories to produce goods, the trend has been to shut down existing ones and build retail malls. The factories were shut down because it seemed more profitable to procure products from developing economies where labor was extremely cheap. Manufacturing jobs were shipped abroad in the strategic scheme of 'outsourcing'. As a result, the Asian manufactures have recorded great economic gains while North America is now saddled with trade deficits. Currently the market driven economy of North America is in such a deep crisis that no one seems to understand how to ameliorate it.

Whether in procurement or marketing, businesses have simply choked and squeezed the blood out of one another. Some retail businesses procured goods at a price that made local producers run aground while boasting huge profits for the applause of shareholders. Others use the strategy of 'ZERO PERCENT INTEREST - NO DOWN PAYMENT - DISCOUNT SALE' to deceive unsuspecting customers. These schemes breed confidence with shareholders who earn huge dividends while dishing out fantastic salaries to their corporate executives.

Honest and fair are two words which have become a taboo for most corporate entities. Dishonesty and unfairness have been redefined with the words 'strategic sale' and 'strategic acquisition' respectively. Whether in the process of sales or procurement it is important that we understand the concept of empowering others. "And if you sell anything to your neighbor or buy from your neighbor's hand, you shall not oppress one another" Leviticus 25:14. We should not sell in such a way that exploits unsuspecting customers or buy in such a way that runs suppliers out of business. The concept of establishing businesses to bring about socio-economic prosperity of society is the way forward for any economy. Of course, it may not be practically possible to sell this philosophy to many entrepreneurs, but then those who buy the concept would be able to survive the test of time. In the season of judgment, the distinction between those whose concept of business is just and unjust would become evident. The businesses established with a godly philosophy of empowering people would emerge as industry leaders.

Whatever we buy and how we trade off goods and services either invokes the blessings of the spirit of wealth or the curse of mammon. All that we see here on earth that can be classified as riches originated from God. "The earth is the LORD's, and all its fullness, The world and those who dwell therein. For He has founded it upon the seas, and established it upon the waters. Who may ascend into the hill of the LORD? Or who may stand in His holy place? He who has clean hands and a pure heart, who has not lifted up his soul to an idol, nor sworn deceitfully. He shall receive blessing from the LORD, and righteousness from the God of his salvation" Psalm 24:1-5. All of creation was founded based on God's word and that is how they are sustained. This includes all human beings as well as material things. The blessing of the Spirit of wealth assigns itself to those who engage divine principles in how they trade off creation. In the same way, the curse of mammon assigns itself to those who fraudulently amass riches.

Though it may not seem like a smart and lucrative way of doing business, endeavoring to engage divine principles is the only way to build wealth and sustainable prosperity. The apostle Paul admonishes in Romans 8:18-25, "For I consider that the sufferings of this present time are not worthy to be compared with the glory which shall be revealed in us. For the earnest expectation of the creation eagerly waits for the revealing of the sons of God. For the creation was subjected to futility, not willingly, but because of Him who subjected it in hope; because the creation itself also will be delivered from the bondage of corruption into the glorious liberty of the children of God. For we know that the whole creation groans and labors with birth pangs together until now. Not only that, but we also who have the firstfruits of the Spirit, even we ourselves groan within ourselves, eagerly waiting for the adoption, the redemption of our body. For we were saved in this hope, but hope that is seen is not hope; for why does one still hope for what he sees? But if we hope for what we do not see, we eagerly wait for it with perseverance." Although science classifies only human beings, plants and animals as living things, while precious minerals and real estate are classified as non-living things, the scripture describes all of

God's creation as creatures. All of God's creation are aware of the competition taking place between the just and the unjust over their ownership. The scripture says that all creation was subjected to a curse when Adam sinned in the Garden of Eden. Through Jesus Christ however, it is possible as a human being to experience deliverance from the curse upon Adam and all his descendants. Furthermore, it is possible to change the status of created things from 'cursed' to 'blessed' based on ownership. The scripture above points out that created things are craving to be released from the curse of sin. They are hoping that the sons of God would come and deliver them from the hands of cursed ownership. Nothing that God created wants to remain under cursed ownership. Houses, vehicles, gold, precious jewelry and every material substance that is desirable to man but currently owned by the unjust, are crying to God for change of ownership. So long as they are owned by the unjust, they are in bondage and subject to decay. They become blessed only when they are owned by the just.

Although the process of adopting divine principles in our sales and procurement may not look like a smart way of doing business, it eventually pays off because we get to enjoy the last laugh in the face of our competitors. Marketing and procurement are platforms that determine the direction for wealth transfer. To become permanent recipients of wealth, it is important that we do not exchange our wealth for a curse. When your sales or procurement strategies rob people and throw them out of business, you trade your wealth for curses.

The Tenth Law of Money – I must have a Plan for Money before getting it

Whether we own a business or not, the mindset that makes the best of money is to mentally position ourselves as the Chief Executive Officer of a multi-million-dollar enterprise. We must have a plan for the next one dollar that comes our way, the next ten dollars, the next hundred dollars, the next thousand dollars, the next ten thousand dollars, the next hundred thousand dollars, the next million dollars, the next ten million dollars, the next hundred million dollars and so on. Any money that comes your way for which you do not have a definite plan is already lost. Whenever money precedes a plan, it tends to be wasted. Money speaks to us because it is a spirit and seeks a resting place. Wealth is the resting place of money. Perfect wealth is money to the seventh dimension. Simply put, it is wealth owned by the righteous. Money acquired in righteousness and administered by divine covenant, transitions to wealth.

In crafting a plan for money, it is important to maintain the mindset of a business entity. This is because as a human being your life is either profitable or in a deficit. When you are profitable, you become wealthy with a lot of resources at your disposal. However, when you are in deficit, you are constantly indebted to others. If you cannot balance your books as an individual, how can you run an enterprise profitably? Chances are that you may end up as a business failure, unless you are able to develop the skills for generating profit from all resources available to you. "Be diligent know the state of your flocks and attend to your herds. For riches are not forever, neither does a crown endure to all generations. When the hay is removed, and the tender grass shows itself, and the herbs of the mountains are gathered in. The lambs will provide your clothing and the goats the price of a field. You shall have enough goats' milk for your food, for the food of your household, and the nourishment of your maidservants" Proverbs 27:23-27. There are six areas of planning that require us to strategize: Mission, Human Resource, Corporate Resource, Production, Marketing and Financial Management. To create a stronghold which is the resting place for wealth, it is necessary that you engage strategies in these six aspects of business.

Mission - "For riches are not forever, neither doth a crown endure for generations." The words 'forever' and 'generations' speak to the essence of stewardship of time. Money-flow responds to time change. There is a time to sow and a time to reap, a time to keep and a time to throw away and so on. Time as an activity determines what kind of supernatural favor we enjoy at every point. When I finished developing the wealth deployment intra-internet system that was used by the Christian Chamber of Commerce in 2007, I began to prepare for a marketing campaign. At a prayer meeting which we convened weekly at our office there was a prophetic word to the contrary. Though it was late in the summer, the prophetic word stated that the marketing campaign would flourish in spring the next year. Upon hearing that word I immediately suspended my plans for the takeoff of the campaign. It happened that in the following winter, opportunities began to open by themselves across the nation. We pursued these opportunities and by the end of that year we had developed seven regional centers for our operations. Best of all, securing funds to run our operations was completely stress free. It was as though the money we needed always knew when to show up.

The short-, medium- and long-term plans of a business must resonate with the times and seasons which we are privileged to discern through fellowship with God. Fellowship with God, takes place during the seasons He has set for divine visitation. The seasons are: The Sabbath; Passover; First-fruits; Pentecost; Trumpets; Atonement and Tabernacles. During these feasts, God blesses those who fulfill the requirements for a visitation, with insight into the aspects of our endeavors where He intends to favor us. "Thus says the LORD: 'In an acceptable time I have heard you, and in the day of salvation I have helped you…" Isaiah 49:8a. There is a time for instance when God hears our prayer, while there is a time when He stretches out His divine hand to help us out. These two instances which are opposite, together constitute a stewardship. Stewardship may begin as a time of a specific challenge. Those who are willing to seek and pursue divine wisdom to ameliorate that challenge often reap the rewards when the time changes. The stewardship of Pharaoh's dream was fourteen years in total. The first seven years was one framework of time after which there was time change for the second seven years. When the Egyptians were harvesting the yields of the first seven years of abundance, they failed to engage the wisdom of Joseph. According to Joseph's counsel they should have bought corn and stored it. Though they cultivated crops, they did not go the extra mile to align their mission with time. Time change proved them foolish and ran them all out of business.

As an individual or corporate entity, you must seek to understand the times and seasons. Though you may be currently enjoying a certain level of prosperity, failure to conform to the times may result in a reversal of prosperity. You determine your long-term plan by prayerfully seeking a vision from God. A vision is the ultimate end of purpose. It is the dimension to which God has promised to elevate you. Your medium-term goals are determined by breaking the entire vision into objectives. Every objective must be specific, measurable, achievable, flexible and the platform to attain the next in line. The first objective is the one that you already have the resources to accomplish. This achievable objective becomes your short-term goal. Each goal you achieve should increase your potential to accomplish the next.

Human Resource - "Be diligent to know the state of your flocks and attend to your herds." Primarily there are two kinds of people in your world. They are distinguished as either sheep or goats based upon their potential and not necessarily their character. Sheep are those people whose talents incline them to facilitate the production aspects of an enterprise while the goats are marketers. The sheep know how to pay attention to details, help in the design and the actual process of making a product or providing a service. These may include your Accountant, Administrator, Engineer, Pharmacologist, Architect, Chef, Beautician etc. On the other hand, your goats are those who may not help you in the process of making the product but have the courage to critic and sell it. Goats are usually annoying in the way they critic a product and may put you off. Their immediate attitude towards the product may discourage you especially if you have spent so much time and resources developing the product. However, if you pay attention to the critical analysis of the goats, it provides you with valuable insights to redesign and make the product perfect. It is only when the goats are entirely pleased with the product that you may begin full scale production and marketing. When the goats are satisfied with the products, they go full throttle to promote and sell them.

It is important to appraise everyone in your world that includes friends, Church members and family relatives to determine the role they can play in the development of your organization. These people are not related to you by chance; rather they can be harnessed to help you with valuable services as you set yourself up to attain destiny. Make deals with those who want to charge for their services either by negotiating deferred payments or trade your services for theirs. If you start to harness these people properly you prepare yourself to make the best out of your paid employees. Whenever people are not properly positioned to function in their divine potential, they become problematic. Furthermore, their creative abilities are not engaged to enhance overall prosperity of the organization. Appraising your human resources periodically to assess their potential and properly assign their tasks, is a strategy that brings constantly renewed energy to the productivity of the organization. The human resource policies of an organization will determine the level of morale of employees, as well as their length of stay with the organization. A high human resource retention rate is evidence of good policies and vice versa.

Corporate Resource - "You shall have enough goats milk for your food, for the food of your household, and the nourishment of your maidservants." How we buy and who we buy from has a role in determining our ability to sustain wealth. Money flow speaks of where we receive and send our money. Your business will certainly attract customers from everywhere but then you need guaranteed patronage. These are customers who will buy from you no matter what negative public opinion the media or competitors may spread against you. These are the customers from whom you should also procure. Money flow is the reason nations enter into bilateral agreements with each other. The airline industry is familiar with code-sharing agreements where an airline partners with another to share passengers on specific travel routes. Money flow means that you must determine where you intend to spend your money so that ultimately it comes back to empower you.

Negotiating the price and terms for our supplies is key to our corporate resource strategy. In certain instances, we may not be able to negotiate price considerably because it may be determined by a larger market. However, the terms of any supply contract can be negotiated. The need to negotiate the price and terms of supplies is fundamental to our success. To have a procurement advantage we must establish a relationship with those suppliers who understand our needs and are willing to be flexible enough to accommodate unexpected changes in the trends of our industry.

Production - "When the hay is removed, and the tender grass shows itself, and the herbs of the mountains are gathered in." The hay is removed because the former rain is about to manifest. As we have previously learned, the former rain is the seed rain which is significant of divine revelation that teaches us how to invest our life, time and resources. In the same way, 'the herbs gathered in' speak of the latter rain which is God's revelation that teaches us to make profit from our investments. Whether it is former or latter rain revelation, we receive the wisdom of God through fellowship with Him.

The seasons of divine visitation were structured to coincide with the agricultural practices of Israel and thereby established the relationship between their spiritual and financial purposes. The Sabbath for instance, was not just to give them physical rest after six days of work, but to provide the framework for spiritual renewal through fellowship with God. The Passover provided a framework for divine protection and wisdom; First-fruits provided an opportunity for supernatural increase; Pentecost provided an opportunity for a renewed anointing; Trumpets provided an opportunity to establish spiritual order and divine favor in their endeavors; Atonement provided an opportunity for alleviation of sins and to end curses; Tabernacles was a forum for repositioning in purpose and the promises of God pertaining to their divine destiny.

After every six years, the Israelites were expected to observe the Seventh-year Sabbath. They did not cultivate the land in this seventh year and allowed the land to rest. In this way, the land recuperated for one full year. In the eighth year they could resume farming their land. To facilitate the sustenance of the Israelites during the seventh year, God supernaturally orchestrated a bumper harvest in the sixth year. This harvest would carry them through the seventh and eighth year until the ninth year when they could harvest from the eighth-year crops. The Seventh-year Sabbatical is significant of occasions when we must attend Holy Ghost inspired conventions. At these times we retire from work and seek the mind of God for our lives and endeavors. This is how we are renewed spiritually with revelation to advance and make progress in our endeavors.

The destiny of a human being is like a jigsaw puzzle. Our entire destiny picture is split into several pieces, and each piece is the revelation God gives us during a visitation. We get precise revelation from God, as and when it is needed for aligning our works to the supernatural process. The more we fellowship with God, the more we get the picture and a better grasp of our destiny. Ultimately, by the end of our lifespan on earth we should have fulfilled all that is divinely expected of us, and experienced all that God has promised us. It is through fellowship that we get the blueprint of our production strategies. There is a process of production or providing professional services that makes great impact.

Marketing - Goodwill advertising and standard pricing are key to our marketing strategy. Instead of spending huge sums of money on persuasive advertising which sometimes yields diminishing returns, it is important to invest in goodwill advertising. First, it is cheaper and never a nuisance to the public. Second, goodwill advertising is a seed to the disadvantaged in the community and comes back to us as supernatural favor. When Boaz allowed Ruth to glean his fields, hardly did he know that this act of goodwill would invoke the blessing of divine favor and make him a direct ancestor of King David and Jesus Christ the Messiah.

Standard pricing means that you do not use the gimmick of sale discounts and hidden conditions to lure and exploit customers. Simply price your product with a fair margin of profit and let those who can afford buy when they can. The sales gimmick is the reason so many individuals and businesses are financially bankrupt. Our marketing strategy must aim at customer retention by providing them with value for their money whenever they buy from us. This is the reason why though highly priced, quality vehicle brands like Rolls Royce, BMW and Mercedes Benz have continued to thrive for generations.

A good marketing strategy must adequately address the reality of competition. We bid for contracts as well as compete with other producers and service providers. To win a war there is need for a strategic plan. Every strategic plan to outwit competition must be three-dimensional. It must enshrine the concepts of ambush, bulwark and besiegement.

Ambush means surprise attack. Surprise attacks are short-term strategies that indulge creativity. It is essential that you continue to add value to your product, making it more useful to the consumer. Research and Development is key to remain competitive.

Bulwark is a strong attack and defense position for the business. These strong positions are medium-term strategies structured into your business to counteract any surprises from your competitors. You must anticipate potentially competing products in the market and stay ahead or at least keep pace with industry trends.

Besiegement is a long-term strategy that aims at positioning your business as head of the industry. It takes cognizance of the overall future of the organization, builds formidable alliances and establishes itself through goodwill to provide a lasting impact on society.

Financial Management – "The lambs will provide your clothing and the goats the price of a field." While clothing in this scripture speaks of liabilities in a business, the field speaks of assets. Liabilities are those recurrent expenditures such as utilities, inventory, rents and salaries. Assets are permanent expenditures such as real estate, vehicles and equipment. All income must have a predetermined direction. For instance, a business with small and large customers may decide which revenue would be directed towards liabilities or for assets.

The ratio of Liabilities to Assets tells the financial strength of a business. If the liabilities are greater than the assets, it shows weakness and vice versa. The liability-asset ratio must always favor assets. If this is not the case, the business must aim at gradually reducing its liabilities in favor of what is invested into assets. The tilt of liability-asset ratio speaks to the sustained profitability of an enterprise.

Rewarding Stakeholders
Those who helped make your vision a reality are your partners. They must be properly rewarded. Usually, many

people resign from an organization when they do not see a future for themselves there. The sense of ownership and partnership is crucial to maintaining highly talented people in your organization. Your business must dedicate a certain percentage of its profit to those who are committed to making the dream come true. This reward strategy must be clearly defined and progressive so that all the members of your team can be motivated accordingly.

Our choice of partners and investors must align with the plowing principle. "You shall not plow with an ox and a donkey together" Deuteronomy 22:10. Unequal yoking takes place when two different kinds of animals are harnessed by a yoke to accomplish work. Though they may look the same outwardly, the bone structure of one animal may place it in advantage over the other. "Do not be unequally yoked together with unbelievers. For what fellowship has righteousness with lawlessness? And what communion has light with darkness? And what accord has Christ with Belial? Or what part has a believer with an unbeliever? And what agreement has the temple of God with idols? For you are the temple of the living God. As God has said: "I will dwell in them and walk among them. I will be their God, and they shall be My people" 2 Corinthians 6:14-18. Partnership with an unbeliever to engage in business is considered as unequal yoking. First, the fundamental principles that underline our value system for engaging in work as well as our cycles of prosperity are entirely different. Most unbelievers can be classified as blind investors. This is because their choice of investment and strategic counsels tends exclusively towards maximized financial rewards as opposed to inheritance. Assuming you have such people as members of your board of directors, their resolutions would choke out the divine agenda for your enterprise. Second, when a believer partners with an unbeliever in an investment, it becomes impossible to draw the clear distinction of how they can be blessed of God. The spirit of the blessing of wealth cannot assign itself to the same resources jointly owned by unbelievers. Such a business is automatically considered a blind investment. Publicly traded stocks and Mutual Funds are typical examples of blind investments. On the other hand, it is possible to raise loans also referred to as bonds from unbelievers who would receive a specific rate of interest for their investment. Only believers who share the same values as us may be considered shareholders of our business.

Potential Investors

When tax collectors came to Jesus Christ to demand his taxes, the scripture says that He told Peter to go and catch fish. Peter obeyed the instruction and found money in the mouth of the first fish he caught. With this money he paid the taxes to cover himself and for Jesus Christ. There are four elements of this miracle that reveal the wisdom by which Jesus solved this challenge. To fulfill the instruction from Jesus, Peter needed a bait, a hook, the sea and the fish.

Fish – When Jesus Christ met Peter for the first time, Peter was a fisherman who had become frustrated in his attempt to catch fish that day. Jesus requested for Peter to make his work tools available for a seashore evangelistic crusade after which, Jesus instructed Peter to make a renewed attempt to catch fish. To the amazement of Peter so many fish are caught, and he required the help of other fishermen in the area to get the fish to shore. Jesus invited Peter to become his disciple and become a fisher of men. Peter obeyed and submitted to the leadership of Jesus.

On this day, when they had to pay taxes, there seemed to be no money in their coffers. Jesus Christ tells Peter to go and catch fish, and the first fish would have money in its mouth that would be enough to meet the need. Though Peter is a fisherman by profession, by this time, Jesus had schooled Peter on how to catch men like fish. A fish with money in its mouth is significantly a potential investor.

Sea – The Sea is the habitat for fishes. It is their community where they reside. Since we have defined the fish as an investor then the sea is a community of investors. It is a pool of potential investors. This is usually a group of like-minded people who share common aspirations or goals. There is always a center of gravity that keeps them together and garners their commitment. An example is the Church, Chamber of Commerce or Business Networks. Another common example of the sea is when a group of rich friends informally host activities to have fun and stay connected. Essentially you must belong to a community of people who are investment oriented, share the same values so that you can leverage opportunities from one another. The critical ingredient that sustains a healthy relationship with your pool of potential investors is your integrity. You must think of the sea as your personal aquarium or fishpond, which you are obliged to maintain. Your character of integrity and resourcefulness to the needs of others within the community is an investment that brings return when you are in need.

Bait – Fish do not get trapped easily without a bait. The bait is what lures the fish towards the trap set for it. The fish recognizes the bait as an opportunity to feed itself, so it immediately moves towards it. Then of course it gets trapped. Investors would not pay attention to you unless you have what looks like a good investment opportunity. Organizations and individuals with financial resources are constantly seeking the most lucrative investment opportunities, and so if you can package your product with a plan that is feasible enough, they will invest.

Hook – The hook is what traps the fish so it cannot escape your grip. When a prospective investor comes your way and gives you some attention, there must be hooks set in place to ensure that they do not walk away from your proposition. The only reason you present an investment opportunity to a prospective investor is because you are seeking a commitment of their financial resources to your proposal. Your proposal must be so convincing, such that they do not walk away without making a commitment. If they were attracted by the bait, they must not escape the hook.

Entertainment-Sports, Fashion, Decorations, Aviation, Maritime-Oceanography, Transport-Shipping, Finance are industries that gender to the economic system of Capitalism.

Harness

Chapter Nineteen

Aligned

"And of the angels He says: "Who makes His angels
spirits and His ministers a flame of fire." But to the Son
He says: "Your throne, O God, is forever and ever; a
scepter of righteousness is the scepter of Your kingdom.
You have loved righteousness and hated lawlessness;
Therefore God, Your God, has anointed You with the oil
of gladness more than Your companions"
Hebrews 1:7-9

At a school campus on a hill, a minister friend had invited
various ministries to participate in a summer camp
meeting. I was scheduled to speak on the opening night,
so I arrived quite early at the residence assigned to the
ministers. My friend who was the host helped me settle in
and requested that I accompany him to the auditorium
where the event was to take place. When we entered, it
had been arranged with chairs and all the equipment for
the services. The Holy Spirit whispered to me saying, "My

Presence is not here." I became frightened because this would frustrate my ministry in the hall that evening. I asked the Holy Spirit, "Why?" And He answered, "Look at the chairs". Upon paying close attention I realized that the rows and columns were not perfectly aligned. I told the host to get us some help to rearrange the chairs. As we started fixing the columns, strangely I could see the presence of God coming in to rest upon wherever the columns and rows were perfectly aligned. That evening when I ministered the glory of God visited in such an awesome way with signs, wonders and miracles. The following morning the ministers residing with me in the same building gathered in the dining room for breakfast. Every one of these ministers had an unusually cold attitude. Then at a point one of them mustered courage and asked me, "Ken why did you do what you did last night?" Surprised at the question, I asked, "What did I do?' Then he said, "Look at my notes, you preached my entire message yesterday." Then another minister also retorted, "You preached my message yesterday and now I don't know what to speak on today." These two ministers who accused me were slated to speak that day and felt that the standard that had been set on the opening night session was too high. They had become intimidated and did not feel confident enough to match the expectations of the attendees. Instead of seeking God to know and align with His presence for their sessions, they resorted to blaming me, so their ministry that day lacked the fervency of the divine presence.

Aligned is to have an inherent hearing of the sounds of heaven so we can be in unison. It is like how a musical orchestra engages the harmony of instruments and voices to produce pleasant music. Everyone in the choir must have hearing ears so they can resonate with each other. The object of fellowship in the tabernacle of Moses that aligned us with the sounds of heaven was the altar of incense. Revelatory worship was offered to God in the tabernacle of Moses at the Altar of Incense. These four spices, frankincense, onycha, stacte and galbanum were tempered into a perfume and the fragrance filled the atmosphere of the Holy Place as well as the Most Holy Place. "And the Lord said to Moses: "Take sweet spices, stacte and onycha and galbanum, and pure frankincense with these sweet spices; there shall be equal amounts of each. You shall make of these an incense, a compound according to the art of the perfumer, salted, pure, and holy. And you shall beat some of it very fine, and put some of it before the Testimony in the tabernacle of meeting where I will meet with you. It shall be most holy to you. But as for the incense which you shall make, you shall not make any for yourselves, according to its composition. It shall be to you holy for the Lord. Whoever makes any like it, to smell it, he shall be cut off from his people" Exodus 30:34-38.

Frankincense is significant of inspired sanctification. Sanctification is from the Greek 'Hagaios' which means to be set apart, holy and pure. It is the essence of the nature of God that makes us different from others. Here, we are prompted to abstain from certain practices that make us flawed in relation to God's word. In addition to personal revelation, there are three frameworks by which the Holy Spirit inspires our sanctification. "Wives, submit to your own husbands, as is fitting in the Lord. Husbands, love your wives and do not be bitter toward them" Colossians

3:18&19. The scriptural prescription for the relationship between a husband and wife is love and submission. This is the 'partnership framework' by which the Holy Spirit sanctifies us so we can become heirs of the grace of life. The journey of destiny may require that we partner with others to obtain our inheritance. Biblical prescriptions for marriage serve as a model for partnering with those who God assigns for us to work with in pursuit of divine destiny. Submission and honor are virtues that foster spouses to inspire sanctification with each other. In the same way, submission and honor from both spouses make marriage work, these values are the bedrock for successful missions, ministry or business partnership. "Children, obey your parents in all things, for this is well pleasing to the Lord. Fathers, do not provoke your children, lest they become discouraged" Colossians 3:20&21. The relationship between parents and children is a 'mentoring framework'. Here, parents inspire sanctification with their children who learn obedience in the process. Parents must not provoke their children because this is discouraging. In our journey of destiny, God intends that we enter mentoring relationships where we first serve as proteges and ultimately mentor others. In the same way that fathers ultimately provide an inheritance to their children, mentoring relationships gives the believer access to their inheritance in Christ. "Bondservants, obey in all things your masters according to the flesh, not with eyeservice, as men-pleasers, but in sincerity of heart, fearing God. And whatever you do, do it heartily, as to the Lord and not to men, knowing that from the Lord you will receive the reward of the inheritance; for you serve the Lord Christ. But he who does wrong will be repaid for what he has done, and there is no partiality" Colossians 3:22-25.

Servants and masters are significant in the working relationship between employees and employers. This is a 'professional framework' where we may be working with believers or unbelievers and yet the scripture sets the standards of 'no eyeservice, no men-pleasing, but serving with sincerity from the heart'. Wherever we are employed, we are expected to work with a mindset of serving our Lord Jesus Christ because He sanctifies us in the process. He takes responsibility for blessing us with our inheritance if we serve with this godly mindset.

Onycha is the second component of the incense of worship, and this is the roar of inspired intercession. The Holy Spirit stands in the gap for the believer to make intercession according to the will of God. "Likewise, the Spirit also helps in our weaknesses. For we do not know what we should pray for as we ought, but the Spirit Himself makes intercession for us with groanings which cannot be uttered. Now He who searches the hearts knows what the mind of the Spirit is, because He makes intercession for the saints according to the will of God" Romans 8:26&27. The Holy Spirit orchestrates a roar from within the believer that announces our dominion to all entities within our space. This roar releases creation from the bondage of the Adamic curse so that we can experience the manifestation of our inheritance in Christ.

Stacte is the third component of the incense of worship, and this is significant of inspired adoration. Here, the Holy Spirit inspires the singing by which we adore God with thanksgiving.

Galbanum is the fourth component of the incense of worship, and this is significant of the inspired fat of offerings. Here, the Holy Spirit inspires us to give specific offerings in specified ways.

Jesus speaks to the essence of true worship which should never be initiated from the carnal mind in the conversation with the Samaritan woman. "But the hour is coming, and now is, when the true worshipers will worship the Father in spirit and truth; for the Father is seeking such to worship Him. God is Spirit, and those who worship Him must worship in spirit and truth" John 4:23&24. True and proper worship is initiated by God, but then we must be willing to offer it when prompted. To be aligned is our resonance with the sounds of heaven to change the atmosphere here on earth. We cannot ignore the occurrences of heaven and yet experience the fullness of the prosperity of the earth as God intends. "The Lord has established His throne in heaven, and His kingdom rules over all. Bless the Lord, you His angels, who excel in strength, who do His word, heeding the voice of His word. Bless the Lord, all you His hosts, you ministers of His, who do His pleasure. Bless the Lord, all His works, in all places of His dominion. Bless the Lord, O my soul!" Psalms 103:19-22. The reign of God with cherubim and seraphim requires our lifestyle of true worship and in unison. To avoid some of the catastrophic events that often manifests to plague our world, everything created by God must be engaged in conformity with His will.

Corporate Character

In the beginning of the seven-year drought in Egypt, the Egyptians spent all their gold to procure food from Joseph and yet the drought raged on unabated. Joseph required them to trade in their livestock for corn supplies. Animals represent the various characteristics of man. Throughout the scriptures, we find various references to animals that depict both divine and human character. For instance, Jesus said in Matthew 10:16, "Behold, I send you out as sheep in the midst of wolves. Therefore, be wise as serpents and harmless as doves." We get the impression that by paying attention to certain animal characteristics, we discover how to become effective in tackling the various challenges that confront us as human beings. "So when the money failed in the land of Egypt and in the land of Canaan, all the Egyptians came to Joseph and said, "Give us bread, for why should we die in your presence? For the money has failed." Then Joseph said, "Give your livestock, and I will give you bread for your livestock, if the money is gone." So they brought their livestock to Joseph, and Joseph gave them bread in exchange for the horses, the flocks, the cattle of the herds, and for the donkeys. Thus he fed them with bread in exchange for all their livestock that year" Genesis 47:15-17. They bought corn from Joseph for survival and to sustain their livestock. After a short while, their money was finished yet they needed to survive. When they came to Joseph, he requested livestock as a means of payment for food. The Egyptians brought their horses, sheep, goats and donkeys to Joseph in exchange for food.

An important factor that may determine the success or failure of an enterprise is corporate character. Corporate character is how the human beings within the organization relate to one another as well as to the outside world. The character exhibited by the human beings who manage goods and services has a strong bearing on the overall prosperity of an organization. This is why an important factor in determining a company's level of customer retention is not necessarily the quality or price of products, but rather the effectiveness of the customer service department. Joseph realized that corporate character in Egypt was appalling. By trading food for their livestock, he was setting new standards for enterprises who would qualify for government contracts and assistance. This concept is the noble basis of the standards set for triple 'A' ratings of companies listed on the financial markets as well as the standards for rating personal credit. Although it is currently perverted in practice, the triple 'A' rating of an organization or the credit score of an individual is supposed to be a measurement of character and determines how much investment or credit they can attract.

There are four living creatures surrounding the throne of Almighty God that gives us insight into how He functions over the universe. "As for the likeness of their faces, each had the face of a man; each of the four had the face of a lion on the right side, each of the four had the face of an ox on the left side, and each of the four had the face of an eagle" Ezekiel 1:10. The creatures had the face of an ox, eagle, lion and man. These faces are features that God revealed to the Prophet Ezekiel so we as humans can understand how He exercises dominion over all creation. At it were, He made us in His image and likeness so we can function like Him.

Ox - The ox is generally humble in nature. In the same family of animals with such a nature are the lamb and the donkey. These animals are known to carry out instructions without rebelling. "Hear, O heavens, and give ear, O earth! For the LORD has spoken: I have nourished and brought up children, and they have rebelled against Me; The ox knows its owner and the donkey its master's crib; but Israel does not know, My people do not consider" Isaiah 1:2&3. Rebelliousness to authority does not resonate with divine character. Essentially if people cannot function within the framework of instruction, then failure is inevitable. Everyone who is a part of your team must understand the essence of humility. "Therefore lay aside all filthiness and superfluity of naughtiness, and receive with meekness the implanted word, which is able to save your souls" James 1:21. An organization functions effectively when its members pay attention to instruction and carry them out accordingly. People must be trained and retrained until their actions are consistent with the set standards of the organization. Everyone who is a part of your team must understand the premise of training and compliance from the very onset when they join you. Rules and regulations must be set for members of your team. This way, there is a definite framework for operating according to a set standard. Do not assume that people would do the right thing because they have a college degree or work experience. Organizations fail because people do not conform to standards. For instance, it is a well-known fact that during the First World War, though the United States Army was more equipped than the Japanese, the American soldiers were careless. The Japanese on the other hand had been trained to check, double check and recheck equipment before engagement. In this way, the Japanese avoided a lot of accidents and equipment failures responsible for several catastrophic losses of the US Army.

Productivity is high when everyone in the team is effectively fulfilling their specific roles in accordance with the plan. The attribute of the ant comes into play here. "Go to the ant, you sluggard! Consider her ways and be wise. Though having no captain, overseer or ruler, provides her supplies in the summer, and gathers her food in the harvest. How long will you slumber, O sluggard? When will you rise from your sleep? A little sleep, a little slumber, A little folding of the hands to sleep, So shall your poverty come on you like a prowler, And your need like an armed man" Proverbs 6:6-11. The ant is one of the most brilliant and fascinating creatures on planet earth. As little as they are in size, it is a great wonder how they can erect massive ant hill structures. Their ability to achieve greatness despite their unassuming features is the reason why as human beings we have no excuse to remain in a state of lack and mediocrity. The ant is a self-motivated leader, supervisor and ruler.

As a leader, the ant is a visionary who understands the times and seasons. Summer is the season of harvest when food is in abundance while food is scarce in the winter. The ant therefore has a plan that is consistent with the annual sequence of seasons. Every employee in your organization must know what goal they are expected to attain within the context of the overall vision. It stimulates a drive in every employee and enables them to function as self-motivated leaders.

As a supervisor, the ant breaks down the overall vision into various divisions. A corporation usually has various departments and units responsible for the functions of the organization. Each department is structured in such a way that all together they achieve the overall vision of the organization. In the same way, every employee must be taught the dynamics of how to set and achieve objectives. First, an objective must be specific, which means that it must be possible to define it with one or two words. Secondly, an objective must be measurable, which means it should be quantified in length, time or degree. Thirdly, an objective must be achievable, which means that we must have access to the resources for accomplishing it. Fourthly, an objective must be flexible such that there are alternative ways of achieving it. Finally, an objective must be the platform for achieving the next goal. When members of your team understand how to set and achieve goals, they become effective supervisors.

As a ruler, the ant has rules that guide its work. Without rules there are no boundaries and people become disorderly. Divine principles must form the basis of all corporate policy. Everyone in the team must learn how to craft policies out of divine principles. "Your word is a lamp to my feet and a light to my path" Psalm 119:105. Rules that do not align with divine principles always open the door to evil. Team members usually get frustrated, look out for loopholes in the system and cut corners. When a policy is established, it must include enforcement procedures so that it can be upheld effectively in corporate practice. Upholding divine principles is the key to efficiency and phenomenal achievements.

Eagle - The eagle is a highly focused, destiny-minded bird. Though it has wings like other birds, it usually does not fly from one place to another by the strength of its wings. Rather it waits patiently for the wind blowing towards its destination and yields its wings to soar on the strength of the wind. In this way, the eagle achieves great heights that other birds are not known to attain. The heights of achievement divinely designed for us are always beyond our own ability to attain. Isaiah 40:28-31 says, "Have you not known? Have you not heard? The everlasting God, the LORD, The Creator of the ends of the earth, neither faints nor is weary. His understanding is unsearchable. He gives power to the weak, And to those who have no might He increases strength. Even the youths shall faint and be weary, and the young men shall utterly fall. But those who wait on the LORD Shall renew their strength; They shall mount up with wings like eagles, they shall run and not be weary, they shall walk and not faint."

The tendency to depend on our own resources and strength to accomplish our goals is the way most of us are accustomed to pursuit. However, to attain the great goals of our divine assignment, we need supernatural strength. We need the strength of the Holy Spirit. "The wind blows where it wishes, and you hear the sound of it, but cannot tell where it comes from and where it goes. So is everyone who is born of the Spirit" John 3:8. The word 'wind' in this scripture is from the Greek word 'pneuma'. 'Pneuma' is the same Greek word that is used in reference to the Spirit of the living God. Just as the wind is an extraordinary help for the eagle, the Spirit of God provides supernatural help for those working towards divine destiny.

Another peculiar characteristic of the eagle is that it feeds on live prey. The eagle does not eat prey that is already dead. Most often it targets fish swimming in a river and moves at a higher speed to catch it. Live food is significant of divine revelation that consists of prophecy, visions, dreams, intuition and the audible voice of the Holy Spirit. Every move we make must align with the divine objectives set for us. At every point in time, there is a specific divine favor that is unleashed on us. We need to align all our objectives with divine timing to enjoy divine favor. When we do the right thing at the right time, the result is always miraculous.

Financial speculation is the bedrock of financial markets across the world. Economic analysis and forecasts determine the movement of investments in the world of commerce. Often, in the light of unforeseen circumstances all the mechanisms for predicting trends leave investors in disarray. To always have a leading edge, we must seek to discern the times by being faithful to fellowship at the appointed times. Aligning our operations to conform to the spiritual seasons, gives us the advantage of receiving divine revelations that strategically position us beyond any kind of speculation. In essence spiritual conventions must be factored into our corporate calendar so we can experience the empowerment of the Holy Spirit.

Lion - The lion is a strategic hunter. It makes war with a flock of animals and overpowers its prey. Despite its great strength the lion does not randomly hunt for prey. "The young lions roar after their prey and seek their food from God. When the sun rises, they gather together and lie down in their dens" Psalm 104:21&22. Knowing that the lion is a predator, the animals that are potential prey stay far away from the lion. The conspiracy to keep away from the lion is such that the lion could end up starving for lack of prey. It leaves the lion no choice than to depend upon God for a prey. The lion roars to seek prey and this roar is so strong it causes the earth to quake. Those animals that are hiding become startled by the roar and eventually start running in a direction away from the roar. This sound from the movement of the prey gives the lion an inkling as to the direction of their position. The lion pursues by targeting only one prey among the group and wears it out until it is overpowered.

The roar of the lion is significant of warfare prayer. Those material resources that God promises the believer are often in the hands of the wicked. This is evident as the magnitude of obstacles that come our way whenever we attempt to pursue a divine purpose. These hurdles can be overcome through spiritual warfare. Learning not to give up when there is legislation or bureaucratic obstacles to our endeavors is key to attaining great victories. "Likewise the Spirit also helps in our weaknesses. For we do not know what we should pray for as we ought, but the Spirit Himself makes intercession for us with groaning which cannot be uttered" Romans 8:26. When challenges confront us, the Holy Spirit flows into our lives as arrows to overcome them. Warfare prayer is the key to surmounting obstacles that come our way. Also, whenever we are confronted with unexplainable losses and challenges, instead of apportioning blame, we must learn to mobilize our human resources and resort to warfare prayer.

Man - Man was made in the image and likeness of God to exercise dominion over all other created things. The four living creatures that surround the throne of God gives us insight into the character of the Most High God, and how He functions as ruler of the universe. Jesus Christ came to earth as an exhibit of the perfect man. He was the diligent ox, going about the business of the Father with the focus of an eagle, strong as the lion of the tribe of Judah and healing the oppressed out of compassion. In the same way, we must learn to function in humility, purpose, warfare and to impact our world through compassion. Because we lack insight into our full leadership potential, we mostly exhibit qualities that are self-centered and self-destructive. The result is that there is so much evil and animosity in our world. The Prophet Isaiah gives insight on how the ministry of Jesus Christ will function to overcome the vices most common in society.

"There shall come forth a Rod from the stem of Jesse, and a Branch shall grow out of his roots. The Spirit of the LORD shall rest upon Him, the Spirit of wisdom and understanding, the Spirit of counsel and might, the Spirit of knowledge and of the fear of the LORD. His delight is in the fear of the LORD, and He shall not judge by the sight of His eyes, nor decide by the hearing of His ears; But with righteousness He shall judge the poor, and decide with equity for the meek of the earth; He shall strike the earth with the rod of His mouth, and with the breath of His lips He shall slay the wicked. Righteousness shall be the belt of His loins, and faithfulness the belt of His waist. "The wolf also shall dwell with the lamb, the leopard shall lie down with the young goat, the calf and the young lion and the fatling together; and a little child shall lead them. The cow and the bear shall graze; their young ones shall lie down together; and the lion shall eat straw like the ox. The nursing child shall play by the cobra's hole, and the weaned child shall put his hand in the viper's den. They shall not hurt nor destroy in all My holy mountain, for the earth shall be full of the knowledge of the LORD as the waters cover the sea" Isaiah 11:1-9.

Operating under divine inspiration is the key to harnessing our leadership potential. The fruit of the Spirit is how the Holy Spirit inspires us to cultivate virtues of love, joy, peace, kindness, gentleness, self-control and patience. If these virtues are engaged to underscore our corporate character, the potential for sustainable success is inevitable. It will potentially create an atmosphere where people of diverse backgrounds and characteristics can work together harmoniously to achieve divine objectives. The wolf would not hurt the lamb, the leopard would fraternize with the goat, the lion would not intimidate the calf, and the bear would not attack the cow. It is possible to establish peaceful co-existence among people who may never have worked together to achieve any results. The inspiration of the Holy Spirit equips us to develop strategic relationships with people exhibiting extremely diverse characters. The more we endeavor to achieve a harmonious work environment as well as engage compassion in relation to clients and customers, the more we increase our capacity to accommodate a harvest of prosperity.

Certain industries like Non-profits enshrine the economic system of Communism.

Harness

Chapter Twenty

Comprehended

"For though we walk in the flesh, we do not war according to the flesh. For the weapons of our warfare are not carnal but mighty in God for pulling down strongholds, casting down arguments and every high thing that exalts itself against the knowledge of God, bringing every thought into captivity to the obedience of Christ, and being ready to punish all disobedience when your obedience is fulfilled" 2 Corinthians 10:3-6

One morning in 2002, I was divinely led to present a sales pitch to a salt mining company. Together with two friends, we had an oil marketing company dealing with fuels and lubricants. I met with the procurement manager of this salt mining company and offered them our products with a credit facility. He accepted my offer, and I supplied this company with their requisitions. When it was time for payment I went to their offices, and the check was prepared which had to be signed by the Chief Executive

Officer. After a brief period of waiting, the procurement manager informed me that the Chief Executive Officer wanted to meet with me. While waiting to meet him at the office of his secretary, I overhead his conversation with another person that revealed he was a Christian believer. At his office he asked me why I came to extend them products on credit. It was a period when this salt mining company was experiencing financial liquidity issues. All their heavy-duty equipment were not working for lack of fuel and lubricants. He was trusting God for a breakthrough when I made them an offer that got them working. This is the reason he was curious to meet me.

To comprehend is to understand how the cohorts of the kingdom of darkness inspire humans. The demonic forces of darkness are structured in a hierarchy that tallies with the faculties of the human mind. Seducing spirits aim at the human conscience, demonic powers target the emotions, principalities influence the intellect, and Satan inspires the will of man. The veil in the tabernacle of Moses was the point where one comprehended the kingdom of darkness. "And he made a veil of blue, purple, and scarlet thread, and fine woven linen; it was worked with an artistic design of cherubim. He made for it four pillars of acacia wood, and overlaid them with gold, with their hooks of gold; and he cast four sockets of silver for them" Exodus 36:35&36. The veil was the curtain that separated the Holy Place from the Most Holy Place. This curtain was made of four colors. The first color was fine linen that signified Jesus Christ our Sanctification by whom we overcome seducing spirits. The second color was scarlet that signified Jesus Christ our Redemption by whom we overcome demonic powers. The third color was blue that depicted Jesus Christ our Sonship by whom we overcome demonic principalities. The fourth color was purple that depicted Jesus Christ our King by whom we overcome Satan.

"And war broke out in heaven: Michael and his angels fought with the dragon; and the dragon and his angels fought, but they did not prevail, nor was a place found for them in heaven any longer. So the great dragon was cast out, that serpent of old, called the Devil and Satan, who deceives the whole world; he was cast to the earth, and his angels were cast out with him. Then I heard a loud voice saying in heaven, "Now salvation, and strength, and the kingdom of our God, and the power of His Christ have come, for the accuser of our brethren, who accused them before our God day and night, has been cast down. And they overcame him by the blood of the Lamb and by the word of their testimony, and they did not love their lives to the death. Therefore rejoice, O heavens, and you who dwell in them! Woe to the inhabitants of the earth and the sea! For the devil has come down to you, having great wrath, because he knows that he has a short time" Revelations 12:7-12.

Land is the essence of space, domain or territory. The kingdom of darkness is made up of rebellious entities who were cast down from heaven, and so they seek to control man and the earth. They craft schemes by which to exert their dominion over humans.

In the hierarchy of the kingdom of darkness, seducing spirits inspire lust in humans. Demonic powers orchestrate chronic infirmities, oppression of humans as well as catastrophic disruptions of the elements. Demonic principalities inspire culture that perpetuate ungodliness in human communities. Satan being their head, perpetuates poverty and prosecutes us before God to resist our blessings.

During the drought that followed the seven years of abundance, Joseph required that the Egyptians surrender their lands in exchange for food. Land speaks to the physical destiny of man. Man was created and is sustained physically from the dust of the earth. "When that year had ended, they came to him the next year and said to him, "We will not hide from my lord that our money is gone; my lord also has our herds of livestock. There is nothing left in the sight of my lord but our bodies and our lands. Why should we die before your eyes, both we and our land? Buy us and our land for bread, and we and our land will be servants of Pharaoh; give us seed, that we may live and not die, that the land may not be desolate". Then Joseph bought all the land of Egypt for Pharaoh; for every man of the Egyptians sold his field, because the famine was severe upon them. So the land became Pharaoh's. And as for the people, he moved them into the cities, from one end of the borders of Egypt to the other end. Only the land of the priests he did not buy; for the priests had rations allotted to them by Pharaoh, and they ate their rations which Pharaoh gave them; therefore they did not sell their lands. Then Joseph said to the people, "Indeed I have bought you and your land this day for Pharaoh. Look, here is seed for you, and you shall sow the land. And it shall come to pass in the harvest that you shall give one-fifth to Pharaoh. Four-fifths shall be your own, as seed for the field and for your food, for those of your households and as food for your little ones." So they said, "You have saved our lives; let us find favor in the sight of my lord, and we will be Pharaoh's servants." And Joseph made it a law over the land of Egypt to this day, that Pharaoh should have one-fifth, except for the land of the priests only, which did not become Pharaoh's" Genesis 47:18-26. In those days, your land determined your vocation, so you harnessed the potential of the land to generate wealth. If the Egyptians were making the best out of their lands, they would not have sold it for food. There are two reasons why you could be poor when you have land. First, it could be the land is not what God assigned to you and secondly, you may have failed to seek insights of how to work the land.

Though you may afford it, not everything sold as real estate is connected to your prosperity. Whenever you hold on to whatever is not your 'right of inheritance,' it works against you. Often, we procure assets that are not divinely assigned to us simply because we have the means to buy. If we do not discern the opportunity to procure assets, then we may not be able to keep them for a long time. Failure to engage what rightfully belongs to us is the worst tragedy of our existence. Fundamentally, we must know who we are in the eyes of God as well as our potentials. The beginning of wealth is to understand your divine potential and deploy them in the light of given opportunities. Wealth is generated by using who you are to administer what you have. The extent to which you understand who you are determines how best you engage what you have, to build wealth.

Land

All land is endowed with wealth, which must be discovered by its owners. The Arabs were looking for water for survival in the desert soil and discovered crude oil which has generated for them many riches. While some lands are endowed with gold, iron, aluminum or diamonds, some lands simply thrive vegetation or serve as a harbor for sea faring boats. The soil from which God formed us, is designed to prosper us. "And He has made from one blood every nation of men to dwell on all the face of the earth, and has determined their pre-appointed times and the boundaries of their dwellings, so that they should seek the Lord, in the hope that they might grope for Him and find Him, though He is not far from each one of us; for in Him we live and move and have our being, as also some of your own poets have said, 'For we are also His offspring" Acts 17:26-28. Wherever we are pleased to dwell comfortably is usually the design of God. He gives us opportunity and peace to settle in a place where we have the potential to prosper.

When Joseph bought the lands of the Egyptians, he reorganized them according to their potentials. What they had originally failed to do by choice, he mandated them. First, they did not engage the land properly, so he relocated everyone by profiling them to discover their potential. Second, they never gave tithes and offerings to acknowledge divine providence. Now he gave these Egyptians seed to sow and they had to pay twenty percent of all the yield of the land to the Pharaoh. Since the land was now under the control of Joseph, he set the rules that determined how the land would be cultivated. He set new rules that governed cultivation and conservation of land to prevent famine from re-occurring.

The Jubilee

The seventh-year Sabbath of land rest had to be observed by the Israelites to foster sustained prosperity. For failing to observe the seventh-year land rest over a period of 490 years, Israel suffered captivity for 70 years to make up for the default. "And you shall count seven Sabbaths of years for yourself, seven times seven years; and the time of the seven Sabbaths of years shall be to you forty-nine years. Then you shall cause the trumpet of the Jubilee to sound on the tenth day of the seventh month; on the Day of Atonement you shall make the trumpet to sound throughout all your land. And you shall consecrate the fiftieth year and proclaim liberty throughout all the land to all its inhabitants. It shall be a Jubilee for you; and each of you shall return to his possession, and each of you shall return to his family. That fiftieth year shall be a Jubilee to you; in it you shall neither sow nor reap what grows of its own accord, nor gather the grapes of your untended vine. For it is the Jubilee; it shall be holy to you; you shall eat its produce from the field. 'In this Year of Jubilee, each of you shall return to his possession. And if you sell anything to your neighbor or buy from your neighbor's hand, you shall not oppress one another. According to the number of years after the Jubilee you shall buy from your neighbor, and according to the number of years of crops he shall sell to you. According to the multitude of years you shall increase its price, and according to the fewer number of years you shall diminish its price; for he sells to you according to the number of the years of the crops. Therefore, you shall not oppress one another, but you shall fear your God; for I am the LORD your God" Leviticus 25:8-17.

After seven cycles of seventh-year Sabbaths which amounts to forty-nine years, Israel was to celebrate the Jubilee in the fiftieth year. In other words, the Jubilee was to be commemorated every fifty years. All land transactions were conducted in regard to the jubilee. The Israelites were not to sell their land permanently. It could only be leased, and those who had leased out their land automatically received a restoration at the Jubilee. It was an opportunity for Israelites to get back their divine legacy and start again. The Jubilee was structured to give everyone a renewed opportunity to pursue divine destiny. Considering the average life span of man, it is right to deduce that most people may have this opportunity just once or twice in a lifetime.

The Jubilee was a destiny restoration moment, and every Israelite looked forward to it. After going through fifty years of perfect cycles of Sabbaths, people in a generation are privileged to experience the jubilee. It brought liberty to slaves in bondage and debts were automatically cancelled. If we consider all these blessings in perspective, then a man who was in slavery because he owed money to another is not just free from slavery, but free from debt and receives back their land. This sounds like a restored dominion. They got back their land, which was significant of return to their destiny, and also, they were free from slavery, oppression and indebtedness. The full version of the mission statement of our Lord Jesus Christ delivered in His first recorded sermon was a quote from Isaiah 61:1-4, "The Spirit of the Lord God is upon Me, because the

Lord has anointed Me to preach good tidings to the poor; He has sent Me to heal the brokenhearted, to proclaim liberty to the captives, and the opening of the prison to those who are bound; To proclaim the acceptable year of the Lord, and the day of vengeance of our God; To comfort all who mourn, to console those who mourn in Zion, to give them beauty for ashes, the oil of joy for mourning, the garment of praise for the spirit of heaviness; That they may be called trees of righteousness, the planting of the Lord, that He may be glorified." And they shall rebuild the old ruins, they shall raise up the former desolations, and they shall repair the ruined cities, the desolations of many generations." The mission of our Lord Jesus Christ is the default mission for all believers. There are four basic premises that govern the Jubilee: Restitution, Redemption, Release and Restoration. These tally with how the demonic entities of the kingdom of darkness are structured to resist the blessings of the believer. Moreover, it shows how the believer can overcome these demonic entities.

RESTITUTION involves repentance and return. The Jubilee was meant to foster repentance in every Israelite who, because of violation of the scriptures, had become disenfranchised from their space. At the sound of the Jubilee trumpet, every Israelite had to return to their space which they had lost. An instance in the scriptures is the account of Zacchaeus to whom Jesus reached out. "Then Jesus entered and passed through Jericho. Now behold, there was a man named Zacchaeus who was a chief tax collector, and he was rich. And he sought to see who Jesus was, but could not because of the crowd, for he was of short stature. So he ran ahead and climbed up into a sycamore tree to see Him, for He was going to pass that way. And when Jesus came to the place, He looked up and saw him, and said to him, "Zacchaeus, make haste and come down, for today I must stay at your house." So he made haste and came down, and received Him joyfully. But when they saw it, they all complained, saying, "He has gone to be a guest with a man who is a sinner." Then Zacchaeus stood and said to the Lord, "Look, Lord, I give half of my goods to the poor; and if I have taken anything from anyone by false accusation, I restore fourfold." And Jesus said to him, "Today salvation has come to this house, because he also is a son of Abraham; for the Son of Man has come to seek and to save that which was lost" Luke 19:1-10. The Roman authorities had colonized Israel during this time and hired Zacchaeus as a chief tax collector. In those days, these officials exploited the people by estimating their taxes more than what was due, so they could keep back the excess amount for themselves. For that reason, the people loathed the tax collectors and Zacchaeus was no exception. Prompted by what he had heard of Jesus, Zacchaeus who was short in stature climbed a tree to catch a glimpse of Jesus who was passing by on that route. Feeling the yearning of Zacchaeus for salvation, Jesus reached out to him and said, "Zacchaeus, make haste and come down, for today I must stay at your house." This was a call to salvation for which Zacchaeus hurriedly responded. But there was an immediate objection from the crowd, for in their hearts, Zacchaeus did not merit to be blessed by Jesus. Their objection in the narrative signals what happens in the spiritual realm when we get saved, and the kingdom of darkness objects to our being blessed. In executing his duties as a chief tax collector on behalf of the Roman authorities, Zacchaeus had been inspired by seducing spirits to exploit the people financially. Now that Jesus had extended salvation to Zacchaeus, the hearts of the people were resisting his blessings. In the spiritual realm, all those deeds that violate the scriptures are called into account each year on the day of Atonement. This is the heavenly court where the accuser brings a litany of accusations against every human being seeking to be legitimately blessed by God. Zacchaeus rose to the occasion and answered their accusation, "Look, Lord, I give half of my goods to the poor; and if I have taken anything from anyone by false accusation, I restore fourfold." Here, Zacchaeus resorts to practice restitution 'as the word of his testimony' to 'cast down the argument' of his accusers and Jesus accepts this as the basis for his blessing.

Repentance simply means change! You cannot experience financial prosperity in a season of economic hardship, unless you are willing to change your financial direction. The manifestation of famine is evidence of divine judgment on society for their sins and disregard for the principles of righteousness. God is simply saying to society, 'If you change your ways, I will respond by changing your circumstances'. While some may recover from a recession, others may never recover for the rest of their lives. Deliverance from the effects of a recession is entirely based on how you position yourself as an individual, in response to God's call for repentance. Remember it is only when you change, that your circumstances will also change!

Return is the next course of action that proves repentance. When the Israelites came to the Promised Land, every tribe was allocated land that had a relationship with their destiny. Those gifted as goldsmiths were given land rich in gold ore, the shepherds received grasslands, and the vinedressers received forestlands. During difficult times, some Israelites leased their lands and went off to seek greener pastures elsewhere. Today we would say, they liquidated their assets and relocated. Straying away from one's divine heritage to escape a season of financial hardship is usually not the proper antidote. Isaac the patriarch was discouraged by God from the plan to move out of Gerar in the time of famine. As a result, Isaac began to reflect on what could be the possible factors responsible for the drought. He realized that when the Philistines stopped the wells of his father Abraham, he did not fight back to restore them. These were wells for retaining water during rainfall and became the water source during droughts. Once Isaac began to revive these wells, he was able to cultivate crops. Though he received much opposition, he persisted and eventually became very prosperous. (Genesis 26)

Wells are symbolic of generational revelations which keep us connected to generational blessings. Sustainable success is always rooted in one's divine heritage. Most of the time, we become victims of a recession because we get distracted from our heritage. We chase after lucrative jobs that promise us the incentives that we hope would raise our standard of living. We invest in businesses that show trends of high profitability hoping for quick returns. We disinvest our time from family commitments and spiritual assignments at Church to work more hours for money. Like Isaac, we must begin to reflect on some of the prophetic revelations we received in the past. Such revelations could potentially help us navigate our way back to the tracks of prosperity. It is time to return to the job that reflects our divine purpose, a return to our core business as an enterprise, a return to our prophetic role in the family and a return to our divine assignment at Church.

REDEMPTION means to buy back. The Jubilee was an opportunity to buy back what was lost. "The land shall not be sold permanently, for the land is Mine; for you are strangers and sojourners with Me. And in all the land of your possession you shall grant redemption of the land. 'If one of your brethren becomes poor, and has sold some of his possession, and if his redeeming relative comes to redeem it, then he may redeem what his brother sold. Or if the man has no one to redeem it, but he himself becomes able to redeem it" Leviticus 25:23-26. Land is the domain where we are empowered to prosper so we ought to have the 'right of redemption'. The Apostle Paul teaches the Ephesus Church that salvation begins the process of total redemption for the believer. "In Him we have redemption through His blood, the forgiveness of sins, according to the riches of His grace which He made to abound toward us in all wisdom and prudence, having made known to us the mystery of His will, according to His good pleasure which He purposed in Himself, that in the dispensation of the fullness of the times He might gather together in one all things in Christ, both which are in heaven and which are on earth in Him. In Him also we have obtained an inheritance, being predestined according to the purpose of Him who works all things according to the counsel of His will, that we who first trusted in Christ should be to the praise of His glory. In Him you also trusted, after you heard the word of truth, the gospel of your salvation; in whom also, having believed, you were sealed with the Holy Spirit of promise, who is the guarantee of our inheritance until the redemption of the purchased possession, to the praise of His glory" Ephesians 1:7-14. In the same way Israel was saved from bondage in Egypt and headed to the Promised Land, our journey in Christ is a path of redemption.

The story of the birth of Moses through whom God redeemed the Israelites from Egypt paints a picture of how redemption works in us. "And a man of the house of Levi went and took as wife a daughter of Levi. So the woman conceived and bore a son. And when she saw that he was a goodly child, she hid him three months. But when she could no longer hide him, she took an ark of bulrushes for him, daubed it with asphalt and pitch, put the child in it, and laid it in the reeds by the river's bank. And his sister stood afar off, to know what would be done to him. Then the daughter of Pharaoh came down to bathe at the river. And her maidens walked along the riverside; and when she saw the ark among the reeds, she sent her maid to get it. And when she opened it, she saw the child, and behold, the baby wept. So she had compassion on him, and said, "This is one of the Hebrews' children." Then his sister said to Pharaoh's daughter, "Shall I go and call a nurse for you from the Hebrew women, that she may nurse the child for you?" And Pharaoh's daughter said to her, "Go." So the maiden went and called the child's mother. Then Pharaoh's daughter said to her, "Take this child away and nurse him for me, and I will give you your wages." So the woman took the child and nursed him. And the child grew, and she brought him to Pharaoh's daughter, and he became her son. So she called his name Moses, saying,

"Because I drew him out of the water" Exodus 2:1-10. Prior to the birth of Moses, the Pharaoh who was king of Egypt decided to diminish the Israelite population because they had become too numerous and prosperous. He gave an edict that any newborn male of the Israelites be cast into the Nile River. It was around this period that Jochebed, the mother of Moses conceived and gave birth to Moses. Jochebed and Amram, the father of Moses were from the tribe of Levi. This tribe as well as the tribes of Reuben and Simeon were not blessed by their ancestor Jacob. Those from the tribe of Levi were known to be cruel with anger and wrath issues. However, when Jochebed gave birth to Moses, she sensed he was a child with a unique divine purpose and so she resolved to defy the decree of the Pharaoh. She hid him for three months after which she feared that someone might notice her actions and report her to the authorities. I believe she prayerfully sought God for direction. She placed Moses in a basket daubed with asphalt and placed him on the river, while Miriam the sister of Moses watched from a distance. The daughter of Pharaoh came to the river at a time when Moses was crying and felt compassion for him, so she engaged the services of Jochebed to raise Moses as her adopted son. This was how the process of redemption begun for the tribe of Levi as well as the entire Israel from the bondage of Egypt.

The decree of the Pharaoh to cast every newborn Israelite male into the river was an inspiration of blood thirsty demonic powers. Though she had previously conceived and given birth to Aaron and Miriam, Jochebed instinctively knew that Moses was a child that would foster redemption for Israel, so she committed herself to pursue his redemption. The resolve of Jochebed to redeem Moses from being sacrificed to the river god was the 'word of her testimony' that 'cast down the ambitious goals' of the enemy.

As Christians, the process of our salvation begins with the redemptive work of Christ on the cross of Calvary. This is a replica of the way Moses brought the Israelites out of Egypt. As a sign from God to let the Israelites go free, God allowed Moses to confront the Pharaoh of Egypt with ten plagues of divine judgment. The Pharaoh did not succumb to this demand until the final plague that resulted in the death of all the firstborn of the Egyptians. Since the first born was symbolic of Egypt's future, this judgment was the ultimate blow that compelled the Pharaoh to let the Israelites go free.

This divine judgment that secured freedom for the Israelites came at a price. God demanded the firstborn of every Israelite family as a spiritual token for the firstborn of the Egyptians who had been killed. The firstborn of all Israelite families would have to serve God as priests. Since this would deny the Israelites the opportunity to have their firstborn carry on the family heritage, God substituted them with the members of the tribe of Levi (Exodus 13, Numbers 3:40-41). By this, every Israelite family could keep their first born. This meant that the Israelites must give the first-fruits of their harvests to the Levites who served as priests of God. The blood of the Passover lamb with which the Israelites marked their door post for protection from the destruction angel, is symbolic of the blood of Jesus Christ.

Usually during an economic recession, prices escalate for most goods and services. Unfortunately, wages may remain the same so there is tremendous pressure on our finances. People have limited resources to meet the overwhelming cost of living. In such times, complaining alone or waiting for the government to turn things around is certainly not our antidote. A season of economic recession is significant of famine in the scriptures which also indicated God's judgment. God's judgment convicts the wicked of what they deserve and acquits the righteous. There is a shift in the spiritual realm so that the wealth of the wicked gravitates towards the righteous. However, the righteous must be in the position to redeem what becomes available to them.

RELEASE is one the premises of the mission of our Lord Jesus Christ. "So He came to Nazareth, where He had been brought up. And as His custom was, He went into the synagogue on the Sabbath day, and stood up to read. And He was handed the book of the prophet Isaiah. And when He had opened the book, He found the place where it was written: "The Spirit of the Lord is upon Me, because He has anointed Me to preach the gospel to the poor; He has sent Me to heal the brokenhearted, to proclaim liberty to the captives and recovery of sight to the blind, to set at liberty those who are oppressed; To proclaim the acceptable year of the Lord" Luke 4:16-19. Notice that the functions of the anointing of the Holy Spirit upon Jesus was to exert release from various forms of oppression. An instance in the scriptures that highlights this is the period when the Midianites oppressed the Israelites. "Then the children of Israel did evil in the sight of the Lord. So the Lord delivered them into the hand of Midian for seven years, and the hand of Midian prevailed against Israel. Because of the Midianites, the children of Israel made for themselves the dens, the caves, and the strongholds which are in the mountains. So it was, whenever Israel had sown, Midianites would come up; also Amalekites and the people of the East would come up against them. Then they would encamp against them and destroy the produce of the earth as far as Gaza, and leave no sustenance for Israel, neither sheep nor ox nor donkey. For they would come up with their livestock and their tents, coming in as numerous as locusts; both they and their camels were without number; and they would enter the land to destroy it. So Israel was greatly impoverished because of the Midianites, and the children of Israel cried out to the Lord" Judges 6:1-6. "Now the Angel of the Lord came and sat under the terebinth tree which was in Ophrah, which belonged to Joash the Abiezrite, while his son Gideon threshed wheat in the winepress, in order to hide it from the Midianites. And the Angel of the Lord appeared to him, and said to him, "The Lord is with you, you mighty man of valor!" Gideon said to Him, "O my lord, if the Lord is with us, why then has all this happened to us? And where are all His miracles which our fathers told us about, saying, 'Did not the Lord bring us up from Egypt?' But now the Lord has forsaken us and delivered us into the hands of the Midianites." Then the Lord turned to him and said, "Go in this might of yours, and you shall save Israel from the hand of the Midianites. Have I not sent you?" So he said to Him, "O my Lord, how can I save Israel? Indeed my clan is the weakest in Manasseh, and I am the least in my father's house." And the Lord said to him, "Surely I will be with you, and you shall defeat the Midianites as one man" Judges 6:11-16. "Now it came to pass the same night that the Lord said to him, "Take your father's young bull, the second bull of seven years old, and tear down the altar of Baal that your father has, and cut down the wooden image that is beside it; and build an altar to the Lord your God on top of this [h]rock in the proper arrangement, and take the second bull and offer a burnt sacrifice with the wood of the image which you shall cut down." So Gideon took ten men from among his servants and did as the Lord had said to him. But because he feared his father's household and the men of the city too much to do it by day, he did it by night" Judges 6:25-27. "Then all the Midianites and Amalekites, the people of the East, gathered together; and they crossed over and encamped in the Valley of Jezreel. But the Spirit of the Lord came upon Gideon; then he blew the trumpet, and the Abiezrites gathered behind him. And he sent messengers throughout all Manasseh, who also gathered behind him. He also sent messengers to Asher, Zebulun, and Naphtali; and they came up to meet them" Judges 6:33-35. "Then Jerubbaal (that is, Gideon) and all the people who were with him rose early and encamped beside the well of Harod, so that the camp of the Midianites was on the north side of them by the hill of Moreh in the valley. And the Lord said to Gideon, "The people who are with you are too many for Me to give the Midianites into their hands, lest Israel claim glory for itself against Me, saying, 'My own hand has saved me.' Now therefore, proclaim in the hearing of the people, saying, 'Whoever is fearful and afraid, let him turn and depart at once from Mount Gilead.'"And twenty-two thousand of the people returned, and ten thousand remained. But the Lord said to Gideon, "The people are still too many; bring them down to the water, and I will test them for you there. Then it will be, that of whom I say to you, 'This one shall go with you,' the same shall go with you; and of whomever I say to you, 'This one shall not go with you,' the same shall not go." So he brought the people down to the water. And the Lord said to Gideon, "Everyone who laps from the water with his tongue, as a dog laps, you shall set apart by himself; likewise everyone who gets down on his knees to drink." And the number of those who lapped, putting their hand to their mouth, was three hundred men; but all the rest of the people got down on their knees to drink water. Then the Lord said to Gideon, "By the three hundred men who lapped I will save you and deliver the Midianites into your hand. Let all the other people go, every man to his place" Judges 7:1-7. "So Gideon and the hundred men who were with him came to the outpost of the camp at the beginning of the middle watch, just as they had posted the watch; and they blew the trumpets and broke the pitchers that were in their hands. Then the three companies blew the trumpets and broke the pitchers, they held the torches in their left hands and the trumpets in their right hands for blowing and they cried, "The sword of the Lord and of Gideon!" And every man stood in his place all around the camp; and the whole army ran and cried out and fled. When the three hundred blew the trumpets, the Lord set every man's sword against his companion throughout the whole camp; and the army fled to Beth Acacia, toward Zererah, as far as the border of Abel Meholah, by Tabbath. And the men of Israel gathered together from Naphtali, Asher, and all Manasseh, and pursued the Midianites. Then Gideon sent messengers throughout all the mountains of Ephraim, saying, "Come down against the Midianites, and seize from them the watering places as far as Beth Barah and the Jordan." Then all the men of Ephraim gathered together and seized the watering places as far as Beth Barah and the Jordan. And they captured two princes of the Midianites, Oreb and Zeeb. They killed Oreb at the rock of Oreb, and Zeeb they killed at the winepress of Zeeb. They pursued Midian and brought the heads of Oreb and Zeeb to Gideon on the other side of the Jordan" Judges 7:19-25.

The overall significance of Gideon's victory over the Midianites is how the anointing of the Holy Spirit works to release from demonic oppression. First, the choice of Gideon for the assignment was not contingent on his mediocre status in society. Second, Gideon had to destroy and disrupt the culture of fetish worship in his community that invoked demonic activity against the Israelites. Notice that when this was executed, it triggered a rally of the enemy to attack Israel. Third, the anointing of the Holy Spirit inspired Gideon to blow the trumpet to mobilize Israel for battle. Thirty-two thousand Israelites who were intuitive responded and gathered around Gideon, but these were too many in the eyes of God. Gideon was prompted to encourage those who were fearful and hence not instinctive to return home. Twenty-two thousand returned to their homes and only ten thousand remained. To determine those who were perceptive, Gideon was prompted to take them to the brook for a drink. Only three hundred demonstrated perception and so the rest were dismissed. Finally, the strategy was simple, empty pitchers with a concealed lamp and trumpets were assigned to each of these three hundred soldiers. They were to follow the lead of Gideon, so when he blew his trumpet they blew, and when he broke his pitcher, they broke theirs to unveil the lamp. Breaking their pitchers produced the sound of their brokenness while the light of the lamp unveiled their perception, and the sound of their trumpets was their alignment with angelic forces. The ensuing victory over the Midianites was not contingent on a large human military force of might, rather it was the anointing of the Holy Spirit at work through Gideon. "And the Lord of hosts will stir up a scourge for him like the slaughter of Midian at the rock of Oreb; as His rod was on the sea, so will He lift it up in the manner of Egypt. It shall come to pass in that day that his burden will be taken away from your shoulder, and his yoke from your neck, and the yoke will be destroyed because of the anointing oil" Isaiah 10:26-27. It is in reference to the victory of Gideon over the Midianites that Isaiah the prophet reveals that yokes and burdens of oppression are destroyed by the anointing. While the cultural mindset of our world, which is a dictate of principalities, portends that success is only possible where there are numerous people and vast amounts of resources, with us believers, it is the anointing of the Holy Spirit that fosters our success. Gideon's resolve to follow the leading of the Holy Spirit was 'the word of his testimony' by which he 'took captive every ungodly thought, subjecting it to the obedience of Christ', and overcame the enemy to foster release of God's people from oppression.

The release was practiced as the seventh-year sabbatical at which time the Israelites would desist from cultivating their fields. The word release was made up of the prefix 're', which means to do it again, and the word 'lease'. Release simply means 'to lease again'. Today we lease cars, houses, furniture, and equipment for domestic and industrial use. When the lease period expires, we return the items, and they are most often re-leased again to others. As children of God, we know that everything we possess is a blessing from God. In other words, whatever we have is a lease to us that is orchestrated by divine providence. The premise of release is designed to make us conscious of our stewardship of God's resources. "At the end of every seven years, you shall grant a release of debts. And this is the form of the release: Every creditor who loaned anything to his neighbor shall release it; he shall not require it of his neighbor or his brother, because it is called the LORD's release" Deuteronomy 15:1&2. The statement "at the end of every seven years you shall grant a release of debts" simply means, 'under the inspiration of the Holy Spirit, you shall release what is owed to you by others.' Let us say for instance, that Jill owed you two hundred dollars, the Holy Spirit may impress upon your heart to write off the debt. In this way you give Jill the opportunity to continue her stewardship of the money.

During times of economic hardship, it is not uncommon for the Holy Spirit to require us to release resources that we may require for our survival. The scripture records a story of how there was a famine in Israel and God had told Elijah to go to Zarephath where He had commanded a widow to sustain him. When Elijah arrived, he met this widow and asked her for a cup of water. As the woman was about to go for it, he asked her for a piece of bread. She told Elijah that she did not have bread except a little flour and oil with which she was about to bake a last meal for herself and her son. Elijah encouraged her not to fear, but to firstly bake him the bread so that the miracle of supernatural release could take place (1 Kings 17:7-16).

As stewards of God's resources, we are expected to administer them according to divine inspiration. Stewardship requires the virtue of faithfulness. "Let a man so consider us, as servants of Christ and stewards of the mysteries of God. Moreover it is required in stewards that one be found faithful" 1 Corinthians 4:1-2. Managing our resources according to scriptural principles and divine inspiration, is the key to increasing. Hoarding our resources is certainly not the way out of financial hardship. Mounting unnecessary pressure on those indebted to us, invokes the displeasure of God. What we need during a time of economic hardship is divine favor that orchestrates supernatural increase. The key here is to begin to administer our resources diligently by divine conviction, and the hand of God would reward our faithfulness with the blessings of increase.

RESTORE means to bring something to its proper condition. "And they shall build the old ruins, they shall raise up the former devastations, and they shall repair the waste cities, the desolations of many generations" Isaiah 61:4. Old ruins, former devastations, waste cities and desolations of many generations represent the spiritual portrait of many people. However, the Jubilee was designed to fix this spiritual state that influences our physical affairs. To change Abraham's spiritual state, God reached out to him with a covenant proposition. "Now the Lord had said to Abram: "Get out of your country, from your family and from your father's house, to a land that I will show you. I will make you a great nation; I will bless you and make your name great; and you shall be a blessing. I will bless those who bless you, and I will curse him who curses you; and in you all the families of the earth shall be blessed" Genesis 12:1-3. Abraham agreed to the proposition, but took along his nephew Lot and left his country. However, after a while when the Lord blessed them both, a strife ensued between the herdsmen of Abraham and Lot. To resolve this Abraham resorted to implement the fullness of God's original covenant proposition. "So Abram said to Lot, "Please let there be no strife between you and me, and between my herdsmen and your herdsmen; for we are brethren. Is not the whole land before you? Please separate from me. If you take the left, then I will go to the right; or, if you go to the right, then I will go to the left." And Lot lifted his eyes and saw all the plain of Jordan, that it was well watered everywhere (before the Lord destroyed Sodom and Gomorrah) like the garden of the Lord, like the land of Egypt as you go toward Zoar. Then Lot chose for himself all the plain of Jordan, and Lot journeyed east. And they separated from each other. Abram dwelt in the land of Canaan, and Lot dwelt in the cities of the plain and pitched his tent even as far as Sodom. But the men of Sodom were exceedingly wicked and sinful against the Lord" Genesis 13:8-13. Lot chose the direction of Sodom while Abraham headed in the opposite direction and settled by the Terebinth trees which were at Hebron. The business decision of Lot to head toward Sodom was because the land there was rich with green pasture. However, Lot did not know of the deplorable spiritual condition of the people of Sodom. Worst of all, they were in rebellion toward a super king known as Chedorlaomer. "Twelve years they served Chedorlaomer, and in the thirteenth year they rebelled. In the fourteenth year Chedorlaomer and the kings that were with him came and attacked the Rephaim in Ashteroth Karnaim, the Zuzim in Ham, the Emim in Shaveh Kiriathaim, and the

Horites in their mountain of Seir, as far as El Paran, which is by the wilderness. Then they turned back and came to En Mishpat (that is, Kadesh), and attacked all the country of the Amalekites, and also the Amorites who dwelt in Hazezon Tamar. And the king of Sodom, the king of Gomorrah, the king of Admah, the king of Zeboiim, and the king of Bela (that is, Zoar) went out and joined together in battle in the Valley of Siddim against Chedorlaomer king of Elam, Tidal king of nations, Amraphel king of Shinar, and Arioch king of Ellasar, four kings against five. Now the Valley of Siddim was full of asphalt pits; and the kings of Sodom and Gomorrah fled; some fell there, and the remainder fled to the mountains. Then they took all the goods of Sodom and Gomorrah, and all their provisions, and went their way. They also took Lot, Abram's brother's son who dwelt in Sodom, and his goods, and departed. Then one who had escaped came and told Abram the Hebrew, for he dwelt by the terebinth trees of Mamre the Amorite, brother of Eshcol and brother of Aner; and they were allies with Abram. Now when Abram heard that his brother was taken captive, he armed his three hundred and eighteen trained servants who were born in his own house, and went in pursuit as far as Dan. He divided his forces against them by night, and he and his servants attacked them and pursued them as far as Hobah, which is north of Damascus. So he brought back all the goods, and also brought back his brother Lot and his goods, as well as the women and the people. And the king of Sodom went out to meet him at the Valley of Shaveh (that is, the King's Valley), after his return from the defeat of Chedorlaomer and the kings who were with him. Abram and Melchizedek Then Melchizedek king of Salem brought out bread and wine; he was the priest of God Most

331

High. And he blessed him and said: "Blessed be Abram of God Most High, Possessor of heaven and earth; and blessed be God Most High, Who has delivered your enemies into your hand." And he gave him a tithe of all" Genesis 14:4-20. Assuming Abraham had not parted ways with Lot, it is possible that with their collective need of green pastures for their herds, he would have succumbed to the business decision to go and reside near Sodom. Abraham's obedience to the divine covenant, led him in a different direction where God empowered him such that he could mobilize his household to go and rescue Lot as well as the people of Sodom and their goods from Chedorlaomer's alliance. The kings of Sodom and Gomorrah had fled the battlefield in defeat but were surprised to hear that Abraham had routed Chedorlaomer's alliance of super kings and recovered their people and goods. They convened at the palladium of kings to meet and celebrate Abraham who at the time was an unknown hero. It was at this forum that Melchizedek appeared with bread and wine in exchange for the tithes of Abraham. This was to show the kings of Sodom and Gomorrah how Abraham had been divinely empowered for the great rescue. "For this Melchizedek, king of Salem, priest of the Most High God, who met Abraham returning from the slaughter of the kings and blessed him, to whom also Abraham gave a tenth part of all, first being translated "king of righteousness," and then also king of Salem, meaning "king of peace," without father, without mother, without genealogy, having neither beginning of days nor end of life, but made like the Son of God, remains a priest continually. Now consider how great this man was, to whom even the patriarch Abraham gave a tenth of the spoils" Hebrews 7:1-4. Melchizedek was Jesus Christ appearing before His time to demonstrate the essence of the covenant relationship with Abraham. This is the same way by which the Lord Jesus Christ celebrated the last supper with the disciplines. "And as they were eating, Jesus took bread, blessed and broke it, and gave it to the disciples and said, "Take, eat; this is My body." Then He took the cup, and gave thanks, and gave it to them, saying, "Drink from it, all of you. For this is My blood of the new covenant, which is shed for many for the remission of sins" Matthew 26:26-28. We subscribe to the New Covenant by participating in His body that was broken for us, as well as His blood that was shed for us on the cross. Our commitment is our tithes which we yield as a token to this covenant. Notice that it was the alliance of Lot with the people of Sodom that got him in trouble with the alliance of Chedorlaomer. However, it was the alliance of Abraham with the Lord Jesus Christ that rescued Lot. Assuming Abraham had not been in covenant with Jesus Christ, he would not have been supernaturally empowered and would possibly have perished with Lot. Abraham's resolve to obey the divine covenant was 'the word of his testimony' by which he 'punished' the alliance of the enemy and fostered the restoration of Lot.

Locust invasion was among the plagues unleashed upon the Egyptians who were not in Goshen where the Israelites were experiencing preferential treatment of divine protection. The prophet Joel describes the locust invasion like this. "That which the palmerworm hath left hath the locust eaten; and that which the locust hath left hath the cankerworm eaten; and that which the cankerworm hath left hath the caterpillar eaten" Joel 1:4. The palmerworm, cankerworm, caterpillar and locust are all four stages of metamorphosis in the development of a locust from egg to adult. During a locust invasion all four creatures target various aspects of vegetation in their path. Each group focuses their attack either on the plant stem, the leaves, the flowers or the fruit. In Matthew chapter 13, Jesus describes the four points at which the devil attacks us so that we may not be fruitful in our endeavors. First, he attacks the seed sown (or plant stem) by stealing the word from our hearts. Second, he attacks the ability to produce leaves which is significant of lack of understanding. Third, he attacks the flowering stage with thorns of worldly temptations. Finally, he attacks the fruit, potentially reducing the harvest from hundred-fold to sixty-fold or even thirty-fold.

The good news is that though the devil has assigned the palmerworm, caterpillar, cankerworm and adult locust to attack us at all four stages in the process of success, God promises us restoration from all of them. "Be glad then, ye children of Zion, and rejoice in the LORD your God: for he hath given you the former rain moderately, and he will cause to come down for you the rain, the former rain, and the latter rain in the first month. And the floors shall be full of wheat, and the vats shall overflow with wine and oil. "And I will restore to you the years that the locust hath eaten, the cankerworm, and the caterpillar, and the palmerworm, my great army which I sent among you" Joel 2:23-25. Rain is significant of divine revelation. Effectively, God sows a seed of divine revelation into the heart of the believer. If we do not doubt the power of God's word and believe it, we overcome seducing spirits. Second, if we endeavor to seek further insight into the divine revelation, we overcome the attack of demonic powers. Third, if we can overcome the allure of barren worldly cultures and stay focused on the pursuit of divine revelation, we overcome the attack of principalities. Finally, perseverance is the quality that enables us to overcome the attack of Satan.

Belief, understanding, focus and perseverance are the four weapons to overcome the demonic invasion of the palmerworm, caterpillar, cankerworm and adult locust. To experience restoration, we must believe, understand, focus and persevere with the premises of restitution, redemption, release and restoration.

Feudalism is the economic system underlining the Real Estate industry.

Chapter Twenty-one

Conviction

"If you really fulfill the royal law according to the
Scripture, "You shall love your neighbor as yourself," you
do well; but if you show partiality, you commit sin, and
are convicted by the law as transgressors. For whoever
shall keep the whole law, and yet stumble in one point,
he is guilty of all. For He who said, "Do not commit
adultery," also said, "Do not murder." Now if you do not
commit adultery, but you do murder, you have become a
transgressor of the law. So speak and so do as those who
will be judged by the law of liberty. For judgment is
without mercy to the one who has shown no mercy.
Mercy triumphs over judgment" James 2:8-13

For ten years, each year I have conducted a program
daubed 'Atonement' in the fall season during the feasts of
Trumpets, Atonement and Tabernacles. Ramping up to
'Atonement 2024', I sought the Lord in prayer for the
theme of the coming year. Interestingly, He indicated to

me that there are 'dark times' in the horizon. However, for the first time the Lord gave two scriptures instead of one to show what He would do for His people. First, He indicated that like the end of Job's trials, the trials of His people were coming to an end. Second, like the blessing He gave King Solomon at the onset of his reign, He would coronate His people. We are in the summer of 2025 and as I write this book the whole world is gripped with economic uncertainty and untold hardships, there are protests all over United States, the war between Russia and Ukraine is raging, Hamas is still holding some of the hostages it took away from Israel captive and Israel is engaged in a war with Iran that threatens the stability of the middle east. During all these global events that are evidence of dark times, the Holy Spirit has started manifesting a revival in our local Church. For several weeks beginning from the Sunday following Mother's Day, an unusual presence of the Lord visits our Sunday morning services during praise and worship so that I am unable to minister as usual, but then there is a glorious ministry of the Holy Spirit to God's people. On the first Sunday of this occurrence, the Holy Spirit said to me that everyone should bring a 'SACRIFICE'. 'Justice' is the theme of this revival, and the scriptures the Lord gave of what He is doing resembles the restoration of Job and the wisdom of King Solomon. This revival is intended to address the current apathy as well as carnality that have embroiled Christians across the globe.

First, let us look at the instance of Job. "And so it was, after the Lord had spoken these words to Job, that the Lord said to Eliphaz the Temanite, "My wrath is aroused against you and your two friends, for you have not spoken of Me what is right, as My servant Job has. Now therefore, take for yourselves seven bulls and seven rams, go to My servant Job, and offer up for yourselves a burnt offering; and My servant Job shall pray for you. For I will accept him, lest I deal with you according to your folly; because you have not spoken of Me what is right, as My servant Job has." So Eliphaz the Temanite and Bildad the Shuhite and Zophar the Naamathite went and did as the Lord commanded them; for the Lord had accepted Job. And the Lord restored Job's losses when he prayed for his friends. Indeed the Lord gave Job twice as much as he had before. Then all his brothers, all his sisters, and all those who had been his acquaintances before, came to him and ate food with him in his house; and they consoled him and comforted him for all the adversity that the Lord had brought upon him. Each one gave him a piece of silver and each a ring of gold. Now the Lord blessed the latter days of Job more than his beginning; for he had fourteen thousand sheep, six thousand camels, one thousand yoke of oxen, and one thousand female donkeys. He also had seven sons and three daughters. And he called the name of the first Jemimah, the name of the second Keziah, and the name of the third Keren-Happuch. In all the land were found no women so beautiful as the daughters of Job; and their father gave them an inheritance among their brothers. After this Job lived one hundred and forty years, and saw his children and grandchildren for four generations. So Job died, old and full of days" Job 42:7-16. Preamble to this divine judgment that ended the trials of Job, Satan had presented an accusation against him on a Day of Atonement. "Now there was a day when the sons of God came to present themselves before the Lord, and Satan also came among them. And the Lord said to Satan,

"From where do you come?" So Satan answered the Lord and said, "From going to and fro on the earth, and from walking back and forth on it." Then the Lord said to Satan, "Have you considered My servant Job, that there is none like him on the earth, a blameless and upright man, one who fears God and shuns evil?" So Satan answered the Lord and said, "Does Job fear God for nothing? Have You not made a hedge around him, around his household, and around all that he has on every side? You have blessed the work of his hands, and his possessions have increased in the land. But now, stretch out Your hand and touch all that he has, and he will surely curse You to Your face!" And the Lord said to Satan, "Behold, all that he has is in your power; only do not lay a hand on his person." So Satan went out from the presence of the Lord. Now there was a day when his sons and daughters were eating and drinking wine in their oldest brother's house; and a messenger came to Job and said, "The oxen were plowing and the donkeys feeding beside them, when the Sabeans raided them and took them away, indeed they have killed the servants with the edge of the sword; and I alone have escaped to tell you!" While he was still speaking, another also came and said, "The fire of God fell from heaven and burned up the sheep and the servants, and consumed them; and I alone have escaped to tell you!" While he was still speaking, another also came and said, "The Chaldeans formed three bands, raided the camels and took them away, yes, and killed the servants with the edge of the sword; and I alone have escaped to tell you!" While he was still speaking, another also came and said, "Your sons and daughters were eating and drinking wine in their oldest brother's house, and suddenly a great wind came from across the wilderness and struck the four corners of the house, and it fell on the young people, and they are dead; and I alone have escaped to tell you!" Then Job arose, tore his robe, and shaved his head; and he fell to the ground and worshiped. And he said: "Naked I came from my mother's womb, and naked shall I return there. The Lord gave, and the Lord has taken away; Blessed be the name of the Lord." In all this Job did not sin nor charge God with wrong" Job 1:6-22. Satan secured a mandate to orchestrate trials against Job, so he lost his businesses, possessions and children as well as his health. Three of Job's friends heard of his situation and came to visit him. Each of them gave a discourse of why they thought Job was undergoing his unusual challenges. Most of what they said was an accusation that implied that Job had secretly violated the commands of God. However, they were all wrong in their assertions and had no clue what was taking place with Job. In Job's own words, we understand why he was tried, "For the thing I greatly feared has come upon me, and what I dreaded has happened to me. I am not at ease, nor am I quiet; I have no rest, for trouble comes" Job 3:25&26. Job was saddled with inherent fear that often motivated his way. This was how Satan secured a mandate to orchestrate the trials that beset Job. At the end of the trial God convicted these three friends for wrongly accusing Job and counselled them to go and offer seven rams and seven bulls so Job could intercede for them. The seven rams signify a sacrifice of spiritual service, while the seven bulls are a financial commitment, and both are predicated by divine conviction. When Eliphaz, Bildad and Zophar obeyed, and Job interceded, the Lord accepted their sacrifice. This triggered a restoration in the community, and all those who had distanced themselves from Job because of his trials returned with each bearing a piece of silver and gold rings for Job. The silver piece tallied with the seven rams while the gold rings represented the seven bulls God required of Job's friends. All sorts of restoration blessings started manifesting with all those who committed to a spiritual and financial sacrifice by divine conviction.

Next let us look at the blessing of God that came upon King Solomon, "Now the king went to Gibeon to sacrifice there, for that was the great high place: Solomon offered a thousand burnt offerings on that altar. At Gibeon the Lord appeared to Solomon in a dream by night; and God said, "Ask! What shall I give you?" And Solomon said: "You have shown great mercy to Your servant David my father, because he walked before You in truth, in righteousness, and in uprightness of heart with You; You have continued this great kindness for him, and You have given him a son to sit on his throne, as it is this day. Now, O Lord my God, You have made Your servant king instead of my father David, but I am a little child; I do not know how to go out or come in. And Your servant is in the midst of Your people whom You have chosen, a great people, too numerous to be numbered or counted. Therefore give to Your servant an understanding heart to judge Your people, that I may discern between good and evil. For who is able to judge this great people of Yours?" The speech pleased the Lord, that Solomon had asked this thing. Then God said to him: "Because you have asked this thing, and have not asked long life for yourself, nor have asked riches for yourself, nor have asked the life of your enemies, but have asked for yourself understanding to discern justice, behold, I have done according to your words; see, I have given you a wise and understanding heart, so that there has not been anyone like you before you, nor shall any like you arise after you. And I have also given you what you have not asked: both riches and honor, so that there shall not be anyone like you among the kings all your days. So if you walk in My ways, to keep My statutes and My commandments, as your father David walked, then I will lengthen your days." Then Solomon awoke; and indeed it had been a dream. And he came to Jerusalem and stood before the ark of the covenant of the Lord, offered up burnt offerings, offered peace offerings, and made a feast for all his servants" 1 Kings 3:4-15. King Solomon was King David's son by Bathsheba. The events surrounding how Bathsheba became wife to King David was distasteful to many in Israel, so it is likely that growing up in the palace, Solomon was shunned by others in the royal family. Worst of all, they may have heard rumors that King David intended him to be the heir of the throne. In his old age while King David had become sickly, Solomon's half-brother by name Adonijah attempted to usurp the throne. Adonijah mobilized all those whom he figured were discontented with King David as well as members of the royal household to coronate him as king over Israel. However, while they were feasting in celebration of Adonijah, King David got hint of their scheme and installed Solomon as king. Some of the discontent of the royal household about King Solomon was legitimate. He was not as mature as some of the other princes who were older, skillful and experienced, and this is why at the onset of his reign he went and offered a thousand animals as sacrifice to God. Offering an animal required the offeror to lay hands on it as an essence of ownership. King Solomon was drained laying hands on a thousand animals, and the last animal was when his entire strength was drained out.

He probably could not stand anymore and went straight to sleep. King Solomon experienced a divine encounter where he was told to make a request. Essentially this was a blank check, and his request unveiled his concerns as a young king. "You have shown great mercy to Your servant David my father, because he walked before You in truth, in righteousness, and in uprightness of heart with You; You have continued this great kindness for him, and You have given him a son to sit on his throne, as it is this day. Now, O Lord my God, You have made Your servant king instead of my father David, but I am a little child; I do not know how to go out or come in. And Your servant is in the midst of Your people whom You have chosen, a great people, too numerous to be numbered or counted. Therefore give to Your servant an understanding heart to judge Your people, that I may discern between good and evil. For who is able to judge this great people of Yours?" In his request King Solomon expressed his insufficiency as it pertains to royalty over God's people. His prayer pleased God and so he was blessed with an understanding heart to discern justice.

The Day of Atonement was one day in the year when there was a convening of the court of heaven. Here, Satan shows up with a litany of cases to prosecute people, while Jesus Christ is advocate for all those who observe the prescriptions for that day, and God the Father sits as Judge. This was the occasion in the Old Dispensation where the high priest will offer up sacrifices, sprinkle the blood on the objects of the tabernacle including the veil, and proceed into the Most Holy Place where there was situated the Ark of the Covenant. "And they shall make an ark of acacia wood; two and a half cubits shall be its length, a cubit and a half its width, and a cubit and a half its height. And you shall overlay it with pure gold, inside and out you shall overlay it, and shall make on it a molding of gold all around. You shall cast four rings of gold for it, and put them in its four corners; two rings shall be on one side, and two rings on the other side. And you shall make poles of acacia wood, and overlay them with gold. You shall put the poles into the rings on the sides of the ark, that the ark may be carried by them. The poles shall be in the rings of the ark; they shall not be taken from it. And you shall put into the ark the Testimony which I will give you. "You shall make a mercy seat of pure gold; two and a half cubits shall be its length and a cubit and a half its width. And you shall make two cherubim of gold; of hammered work you shall make them at the two ends of the mercy seat. Make one cherub at one end, and the other cherub at the other end; you shall make the cherubim at the two ends of it of one piece with the mercy seat. And the cherubim shall stretch out their wings above, covering the mercy seat with their wings, and they shall face one another; the faces of the cherubim shall be toward the mercy seat. You shall put the mercy seat on top of the ark, and in the ark you shall put the Testimony that I will give you. And there I will meet with you, and I will speak with you from above the mercy seat, from between the two cherubim which are on the ark of the Testimony, about everything which I will give you in commandment to the children of Israel" Exodus 25:10-22.

The ark of the covenant was positioned in the Most Holy Place. The anointed high priest will come here once every year on the Day of Atonement to get judgment on behalf of God's people. The ark of the covenant was made of three components that are the three factors that determine God's judgment. The gold-plated box contained the ten commandments which signified the logos. Two golden cherubim positioned on the box that signified the rhema. A mercy seat that was on the box between the two cherubim.

The logos factor of judgment was how effective the anointed high priest had engaged the kingdom of darkness using the scriptures. "For though we walk in the flesh, we do not war according to the flesh. For the weapons of our warfare are not carnal but mighty in God for pulling down strongholds, casting down arguments and every high thing that exalts itself against the knowledge of God, bringing every thought into captivity to the obedience of Christ, and being ready to punish all disobedience when your obedience is fulfilled" 2 Corinthians 10:3-6. The anointed high priest was expected to confront the demonic inspired mindsets that plagued the world.

The rhema factor of judgment was how well the anointed high priest had yielded to divinely inspired worship. Angels furnished him with what was taking place in heaven so he could join the symphony of heavenly worship.

The mercy factor of judgment was how the anointed high priest had exercised his prerogative of mercy. "So speak and so do as those who will be judged by the law of liberty. For judgment is without mercy to the one who has shown no mercy. Mercy triumphs over judgment" James 2:12&13. Mercy is the most significant factor of God's judgment. Here we are judged based on how we exercised the privilege of making decisions that change the circumstance of others when we can do so. This is known as our prerogative that everyone can wield in any way they choose. Restitution, redemption, release and restoration are mercy concepts that require our prerogative. They not only stop the kingdom of darkness in their tracks, but foster a turnaround for God's people.

Stephanos and Diadema

In the fifty-year cycle that culminated in the Jubilee, the trumpet was sounded on the Day of Atonement to signal the commencement. While the practice of restitution, redemption, release and restoration were mandates of the jubilee, it signaled an end to forms of slavery, bondage, captivity and disenfranchisement. This ushered God's people into royalty which is not the preserve of a few, rather it is the design of God for everyone. The Jubilee is the year of the 'diadema' where people are crowned with royalty. As we have learned earlier, Kairos are opportune times that are divinely scheduled for lives. Whenever we master a specific function of time, we secure the conqueror crown which is known as 'Stephanos' in the Greek. The 'Diadema' is the royal crowning which is the overall restoration to destiny that comes to us in the Jubilee.

The Jubilee was every fifty years and so you might meet your jubilation twice in your lifetime. Your period to shine as a star may come very early and not come again until you are around the age of sixty. This is why it is important to pay attention to God's word and synchronize with what is required of you. For instance, there may be a time in your life when all you are constantly convicted by the Holy

Spirit to change is your attitude. You must understand that God wants to kill those attitude demons in you so that by the time your life clock turns around, your emotions would be healed. Just as the whole earth is divided into various time zones, all of us are in different time zones and God convicts each of us differently. Although we may all be at the same forum listening to His word, we must always discern what God is saying to us as individuals. Whenever God reveals to us the time, it is composed of divine principles and angelic presence which amounts to divine favor. When you know the time, then you become aware of how to unleash divine favor. For instance, when it is God's time for you to fast, you immediately find the grace to do it. Often, you may have tried to fast without conviction and were unable to do so. This is because there was no favor. God's word from the pulpit, always releases a manifestation of divine favor that we must be diligent to tap into.

Just as much as physical fire has the power to process gold ore into pure gold, time is like a spiritual fire that transforms us. We are refined by the challenges and opportunities of our lifetime. Whether it is mastering the time to speak opposed to the time to keep silence, or the time of war against the time of peace, time refines us thoroughly so that we emerge as a shining star. Our spirit, body and soul must resonate with the character of God the Father, Son and Holy Spirit. This is the essence of baptism. "And Jesus came and spoke to them, saying, "All authority has been given to Me in heaven and on earth. Go therefore and make disciples of all the nations, baptizing them in the name of the Father and of the Son and of the Holy Spirit, teaching them to observe all things that I have commanded you; and lo, I am with you always, even to the end of the age" Matthew 28:18-20. We are immersed completely into the nature of God the Father, Son and Holy Ghost. With our spirit, we relate to the Father as the architect, with our body we relate to the Son who is the maker, and with our soul we relate to the Holy Ghost who is the revealer of truth. The process of attaining this dimension starts when we give our lives to Christ and allow the word to reshape us to conform to the image and likeness of God. Our spirit as human beings is a word of destiny from God. Our body is made from the dust of the earth. Our soul is a license to live on earth. From the first day we exist on this earth, Satan works very hard to ensure that we lose the nature of God that enables us to function in dominion. "Beware lest anyone cheat you through philosophy and empty deceit, according to the tradition of men, according to the basic principles of the world, and not according to Christ. For in Him dwells all the fullness of the Godhead bodily; and you are complete in Him, who is the head of all principality and power" Colossians 2:8-10. Through salvation in Jesus Christ, we begin the rapid process of regaining our lost image. The more we conform to the image of God the Father, Son and Holy Ghost, the more we are restored to our place of dominion.

The rising star becomes a shining star. This is the place of destiny that started with natural birth, salvation in Christ, pursuit of divine purpose and glorification. "And we know that all things work together for good to those who love God, to those who are the called according to His purpose. For whom He foreknew, He also predestined to be conformed to the image of His Son, that He might be the firstborn among many brethren. Moreover whom He predestined, these He also called; whom He called, these He also justified; and whom He justified, these He also glorified" Romans 8:28-30. The process of turning black gold ore into shining pure twenty-four carat gold is a costly and meticulous process. However, the end product is not left in the unattractive depths of the earth, but rather in the palaces of kings and the wealthy. Notice that glory starts with a foreknowing of God. Next, we are predestined with an assignment before we show up here on earth. Then we are saved by Christ and called into purpose. Our steps in line with divine purpose justify us in Christ. With perseverance and in a matter of time, we are glorified with the diadem of a royal crown.

SECTION 3

Dimensions

Every situation that confronts us exists as one or more of the frameworks by which God created the world. In this section of the book, we shall explore how to engage and resolve issues as God intended.

Chapter Twenty-Two

'Let There Be Light'

"In the beginning God created the heavens and the earth. The earth was without form, and void; and darkness was on the face of the deep. And the Spirit of God was hovering over the face of the waters. Then God said, "Let there be light"; and there was light. And God saw the light, that it was good; and God divided the light from the darkness. God called the light Day, and the darkness He called Night. So the evening and the morning were the first day" Genesis 1:1-5.

In the face of the chaos, emptiness and absence of light that shrouded the universe, God called out light to begin the work of creation. The account of light on the first day of creation tallies with how the apostle John records its relevance. "In the beginning was the Word, and the Word was with God, and the Word was God. He was in the beginning with God. All things were made through Him, and without Him nothing was made that was made. In

Him was life, and the life was the light of men. And the light shines in the darkness, and the darkness did not comprehend it" John 1:1-5. Jesus Christ came as the light and taught the Word in such a way that established a clear distinction between light and darkness. The impact of light on man's heart is what fosters repentance and restitution among others.

What is darkness?

Three words are used by the apostle Paul to depict darkness, which are shame, craftiness and deceit. "Therefore, since we have this ministry, as we have received mercy, we do not lose heart. But we have renounced the hidden things of shame, not walking in craftiness nor handling the word of God deceitfully, but by manifestation of the truth commending ourselves to every man's conscience in the sight of God. But even if our gospel is veiled, it is veiled to those who are perishing, whose minds the god of this age has blinded, who do not believe, lest the light of the gospel of the glory of Christ, who is the image of God, should shine on them. For we do not preach ourselves, but Christ Jesus the Lord, and ourselves your bondservants for Jesus' sake. For it is the God who commanded light to shine out of darkness, who has shone in our hearts to give the light of the knowledge of the glory of God in the face of Jesus Christ" 2 Corinthians 4:1-6.

First, 'shame' is from the Greek word 'aischunomai' and is associated with failure. It is a painful feeling of humiliation caused by the consciousness of wrong behavior. We often do not deliberately plan to fail because it is accompanied by the feeling of shame which is not pleasant. The

Ephraimites started as a very prosperous tribe when the Israelites took possession of the Promised Land. However, as the years passed, they were drawn into complacency. "Woe to the crown of pride, to the drunkards of Ephraim, whose glorious beauty is a fading flower which is at the head of the verdant valleys, to those who are overcome with wine! Behold, the Lord has a mighty and strong one, like a tempest of hail and a destroying storm, like a flood of mighty waters overflowing, Who will bring them down to the earth with His hand. The crown of pride, the drunkards of Ephraim, Will be trampled underfoot; and the glorious beauty is a fading flower which is at the head of the verdant valley, like the first fruit before the summer, which an observer sees; he eats it up while it is still in his hand. In that day the Lord of hosts will be for a crown of glory and a diadem of beauty to the remnant of His people, for a spirit of justice to him who sits in judgment, and for strength to those who turn back the battle at the gate" Isaiah 28:1-6.

The Ephraimites were half of the descendants of Joseph who represent instruction for skill development. At this time, however, Isaiah the prophet refers to Ephraim as the crown of pride, drunkards whose glory had faded away. Failure had crept into their endeavors and obliterated their past successes. By their pride, they departed from the legacy whereby God had instructed their ancestor Joseph. As drunkards they constantly relished in vain talk. Their predicament could be reversed only if they turned to God for their legacy. There is a way by which God instructs each human being, and it is incumbent on everyone to find it. He weans us as a child and nurtures us until we attain maturity in the skills of life. This is a lifelong process from which we must never excuse ourselves, so that the light of God would constantly stream into our hearts.

Second, 'craftiness' is from the Greek word 'panougos' and it means trickery. Several acts of magic are tricks to the human eye. The scripture tells of Simon, the sorcerer who bewitched the city of Samaria with his magic until Philip came into town. "Then Philip went down to the city of Samaria and preached Christ to them. And the multitudes with one accord heeded the things spoken by Philip, hearing and seeing the miracles which he did. For unclean spirits, crying with a loud voice, came out of many who were possessed; and many who were paralyzed and lame were healed. And there was great joy in that city. But there was a certain man called Simon, who previously practiced sorcery in the city and astonished the people of Samaria, claiming that he was someone great, to whom they all gave heed, from the least to the greatest, saying, "This man is the great power of God." And they heeded him because he had astonished them with his sorceries for a long time. But when they believed Philip as he preached the things concerning the kingdom of God and the name of Jesus Christ, both men and women were baptized. Then Simon himself also believed; and when he was baptized he continued with Philip, and was amazed, seeing the miracles and signs which were done" Acts 8:5-13. You will notice that Simon astonished the people of Samaria with his magic. They considered him as the great power of God, until they heard the truth of the gospel of Jesus Christ from the lips of Philip. The word of God from Philip was confirmed with miracles that could not be disputed. Magical prowess by which Simon the sorcerer had appealed to the minds of the Samaritans with tricks of magic are developed through the apprenticeship of sorcery. It is a curious art that requires induction training. The apprentice of magic involved interaction with demonic spirits. Magicians collaborate in practice with demonic spirits to amaze spectators at a circus show. Several things that are marketed to us are of no lasting value, and yet we procure and subscribe because of how well they are packaged. Such products and services will continue to wow the world and garner patronage until the light appears to unveil their darkness. Philip came to Samaria bearing the gospel of our Lord Jesus Christ, so that the audiences of Simon the sorcerer will encounter the true light of God. They made a choice that is consistent with what we sincerely crave as humans and got saved. "Now when the apostles who were at Jerusalem heard that Samaria had received the word of God, they sent Peter and John to them, who, when they had come down, prayed for them that they might receive the Holy Spirit. For as yet He had fallen upon none of them. They had only been baptized in the name of the Lord Jesus. Then they laid hands on them, and they received the Holy Spirit. And when Simon saw that through the laying on of the apostles' hands the Holy Spirit was given, he offered them money, saying, "Give me this power also, that anyone on whom I lay hands may receive the Holy Spirit." But Peter said to him, "Your money perish with you, because you thought that the gift of God could be purchased with money! You have neither part nor portion in this matter, for your heart is not right in the sight of God. Repent therefore of this your wickedness and pray God if perhaps the thought of your heart may be forgiven you. For I see that you are poisoned by bitterness and bound by iniquity." Then Simon answered and said, "Pray to the Lord for me, that none of the things which you have spoken may come upon me." So when they had testified and preached the word of the Lord, they returned to Jerusalem, preaching the gospel in many villages of the Samaritans" Acts 8:14-25.

Apostles Peter and John came from Jerusalem to reinforce the work that Philip had started in Samaria. Through the ministry of laying on of hands, the Samarians received the baptism of the Holy Ghost. Simon the sorcerer who had also accepted Jesus Christ as Savior through the ministry of Philip, was amazed at the impartation of the Holy Ghost through the laying on of hands. He made an offer to procure this gift from the apostles. Peter instantly rebuked him, "Your money perish with you, because you thought that the gift of God could be purchased with money!" Many billionaires today are aggressively seeking successful entities to procure so they can make more money. Some of such endeavors were developed by people who went through a lot of trials to become successful, but when the ownership changes with the aim of more profitability, the compromise of legitimate processes begin. "For You, O God, have proved us: You have tried us, as silver is tried. You brought us into the net; You laid affliction upon our loins. You have caused men to ride over our heads; we went through fire and through water: but You brought us out into a wealthy place" Psalms 66:10-12. To attain the highest value, metals such as silver and gold are refined in a furnace at very high temperatures. The only endeavors that would endure the test of time are those for which we persevere holding on to divine instructions. Through perseverance we become one with the light of God's word and so transparent, such that darkness cannot be concealed.

Third, 'deceit' is from the Greek word 'dolos' which means to adulterate. This is to render something poorer in quality by adding another substance, typically an inferior one. It is the lack of integrity in one's way. "Now it came to pass when Samuel was old that he made his sons judges over Israel. The name of his firstborn was Joel, and the name of his second, Abijah; they were judges in Beersheba. But his sons did not walk in his ways; they turned aside after dishonest gain, took bribes, and perverted justice. Then all the elders of Israel gathered together and came to Samuel at Ramah, and said to him, "Look, you are old, and your sons do not walk in your ways. Now make us a king to judge us like all the nations." But the thing displeased Samuel when they said, "Give us a king to judge us." So Samuel prayed to the Lord. And the Lord said to Samuel, "Heed the voice of the people in all that they say to you; for they have not rejected you, but they have rejected Me, that I should not reign over them. According to all the works which they have done since the day that I brought them up out of Egypt, even to this day with which they have forsaken Me and served other gods so they are doing to you also. Now therefore, heed their voice. However, you shall solemnly forewarn them, and show them the behavior of the king who will reign over them" 1 Samuel 8:1-9. There was a legitimate problem in Israel during the era of Samuel the prophet, where his sons who deputized for him as judges were corrupt in their ways. The Israelites approached Samuel to demand a monarchy like the neighboring nations, and this request was displeasing to God. Israel's request was consistent with their history of idolatry and emulating their heathen neighbors in the Promised Land. Samuel was instructed to grant their request as well as advise them of the consequences.

"Nevertheless, the people refused to obey the voice of Samuel; and they said, "No, but we will have a king over us, that we also may be like all the nations, and that our king may judge us and go out before us and fight our battles." And Samuel heard all the words of the people, and he repeated them in the hearing of the Lord. So the Lord said to Samuel, "Heed their voice, and make them a king." And Samuel said to the men of Israel, "Every man go to his city" 1 Samuel 8:19-22. Israel was adamant in their desire to have a king like their neighbors, and so Saul from the tribe of Benjamin was anointed and installed as king. The character of King Saul and how he reigned over Israel, reflected how the hearts of the Israelites had departed from God. While noble initiatives propelled his reign at the beginning, King Saul eventually degenerated into a self-serving opportunist. Many of our initiatives as believers often arise from the need to address issues in a 'smart way'. However, we often forget that God anticipates these problems and designates the appropriate solutions. In the case of Israel, He had given a prophetic word through the blessing that Jacob their ancestor conferred on the tribe of Judah several years earlier. They ought to have sought God for a solution to the leadership issues without suggesting the model of the world. Their quest to emulate their neighbors poisoned their request and landed them a carnal king. While Israel was experiencing the corruption of Samuel's sons, God had started grooming David to become king of Israel. Assuming they had heeded the admonishment of Samuel, they would not have suffered the reign of King Saul. We must be careful of so-called common-sense initiatives for our sophisticated problems that entail corruption. Whatever solutions we learn directly from the world is often a perverted form of something good, so why not seek the purest version. Let us learn to seek the light of God without prejudice of any form.

Shame, craftiness and deceitfulness are the ways the kingdom of darkness veils the minds of those who do not believe the gospel. However, God commands light to shine into the hearts of those who believe in Him. Divine light shows us a way to overcome the schemes of darkness. This light is also the first weight category of divine glory, so it is incumbent upon us to always seek divine light.

The Dimension of Light is where we confront darkness in the mind by praying 'let there be light', and then wait for a divine leading in the heart.

Dimensions

Chapter Twenty-Three

'Let There Be a Firmament to Divide the Waters'

"Then God said, "Let there be a firmament in the midst of the waters, and let it divide the waters from the waters." Thus God made the firmament, and divided the waters which were under the firmament from the waters which were above the firmament; and it was so. And God called the firmament Heaven. So the evening and the morning were the second day" Genesis 2:6-8.

On the second day of creation, God dealt with the 'without form' condition of the universe. Water was everywhere and so He called out the firmament to separate the water such that there was a space between the water above and below. Isaiah the prophet provides significance to this manifestation. "For My thoughts are not your thoughts, nor are your ways My ways," says the Lord. "For as the heavens are higher than the earth, so are My ways higher than your ways, and My thoughts than your thoughts. "For as the rain comes down, and the snow from heaven, and do not return there, but water the earth, and make it bring forth and bud, that it may give seed to the sower and bread to the eater, So shall My word be that goes forth from My mouth; It shall not return to Me void, but it shall accomplish what I please, and it shall prosper in the thing for which I sent it" Isaiah 55:8-11. The waters above the heavens signify divine thoughts and ways, while the waters below speak of human thoughts and ways. God's thoughts and ways are made known to us by revelation. Isaiah uses the manifestation of rainfall and snow to show how divine revelation comes to orchestrate prosperity on the earth. God's word would not return void but accomplish what it is intended. The waters below the heavens speak of human thoughts and ways that are usually the sum of what has been revealed to us in the past. Often, we are stuck in these ways unless we receive fresh revelations that show us the way forward. Moses said, "The secret things belong to the Lord our God, but those things which are revealed belong to us and to our children forever, that we may do all the words of this law" Deuteronomy 29:29. Whatever is revealed to a generation of humans become the legacy for future generations. However, when humans fail to uphold God's word that has been revealed, the consequences are severe. "Now it came to pass, when men began to multiply on the face of the earth, and daughters were born to them, that the sons of God saw the daughters of men, that they were beautiful; and they took wives for themselves of all whom they chose. And the Lord said, "My Spirit shall not strive with man forever, for he is indeed flesh; yet his days shall be one hundred and twenty years." There were giants on the earth in those days, and also afterward, when the sons of God came in to the daughters of men and they bore children to them. Those were the mighty men who were of old, men of renown. Then the Lord saw that the wickedness of man was great in the earth, and that every intent of the thoughts of his heart was only evil continually. And the Lord was sorry that He had made man on the earth, and He was grieved in His heart. So the Lord said, "I will destroy man whom I have created from the face of the earth, both man and beast, creeping thing and birds of the air, for I am sorry that I have made them." But Noah found grace in the eyes of the Lord" Genesis 6:1-8. Adam and Eve did not uphold God's instructions while they lived in the Garden of Eden. Cain did not offer acceptable sacrifices and murdered his brother Abel. Lamech, who was a descendant of Cain, was a murderer. By the tenth generation of humanity there was an unprecedented wickedness taking place on earth. Fallen angels married humans and bred giants that perpetuated all forms of injustices, curses and vilification. It was a literal manifestation of the chaos of water everywhere. This chaos of heaven and earth signifies the absence of redemption where the kingdom of darkness perpetuates all kinds of evil in every space.

The first time it rained was during the flood that God sent to destroy the people of Noah's generation. After the flood, Noah offered a sacrifice to God that activated the cycle of rainfall blessings that we still experience today. "Then Noah built an altar to the Lord, and took of every clean animal and of every clean bird, and offered burnt offerings on the altar. And the Lord smelled a soothing aroma. Then the Lord said in His heart, "I will never again curse the ground for man's sake, although the imagination of man's heart is evil from his youth; nor will I again destroy every living thing as I have done. "While the earth remains, seedtime and harvest, cold and heat, winter and summer, and day and night shall not cease" Genesis 8:20-22. The cycles of the elements and seasons were all activated when Noah offered an acceptable sacrifice to God. Furthermore, God established a covenant with Noah for all humans. "So God blessed Noah and his sons, and said to them: "Be fruitful and multiply, and fill the earth. And the fear of you and the dread of you shall be on every beast of the earth, on every bird of the air, on all that move on the earth, and on all the fish of the sea. They are given into your hand. Every moving thing that lives shall be food for you. I have given you all things, even as the green herbs. But you shall not eat flesh with its life, that is, its blood. Surely for your lifeblood I will demand a reckoning; from the hand of every beast I will require it, and from the hand of man. From the hand of every man's brother I will require the life of man. "Whoever sheds man's blood, by man his blood shall be shed; For in the image of God He made man. And as for you, be fruitful and multiply; Bring forth abundantly in the earth and multiply in it" Genesis 9:1-7. God's covenant entailed a caveat about blood. "But you shall not eat flesh with its life, that is, its blood. Surely for your lifeblood I will demand a reckoning; from the hand of every beast I will require it, and from the hand of man. From the hand of every man's brother I will require the life of man. "Whoever sheds man's blood, by man his blood shall be shed; For in the image of God He made man." Concerning the essence of blood, God told Moses in Leviticus 17:10&11, "And whatever man of the house of Israel, or of the strangers who dwell among you, who eats any blood, I will set My face against that person who eats blood, and will cut him off from among his people. For the life of the flesh is in the blood, and I have given it to you upon the altar to make atonement for your souls; for it is the blood that makes atonement for the soul." The demarcation of the firmament required a framework for bridging the earth and heaven. Blood was designed to bridge this gulf to reconnect man with God. Injustices of the bloodline can result in unfathomable complications that shroud us and may hold us in bondage perpetually. "Then Lamech said to his wives: "Adah and Zillah, hear my voice; Wives of Lamech, listen to my speech! For I have killed a man for wounding me, even a young man for hurting me. If Cain shall be avenged sevenfold, then Lamech seventy-sevenfold" Genesis 4:23&24. Notice that Lamech a descendant of Cain is telling his wives about the consequences of an ancestral bloodline issue. Too many people in our world are bound by bloodline addictions, vices, infirmities and oppressive conditions, for which therapy and medication alone cannot resolve. Jesus Christ taught the disciples God's word, but then without his sacrifice at the cross, humanity could not have experienced the ultimate redemption from all forms of injustice. Jesus laid a path for each one of us to follow through self-denial and the grace to carry our cross. It is expedient that we all find the path of our cross, and be willing to bear the burden that redeems us from all manifestations of injustice.

The sin of Adam and Eve in transgressing against divine instruction, resulted in a curse upon creation. However, Jesus Christ went to the cross and paid the price for us. "Christ has redeemed us from the curse of the law, having become a curse for us: for it is written, "Cursed is everyone who hangs on a tree", that the blessing of Abraham might come upon the Gentiles in Christ Jesus, that we might receive the promise of the Spirit through faith" Galatians 3:13&14. Receiving the blessing of Abraham and the promises of the Spirit entails faith. "Faith is the substance of things hoped for, the evidence of things not seen" Hebrews 11:1. "So then faith comes by hearing, and hearing by the Word of God" Romans 10:17. We see clearly from the scriptures that faith is a path conveyed to us by revelation. This path is unique for every individual believer and entails customized experiences. "For as many as are led by the Spirit of God, these are sons of God. For you did not receive the spirit of bondage again to fear, but you received the Spirit of adoption by whom we cry out, "Abba, Father." The Spirit Himself bears witness with our spirit that we are children of God, and if children, then heirs, heirs of God and joint heirs with Christ, if indeed we suffer with Him, that we may also be glorified together. For I consider that the sufferings of this present time are not worthy to be compared with the glory which shall be revealed in us. For the earnest expectation of the creation eagerly waits for the revealing of the sons of God. For the creation was subjected to futility, not willingly, but because of Him who subjected it in hope; because the creation itself also will be delivered from the bondage of corruption into the glorious liberty of the children of God. For we know that the whole creation groans and labors with birth pangs together until now. Not only that, but we also who have the firstfruits of the Spirit, even we ourselves groan within ourselves, eagerly waiting for the adoption, the redemption of our body" Romans 8:14-23. The way that every believer comes to experience their blessings of inheritance in Christ, is tailored to their unique divine purpose and history. We all ought to be in the process of turning curses into blessings. For this reason, we travail and groan alongside creation to release our inheritance from the bondage of the Adamic curse.

Vilification is character assassination. Words are spoken to poison the minds and hearts of people to trigger disfavor. This was a common occurrence prior to the flood of Noah's era. "But there were also false prophets among the people, even as there will be false teachers among you, who will secretly bring in destructive heresies, even denying the Lord who bought them, and bring on themselves swift destruction. And many will follow their destructive ways, because of whom the way of truth will be blasphemed. By covetousness they will exploit you with deceptive words; for a long time their judgment has not been idle, and their destruction does not slumber. For if God did not spare the angels who sinned, but cast them down to hell and delivered them into chains of darkness, to be reserved for judgment; and did not spare the ancient world, but saved Noah, one of eight people, a preacher of righteousness, bringing in the flood on the world of the ungodly" 2 Peter 2:1-5. To overcome vilification, Noah preached righteousness to his generation. It is obvious that they did not heed his message and so they were destroyed by the flood. "How beautiful upon the mountains are the feet of him who brings good news, who proclaims peace, who brings glad tidings of good things, who proclaims salvation, who says to Zion, "Your God reigns!" Isaiah 52:7. Our witness of the life, death and resurrection of our Lord Jesus Christ dismantles any vilification against us. Though the enemy may inspire people to vilify us to tarnish our reputation, preaching the gospel counteracts the negative narrative. Nicodemus the Pharisee could not reconcile with the vilification of his colleagues concerning Jesus and the miracles that confirmed His message. He came to Jesus secretly at night to seek insights. This is the occasion where Jesus revealed the profound truth about salvation. "Most assuredly, I say to you, unless one is born of water and the Spirit, he cannot enter the kingdom of God. That which is born of the flesh is flesh, and that which is born of the Spirit is spirit. Do not marvel that I said to you, 'You must be born again.' The wind blows where it wishes, and you hear the sound of it, but cannot tell where it comes from and where it goes. So is everyone who is born of the Spirit" John 3:5-8. Here, Jesus brings to relevance the essence of the second day of creation. To be saved, the waters below the firmament must engage the Spirit that is the waters above. In Greek the water below is rendered as 'logos' while the water above the firmament is 'rhema' that is the revelation of the Spirit. Science tells us that whenever negative current meets with positive current power is generated. This is a concept for electricity, engines and the various devices powered by automation. Where logos meet with rhema, power is produced!

The Dimension of Power is where persistent injustices, curses and vilification are overcome, by seeking the leading of the cross of our Lord Jesus Christ.

Chapter Twenty-Four

'Let The Dry Land Appear'

"Then God said, "Let the waters under the heavens be gathered together into one place, and let the dry land appear"; and it was so. And God called the dry land Earth, and the gathering together of the waters He called Seas. And God saw that it was good. Then God said, "Let the earth bring forth grass, the herb that yields seed, and the fruit tree that yields fruit according to its kind, whose seed is in itself, on the earth"; and it was so. And the earth brought forth grass, the herb that yields seed according to its kind, and the tree that yields fruit, whose seed is in itself according to its kind. And God saw that it was good. So the evening and the morning were the third day" Genesis 1:9-13.

God dealt with the 'void' condition of the world by calling forth the dry land. Void is a state of poverty and on this third day, God called the substance of land into manifestation. Then God spoke to the dry land to manifest various forms of vegetation that bear fruit with seed. Land, fruit and seed are the natural elements that correspond with our three-fold existence, body, soul and spirit. "And the Lord God formed man of the dust of the ground and breathed into his nostrils the breath of life; and man became a living being" Genesis 2:7. Every living human enshrines land, fruit and seed which are our potential to overcome poverty.

Land enshrines most of the raw materials for the developments that make life on earth comfortable. When Leah gave birth to Reuben the first born of Jacob, it was as though God was saying, 'Let the dry land appear'. Though Leah perverted Reuben by naming him after her emotional frustration, he eventually discovers his purpose as a physician. Reuben is involved in the practice of medical science for the health of people. From here we see the essence of engineering for clean water, sanitation, plumbing, electricity, heating, air-conditioning, automobiles etc. Scripture records that a king of Israel by the name of King Uzziah, started a scientific era that fostered his prosperity. "Uzziah was sixteen years old when he became king, and he reigned fifty-two years in Jerusalem. His mother's name was Jecholiah of Jerusalem. And he did what was right in the sight of the Lord, according to all that his father Amaziah had done. He sought God in the days of Zechariah, who had understanding in the visions of God; and as long as he sought the Lord, God made him prosper. Now he went out and made war against the Philistines, and broke down the wall of Gath, the wall of Jabneh, and the wall of Ashdod; and he built cities around Ashdod and among the Philistines. God helped him against the Philistines, against the Arabians who lived in Gur Baal, and against the Meunites. Also the Ammonites brought tribute to Uzziah. His fame spread as far as the entrance of Egypt, for he became exceedingly strong. And Uzziah built towers in Jerusalem at the Corner Gate, at the Valley Gate, and at the corner buttress of the wall; then he fortified them. Also he built towers in the desert. He dug many wells, for he had much livestock, both in the lowlands and in the plains; he also had farmers and vinedressers in the mountains and in Carmel, for he loved the soil. Moreover Uzziah had an army of fighting men who went out to war by companies, according to the number on their roll as prepared by Jeiel the scribe and Maaseiah the officer, under the hand of Hananiah, one of the king's captains. The total number of chief officers of the mighty men of valor was two thousand six hundred. And under their authority was an army of three hundred and seven thousand five hundred, that made war with mighty power, to help the king against the enemy. Then Uzziah prepared for them, for the entire army, shields, spears, helmets, body armor, bows, and slings to cast stones. And he made devices in Jerusalem, invented by skillful men, to be on the towers and the corners, to shoot arrows and large stones. So his fame spread far and wide, for he was marvelously helped till he became strong" 2 Chronicles 26:3-15. King Uzziah harnessed the land for water and agriculture. He spurred creativity by engaging engineers to invent machines for warfare and utilities. 'He sought God in the days of Zechariah, who had understanding in the visions of God; and as long as he sought the Lord, God made him prosper'. King Uzziah prospered in his endeavors because he sought God through the prophet Zechariah. However, when he was intoxicated by his accomplishments and became arrogant, he violated the divine presence and ended up as a leper and died in disgrace.

Seed is the root of anything that resurrects and can reproduce itself. It is the spoken word of God intended as the root of whatever ought to bear fruit. Seed is often used to describe the human spirit. Jesus used seed as a metaphor for His death and resurrection. "Most assuredly, I say to you, unless a grain of wheat falls into the ground and dies, it remains alone; but if it dies, it produces much grain" John 12:24. While He was here on earth, Jesus demonstrated the miracle of seed to His followers and so when the New Testament Church was born, the apostles resorted to this premise for tackling the poverty among the believers. "Now the multitude of those who believed were of one heart and one soul; neither did anyone say that any of the things he possessed was his own, but they had all things in common. And with great power the apostles gave witness to the resurrection of the Lord Jesus. And great grace was upon them all. Nor was there anyone among them who lacked; for all who were possessors of lands or houses sold them and brought the proceeds of the things that were sold, and laid them at the apostles' feet; and they distributed to each as anyone had need. And Joses, who was also named Barnabas by the apostles (which is translated Son of Encouragement), a Levite of the country of Cyprus, having land, sold it, and brought the money and laid it at the apostles' feet" Acts 4:32-37. With one heart and soul the disciples committed themselves to the premise of the word as Jesus had taught and demonstrated. Everyone made seed available according to their means and the apostles administered them by the model of Christ. "And as they were eating,

Jesus took bread, blessed and broke it, and gave it to the disciples and said, "Take, eat; this is My body" Matthew 26:26. The bread was blessed, broken and given. First, blessed means to subject something or a person to the requirement of God's word. It entails thanksgiving to God. Second, the bread was broken. This means it was appropriated according to the table of showbread where twelve loaves of bread were assigned as provision for the twelve tribes of Israel. It was the diligence of assignments according to divine covenant stipulations. Third, it was given, which means distribution was made according to the priority of need. In this way, the New Testament Church overcame poverty and experienced phenomenal growth.

Fruit is reward, sustenance and comfort. The human soul craves reward, sustenance and comfort either legitimately or illegitimately. Assuming gold trinkles started falling amid people congregated in a space, there is a high tendency for the occurrence of a stampede. This reality was manifested when miracles of divine providence began to manifest in the New Testament Church at its onset. "Now in those days, when the number of the disciples was multiplying, there arose a complaint against the Hebrews by the Hellenists, because their widows were neglected in the daily distribution. Then the twelve summoned the multitude of the disciples and said, "It is not desirable that we should leave the word of God and serve tables. Therefore, brethren, seek out from among you seven men of good reputation, full of the Holy Spirit and wisdom, whom we may appoint over this business; but we will give ourselves continually to prayer and to the ministry of the word." And the saying pleased the whole multitude. And they chose Stephen, a man full of faith and the Holy Spirit, and Philip, Prochorus, Nicanor, Timon, Parmenas, and Nicolas, a proselyte from Antioch, whom they set before the apostles; and when they had prayed, they laid hands on them. Then the word of God spread, and the number of the disciples multiplied greatly in Jerusalem, and a great many of the priests were obedient to the faith" Acts 6:1-7. Favoritism and prejudice shrouded the glorious manifestations of supernatural providence in the Church. For this reason, a system had to be employed which entailed the installation of deacons in the Church. You will notice the caliber of these deacons were 'seven men of good reputation, full of the Holy Spirit and wisdom'. They were not chosen because they were highly educated and rich but rather deeply spiritual. They were God's choice to handle this situation and so their administration ended the problem and spiritual growth continued unabated.

The Dimension of Fruitfulness is where the appropriate land is sown with the right seed for the required harvest.

Dimensions

Chapter Twenty-Five

'Let There Be Lights in the Firmament'

"Then God said, "Let there be lights in the firmament of the heavens to divide the day from the night; and let them be for signs and seasons, and for days and years; and let them be for lights in the firmament of the heavens to give light on the earth"; and it was so. Then God made two great lights: the greater light to rule the day, and the lesser light to rule the night. He made the stars also. God set them in the firmament of the heavens to give light on the earth, and to rule over the day and over the night, and to divide the light from the darkness. And God saw that it was good. So the evening and the morning were the fourth day" Genesis 1:14-19.

God created the sun, moon and stars on the fourth day of His work to orchestrate time. The challenges and opportunities that we experience in life are all factors of time. "He appointed the moon for seasons; The sun knows its going down He appointed the moon for seasons; The sun knows its going down. You make darkness, and it is night, in which all the beasts of the forest creep about. The young lions roar after their prey, and seek their food from God. When the sun rises, they gather together and lie down in their dens. Man goes out to his work and to his labor until the evening" Psalm 104:19-23. 'Point in time', 'Appointed time' and 'Covenant time' are three-time frames regulated by the sun, moon and stars respectively. While a literal day is a twenty-four-hour period, a spiritual day in the Hebrew is known as 'Yom' and means a point in time which could extend up to several years. "For behold, the day is coming, burning like an oven, and all the proud, yes, all who do wickedly will be stubble. And the day which is coming shall burn them up," says the Lord of hosts, "That will leave them neither root nor branch. But to you who fear My name the Sun of Righteousness shall arise with healing in His wings; and you shall go out and grow fat like stall-fed calves. You shall trample the wicked, for they shall be ashes under the soles of your feet on the day that I do this," Says the Lord of hosts" Malachi 4:1-3. A spiritual day was characterized by some specific challenge or opportunity. This day did not end until the challenge or opportunity expired. Malachi the prophet characterizes this day as when the wicked experiences fire of judgment, but the godly will experience the 'Sun of Righteousness' that is a reference to Christ. While the wicked are plagued with destructive occurrences, the godly who revere the nature of Christ will experience healing. Faithful stewardship of the times of challenges and opportunities is the essence of royalty. "Thus says the Lord: "In an acceptable time I have heard You, and in the day of salvation I have helped You; I will preserve You and give You as a covenant to the people, to restore the earth, to cause them to inherit the desolate heritages; That You may say to the prisoners, 'Go forth,' to those who are in darkness, 'show yourselves.' "They shall feed along the roads, and their pastures shall be on all desolate heights. They shall neither hunger nor thirst, neither heat nor sun shall strike them; For He who has mercy on them will lead them, even by the springs of water He will guide them. I will make each of My mountains a road, and My highways shall be elevated. Surely these shall come from afar; Look! Those from the north and the west, and these from the land of Sinim." Sing, O heavens! Be joyful, O earth! And break out in singing, O mountains! For the Lord has comforted His people and will have mercy on His afflicted" Isaiah 49:8-13. A godly king knows when to engage in dialogue with God concerning specific issues. This spiritual sense is attained through worship. Acknowledgement of God with a sincere heart invokes this privilege upon the king. Furthermore, a king would often have several requests tabled before him for resource allocation. Without a sense of where divine help has been appropriated, he risks deploying resources in the wrong direction. This would result in the irony of several white elephants that hold up resources unnecessarily.

The moon is the lesser light designed to rule the night. Night is synonymous with when the kingdom of darkness plot evil schemes. However, God planned for the light of the moon to signify divine light to evade the schemes of darkness. "He appointed the moon for seasons." Seasons here is a reference to the Hebrew word 'Moed' which are appointed times for divine visitations. Passover is the divine visitation for death to sin and lusts. First-fruit is the divine visitation for resurrection life. Pentecost is the divine visitation for the empowerment of the Holy Spirit. The Feast of Trumpets is the divine visitation for spiritual alignment. Atonement is the divine visitation for terminating curse mandates. Tabernacles is the divine visitation for the promises of God. During these divine visitations, we are equipped with revelation by which we can evade the schemes of the kingdom of darkness. Whenever we encounter a situation and it seems as though we are in a wilderness having no coordinates, we can find our way by stirring up the gifts of the Holy Spirit and honoring divine visitations.

The stars are responsible for signs, wonders and miracles. They are like cabinets where God's covenants are stored, so they manifest signs, wonders and miracles on a schedule for the beneficiaries. Job acknowledges how God works through the function of the stars. "God is wise in heart and mighty in strength. Who has hardened himself against Him and prospered? He removes the mountains, and they do not know when He overturns them in His anger; He shakes the earth out of its place, and its pillars tremble; He commands the sun, and it does not rise; He seals off the stars; He alone spreads out the heavens, and treads on the waves of the sea; He made the Bear, Orion, and the Pleiades, and the chambers of the south; He does great things past finding out, yes, wonders without number" Job 9:4-10. The prophetess Deborah in acknowledgment of how God came through for Israel, in their war against Sisera the commander of the army of Jabin king of Canaan. "The kings came and fought, then the kings of Canaan fought in Taanach, by the waters of

Megiddo; They took no spoils of silver. They fought from the heavens; The stars from their courses fought against Sisera" Judges 5:19&20. Spiritual signs manifest to confirm divine covenants. Wonders are divine interruptions of the natural course of the elements. Miracles are supernatural manifestations that furnish covenant beneficiaries. Essentially, to know what God is doing, when natural patterns of the elements are altered so we can adjust our ways accordingly, we must pay attention to divine covenants, purposes, biblical prophecies as well as present truths.

The Dimension of Royalty is where we reverence His nature at every point in time, fellowship with His presence at the appointed times and are faithful stewards of covenant times.

Dimensions

Chapter Twenty-Six

'Let the Waters Abound With Living Creatures'

"Then God said, "Let the waters abound with an abundance of living creatures, and let birds fly above the earth across the face of the firmament of the heavens." So God created great sea creatures and every living thing that moves, with which the waters abounded, according to their kind, and every winged bird according to its kind. And God saw that it was good. And God blessed them, saying, "Be fruitful and multiply, and fill the waters in the seas, and let birds multiply on the earth" So the evening and the morning were the fifth day" Genesis 1:20-23.

On the fifth day, God called forth fishes and birds into existence from the waters. These creatures are significant of seraphim and cherubim which are angelic beings. They are orderly beings and furnish our true and proper worship of God. There is constant worship taking place in heaven, and so to plugin, we must be sensitive to divine promptings.

Seraphim are assigned to the glory of man. The divine encounter of Isaiah the prophet provides insights of Seraphim. "In the year that King Uzziah died, I saw the Lord sitting on a throne, high and lifted up, and the train of His robe filled the temple. Above it stood seraphim; each one had six wings: with two he covered his face, with two he covered his feet, and with two he flew. And one cried to another and said: "Holy, holy, holy is the Lord of hosts; The whole earth is full of His glory!" And the posts of the door were shaken by the voice of him who cried out, and the house was filled with smoke. So I said: "Woe is me, for I am undone! Because I am a man of unclean lips, and I dwell in the midst of a people of unclean lips; For my eyes have seen the King, The Lord of hosts." Then one of the seraphim flew to me, having in his hand a live coal which he had taken with the tongs from the altar. And he touched my mouth with it, and said: "Behold, this has touched your lips; Your iniquity is taken away, and your sin purged." Also I heard the voice of the Lord, saying: "Whom shall I send, and who will go for Us?" Then I said, "Here am I! Send me." And He said, "Go, and tell this people: 'Keep on hearing, but do not understand; Keep on seeing, but do not perceive.' "Make the heart of this people dull, and their ears heavy, and shut their eyes; Lest they see with their eyes, and hear with their ears, and understand with their heart, and return and be healed." Then I said, "Lord, how long?" And He answered: "Until the cities are laid waste and without inhabitant, the houses are without a man, the land is utterly desolate, the Lord has removed men far away, and the forsaken places are many in the midst of the land. But yet a tenth will be in it, and will return and be for consuming, as a terebinth tree or as an oak, whose stump remains when it is cut down. So the holy seed shall be its stump" Isaiah 6:1-13. In the encounter, Isaiah finds himself in the throne room of heaven and is in awe of the experience. However, he immediately becomes aware of his shortcomings and cries out, "Woe is me, for I am undone! Because I am a man of unclean lips, and I dwell in the midst of a people of unclean lips; For my eyes have seen the King, The Lord of hosts." Interestingly we see how heaven responds to his admission of guilt. "Then one of the seraphim flew to me, having in his hand a live coal which he had taken with the tongs from the altar. And he touched my mouth with it, and said: "Behold, this has touched your lips; Your iniquity is taken away, and your sin purged." Instead of a harsh pronouncement of judgment against Isaiah, his iniquity was purged! Though our shortcomings diminish the glory of God upon our lives, here we see how Seraphim function to restore the glory of Isaiah. The mouth of the prophet symbolized his entire spiritual senses that were defiled at the time. There was a pending divine mission for which reason the prophet needed to be restored with glory. Israel at this time was alienated from God by being irresponsive to God. Isaiah's mission was to shut down their spiritual senses until their destruction was overwhelming. As in the instance of Isaiah, we all have Seraphim assigned to our glory. Jesus alludes to this in Matthew 18:10, "Take heed that you do not despise one of these little ones, for I say to you that in heaven their angels always see the face of My Father who is in heaven." If little children have angels assigned to them, then it is the same for adults. The problem here is that the innocence of little children guarantees their angels are at work on their behalf. However, as we grow as adults, we stop covering our face as is the manner of Seraphim. We start making decisions that violate our spiritual senses and so our angels become dormant. Seraphim cover their feet with two of their wings, which means they are assigned to our ways. Each day we must equip ourselves with the whole armor of God as I taught in chapter fourteen. Furthermore, Seraphim fly with two of their wings. They equip us with the supernatural manifestations that become due for us because of God's covenant.

Cherubim are assigned to the glory of God. When Adam and Eve sinned and were driven out of the Garden of Eden, we see the first mention of Cherubim. "Then the Lord God said, "Behold, the man has become like one of Us, to know good and evil. And now, lest he put out his hand and take also of the tree of life, and eat, and live forever" therefore the Lord God sent him out of the garden of Eden to till the ground from which he was taken. So, He drove out the man; and He placed cherubim at the east of the garden of Eden, and a flaming sword which turned every way, to guard the way to the tree of life" Genesis 3:22-24. After their fall, access to eat from the tree of life would have guaranteed eternity for Adam and Eve, so Cherubim were assigned to protect the tree of life. Another important instance is the design of the Ark of the Covenant in the tabernacle of Moses. "And they shall make an ark of acacia wood; two and a half cubits shall be its length, a cubit and a half its width, and a cubit and a half its height. And you shall overlay it with pure gold, inside and out you shall overlay it, and shall make on it a molding of gold all around. You shall cast four rings of gold for it, and put them in its four corners; two rings shall be on one side, and two rings on the other side. And you shall make poles of acacia wood, and overlay them with gold. You shall put the poles into the rings on the sides of the ark, that the ark may be carried by them. The poles shall be in the rings of the ark; they shall not be taken from it. And you shall put into the ark the Testimony which I will give you. "You shall make a mercy seat of pure gold; two and a half cubits shall be its length and a cubit and a half its width. And you shall make two cherubim of gold; of hammered work you shall make them at the two ends of the mercy seat. Make one cherub at one end, and the other cherub at the other end; you shall make the cherubim at the two ends of it of one piece with the mercy seat. And the cherubim shall stretch out their wings above, covering the mercy seat with their wings, and they shall face one another; the faces of the cherubim shall be toward the mercy seat. You shall put the mercy seat on top of the ark, and in the ark you shall put the Testimony that I will give you. And there I will meet with you, and I will speak with you from above the mercy seat, from between the two cherubim which are on the ark of the Testimony, about everything which I will give you in commandment to the children of Israel" Exodus 25:10-22. Cherubim represented in the structure of the Ark of the Covenant symbolizes divine revelation to us. Usually when God speaks, it is Cherubim that convey to us the message. For this reason, their ministry to us is a significant factor in how we are judged by God.

Overall, the fifth day of creation is our alignment with God and the ministry of angels. "The Lord has established His throne in heaven, and His kingdom rules overall. Bless the Lord, you His angels, who excel in strength, who do His word, heeding the voice of His word. Bless the Lord, all you His hosts, you ministers of His, who do His pleasure. Bless the Lord, all His works, in all places of His dominion. Bless the Lord, O my soul!" Psalms 103:19-22. The entire universe was designed to function as an orchestra of glorious manifestations. God the ruler of the universe, Seraphim, Cherubim, created things as well as man, must align so we can flourish. Man is often the one who tends to be out of alignment. Though we are designed to be the beneficiaries of this arrangement, we end up as victims because of our incoherence. Most of the natural disasters that occur with devastating impact to man's tranquility, are often because of our failure to synchronize with divinity.

The Dimension of Divinity is where we align with angelic ministry to honor God in worship.

Chapter Twenty-Seven

'Let Us Make Man in Our Image and Likeness'

"Then God said, "Let the earth bring forth the living creature according to its kind: cattle and creeping thing and beast of the earth, each according to its kind"; and it was so. And God made the beast of the earth according to its kind, cattle according to its kind, and everything that creeps on the earth according to its kind. And God saw that it was good. Then God said, "Let Us make man in Our image, according to Our likeness; let them have dominion over the fish of the sea, over the birds of the air, and over the cattle, over all the earth and over every creeping thing that creeps on the earth" Genesis 1:24-26.

On the sixth day God created animals from the land as well as man. Animals depict human character potential. They enshrine the creative aspects of human nature. The Father, Son and Holy Spirit resolved to make man in their image and likeness. Man was blessed with dominion over all that God had created. Creating and making are two words that describe the works of God. Create is from the Hebrew word 'bara' and it means to form out of nothing. We notice the phrase 'let there be' consistently during the six days of creation, where God calls out light, the heavens, land, constellations, water creatures and land creatures. 'Asah' is the Hebrew word for 'make', that means to form out of something. This function is used to describe how God intends to form man. "This is the history of the heavens and the earth when they were created, in the day that the Lord God made the earth and the heavens, before any plant of the field was in the earth and before any herb of the field had grown. For the Lord God had not caused it to rain on the earth, and there was no man to till the ground; but a mist went up from the earth and watered the whole face of the ground. And the Lord God formed man of the dust of the ground, and breathed into his nostrils the breath of life; and man became a living being" Genesis 2:4-7. During the six days of creation, the manifestations were either literal or spiritual. For instance, on the third day, land manifested physically but then vegetation did not show up immediately. God intended for man to understand the dimension of fruitfulness, so man was formed first to observe the process. Man was made from the dust of the ground, God spoke purpose into his being and man became a living soul. 'Let Us Make Man In Our Image And Likeness' is the expression that captures the intentions of God for mankind. "And we know that all things work together for good to those who love God, to those who are the called according to His purpose. For whom He foreknew, He also predestined to be conformed to the image of His Son, that He might be the firstborn among many brethren. Moreover, whom He predestined, these He also called; whom He called, these He also justified; and whom He justified, these He also glorified" Romans 8:28-30. Owing to the fall of Adam, we lost our inclination of divine purpose. Salvation through Jesus Christ unveils the predestination of God for the believer. We were with Him, so He foreknew us. He dispatched us to planet earth with a predetermined destiny to conform with the image of Christ. In Christ Jesus we see the manifestation of the model of God's glory, so we know the standard of how we are expected to conform. "Remember the former things of old, for I am God, and there is no other; I am God, and there is none like Me, declaring the end from the beginning, And from ancient times things that are not yet done, saying, 'My counsel shall stand, and I will do all My pleasure,' calling a bird of prey from the east, the man who executes My counsel, from a far country. indeed I have spoken it; I will also bring it to pass. I have purposed it; I will also do it" Isaiah 46:9-11. Divine revelation is how we 'remember the former things of old'. This is when we were with God before our dispatch to the earth. 'Declaring the end from the beginning' is the essence of destiny, where God predestined us to be conformed to the image of Christ. 'Calling a bird of prey from the east, the man who executes My counsel from a far country' is how at some point in our existence here on earth, He calls us to divine purpose, which is the beginning of our journey towards destiny.

Trees in the Garden
"The Lord God planted a garden eastward in Eden, and there He put the man whom He had formed. And out of the ground the Lord God made every tree grow that is

pleasant to the sight and good for food. The tree of life was also in the midst of the garden, and the tree of the knowledge of good and evil. Now a river went out of Eden to water the garden, and from there it parted and became four riverheads. The name of the first is Pishon; it is the one which skirts the whole land of Havilah, where there is gold. And the gold of that land is good. Bdellium and the onyx stone are there. The name of the second river is Gihon; it is the one which goes around the whole land of Cush. The name of the third river is Hiddekel; it is the one which goes toward the east of Assyria. The fourth river is the Euphrates. Then the Lord God took the man and put him in the garden of Eden to tend and keep it. And the Lord God commanded the man, saying, "Of every tree of the garden you may freely eat; but of the tree of the knowledge of good and evil you shall not eat, for in the day that you eat of it you shall surely die" Genesis 2:8-17. After God made man, He took him to the east of Eden and planted a garden while man observed the process. God the Son is the maker of all things, so He was the personality of the Godhead at work here with Adam. The tree of life, tree good for food and tree pleasant to the sight, are the three trees that man was permitted to access. The tree of life signifies our spiritual destiny and shows our spiritual service to God. The tree good for food is our financial destiny, that shows the vocation to which we are called. The tree pleasant to the sight is our emotional destiny and indicates how we are designed to flourish maritally. God the Son called on the Holy Spirit to manifest the river Pison. Pison means to 'grow fat and flourishing'. This river activates seeds that are enshrined in the soil. These seeds are fattened by the river Pison until they are turgid in the soil. This is significant of how we ought to seek our divine destiny potential prayerfully, until we obtain revelation from the Holy Spirit. Next, God the Son called on the Holy Spirit to manifest the river Gihon. Gihon means to 'burst out' and it is how the seed in the soil germinates to become a plant. Third, God the Son called on the Holy Spirit to manifest the river Hiddekel. Hiddekel means arrows. Prior to a plant bearing fruit, all forms of challenges arise from the atmosphere and from creatures. Here, the Holy Spirits equips the believer to overcome adversity that confronts us in our pursuit of destiny. Finally, God the Son called on the Holy Spirit to manifest the river Euphrates. This river fosters the harvest. There is a unique way by which every endeavor becomes fruitful, so it is incumbent on the believer to seek this way. When all these three trees were manifested, suddenly a tree sprung up from the soil which was the tree of the knowledge of good and evil. This tree did not manifest through the instruction of God the Son to the Holy Spirit. It showed up by itself and it signifies the carnal mind. "Because the carnal mind is enmity against God; for it is not subject to the law of God, nor indeed can be. So then, those who are in the flesh cannot please God" Romans 8:7&8. Decisions about how to serve God, vocation for financial prosperity and marriage should never be made without seeking God diligently for divine direction. The Holy Spirit is our counselor who is ever present to foster the manifestations by which we can prosper spiritually, financially and emotionally.

Animals in the Garden

"Out of the ground the Lord God formed every beast of the field and every bird of the air, and brought them to Adam to see what he would call them. And whatever

Adam called each living creature, that was its name. So Adam gave names to all cattle, to the birds of the air, and to every beast of the field" Genesis 2:19-20a. The living creatures were called into existence from water and the land. They were created, that is formed out of nothing and are the essence of the human spirit. Animals signify human character potential. The prophet Isaiah gives us insight of how the animals lived with Adam prior to his fall, as an indication of what should happen in the kingdom of Christ. "The wolf also shall dwell with the lamb, the leopard shall lie down with the young goat, the calf and the young lion and the fatling together; And a little child shall lead them. The cow and the bear shall graze; Their young ones shall lie down together; And the lion shall eat straw like the ox. The nursing child shall play by the cobra's hole, and the weaned child shall put his hand in the viper's den. They shall not hurt nor destroy in all My holy mountain, for the earth shall be full of the knowledge of the Lord as the waters cover the sea" Isaiah 11:6-9. Before the fall, God engaged Adam in the naming of all the animals. All their character potential was inherent in Adam. God the Son molded each animal from the dust of the ground, and Adam saw what potential was manifested and gave their names. The word 'name' means nature and character. Adam gave nature and character to each animal as he perceived them. Though as humans we have either taken the disposition of predators or prey in how we conduct ourselves, it is because of the perversion that started after man's fall. In Christ, we have the privilege for a do-over. "Therefore, from now on, we regard no one according to the flesh. Even though we have known Christ according to the flesh, yet now we know Him thus no longer. Therefore, if anyone is in Christ, he is a new creation; old things have passed away; behold, all things have become new. Now all things are of God, who has reconciled us to Himself through Jesus Christ, and has given us the ministry of reconciliation, that is, that God was in Christ reconciling the world to Himself, not imputing their trespasses to them, and has committed to us the word of reconciliation. Now then, we are ambassadors for Christ, as though God were pleading through us: we implore you on Christ's behalf, be reconciled to God. For He made Him who knew no sin to be sin for us, that we might become the righteousness of God in Him" 2 Corinthians 5:16-21. It is important as believers that we pay attention to the true character potentials in people. We ought to look beyond the perversions to see what God originally intended for everyone. We were never designed to be either predators or prey. The gospel is intended to restore us all to our original character potential and reconcile us to God.

Male and Female

"And the Lord God said, "It is not good that man should be alone; I will make him a helper comparable to him" Genesis 2:18. "but for Adam there was not found a helper comparable to him. And the Lord God caused a deep sleep to fall on Adam, and he slept; and He took one of his ribs, and closed up the flesh in its place. Then the rib which the Lord God had taken from man He made into a woman, and He brought her to the man. And Adam said: "This is now bone of my bones and flesh of my flesh; She shall be called Woman, because she was taken out of Man." Therefore a man shall leave his father and mother and be joined to his wife, and they shall become one flesh. And they were both naked, the man and his wife, and were not ashamed" Genesis 2:20b-25. The decision of the

Godhead to make man in their image and likeness was to foster our dominion. Notice that the Godhead demonstrates counsel in how man is made, and this is the reason man needs counsel to exercise dominion over creation. Interestingly, God starts out by making the male man first, and showed him how the Garden of Eden was planted, and involved him in naming the animals. In all these, God observes that man is alone and needs to exist in the framework of counsel which was the original design. He put Adam to a deep sleep where Adam is in visionary mode. Adam is aware of how God takes his rib and molds the woman. He wakes up from the sleep to find he has a female counterpart manifested. In the same way that he named the animals that God the Son presented to him, he calls her 'Woman' and establishes the precedent for marriage and family. The important point we learn here is how God implemented male and female in a fashion that reveals the essence of counsel and leadership, that are both core to the blessing of dominion. The ideal relationship between a husband and wife must mirror how Jesus worked with the Holy Spirit while on earth. While Jesus Christ manifested leadership by walking in the Word, the Holy Spirit served as Counselor.

The Dimension of Dominion is where we function in our three-fold destiny, harness our character potential and engage counsel in all our endeavors.

Harness

Dimensions

Chapter Twenty-Eight

'And God Blessed Sanctified the Seventh Day'

"Thus the heavens and the earth, and all the host of them, were finished. And on the seventh day God ended His work which He had done, and He rested on the seventh day from all His work which He had done. Then God blessed the seventh day and sanctified it, because in it He rested from all His work which God had created and made" Genesis 2:1-3.

On the seventh day God rested from his works. He sanctified and blessed it, which means that the day was furnished with divine fulfilment. Sanctification is how God's word cleans us from the influences that desecrate us. Romans 3:23 says, "For all have sinned and fall short of the glory of God." Glory is the 'heavy weightiness' of God, and is the ultimate design of God for believers. The glory of each believer is how diligent they have endeavored to incline with God's word. "Therefore, since a promise remains of entering His rest, let us fear lest any of you seem to have come short of it. For indeed the gospel was preached to us as well as to them; but the word which they heard did not profit them, not being mixed with faith in those who heard it. For we who have believed do enter that rest, as He has said: "So I swore in My wrath, 'They shall not enter My rest,'" although the works were finished from the foundation of the world. For He has spoken in a certain place of the seventh day in this way: "And God rested on the seventh day from all His works"; and again in this place: "They shall not enter My rest." Since therefore it remains that some must enter it, and those to whom it was first preached did not enter because of disobedience, again He designates a certain day, saying in David, "Today," after such a long time, as it has been said: "Today, if you will hear His voice, Do not harden your hearts." For if Joshua had given them rest, then He would not afterward have spoken of another day. There remains therefore a rest for the people of God. For he who has entered His rest has himself also ceased from his works as God did from His" Hebrews 4:1-10. The disposition of the heart of man towards God's word is how he becomes sanctified or remains desecrated. We are sanctified by the word of God because we believe and by faith we act on it. God rewards our faith with blessings of glory which is our state of rest from struggles with the enemy. Our level of glory is our divine capacity to be victorious over the schemes of the kingdom of darkness. Every year the anointed high priest would appear in the Most Holy Place to account for his stewardship of the past year, and the judgment that was passed determined the fate of God's people for the coming year.

The Dimension of Glory is where we endeavor to pursue divine promises by faith so that we can increase in blessings of divine glory.

Conclusion

As you traversed the pages of this book, you may have discovered that a particular tribe reflected your dominant potential. Assuming this is the truth about your spiritual identity, there should have been an inner witness for validation. However, if you are conflicted as to which tribe reflects your dominant potential, then I encourage you to prayerfully read each chapter of the book daily until this is ascertained.

The important point is that aside one's dominant potential, the potential of all the twelve tribes are inherent in everyone as recessed potentials. However, it is necessary to ascertain your dominant potential because this is where you want to serve whenever you have options. When you serve in the arena of your recessed potential, you end up being mediocre. Though it is expedient for us all to develop our recessed potential, our dominant potential is where we are empowered to excel.

Our dominant potential is our royalty in Christ and together with insights of the priesthood as well as the tabernacle, is how we are harnessed for significant corporate and individual progress. Anyone who qualifies to head a corporate entity responsible for significant resources in the kingdom economy ought to be Intuitive, Instinctive, Perceptive, Resolute, Aligned, Comprehended and Convicted in their judgments.

References

Online Encyclopedia, www.wikipedia.org
(https://en.wikipedia.org/wiki/Mandrake)
Oral Roberts University input is courtesy of Wikipedia,
https://en.m.wikipedia.org/wiki/Oral_Roberts_Universit
y)
Hebrew – Greek Key Word Study Bible by Spiros
Zhodiates
Wilmington's Guide To The Bible by Dr. H. L. Wilmington
Oxford Languages: https://languages.oup.com/

About the Book

The Israelites were freed from bondage in Egypt through the leadership of Moses the servant of God. They did not leave Egypt in a disorganized manner but were harnessed in orderly ranks as a family of tribes. Under the auspices of God's glory, the entire Israelite community journeyed to the Promised Land and possessed their allotments. No one was left disenfranchised because corporate progress translates into individual progress. Can that be said about the Body of Christ today?

The prophetic destinies of the twelve tribes of Israel unveil our dominant and recessed potentials that ought to be engaged in our endeavors. Altogether these potentials are the basis of our spiritual senses that determine our choices.

This book teaches how the twelve tribes provide insight into our prophetic purposes and the corresponding apostolic foundations for a grasp of basic kingdom economics as well as the dimensions of how God works.

About the Author

Kenneth Walley is the Lead Pastor of New Faith Tabernacle in New Jersey. He is the President of Cibunet, a kingdom interface for planning, analysis, networking and funding. Ken serves as an advisor to several profit and non-profit organizations. 'American Culture in Water, Blood, Oil and Bread' as well as 'Substitutional Arrangement' are among other books he has authored.